KU-605-437

DEATH ON
IRELAND'S EYE

Dean Ruxton tells stories. Old ones, mostly. As an author and digital journalist, he is best known for writing that peers into the dark, fascinating corners of historical crime in Ireland. Dean works for the *Irish Times*, where he writes and curates his archive project 'Lost Leads'. His first book, *When the Hangman Came to Galway*, was published by Gill in 2018. He lives in Dublin.

DEATH ON IRELAND'S EYE

THE VICTORIAN MURDER TRIAL
THAT SCANDALISED A NATION

Dean Ruxton

Gill Books

Gill Books

Hume Avenue

Park West

Dublin 12

www.gillbooks.ie

Gill Books is an imprint of M.H. Gill and Co.

© Dean Ruxton 2022

978 07171 8892 5

Designed and print origination by O'K Graphic Design, Dublin

Edited by Neil Burkey

Proofread by Caroline Twomey

Map by Derry Dillon

Printed by CPI Group (UK) Ltd, Croydon CRO 4YY

This book is typeset in 11/17 pt Adobe Garamond Pro with headings in Modesto
Condensed.

All rights reserved.

No part of this publication may be copied, reproduced or transmitted in any form or by
any means, without written permission of the publishers.

A CIP catalogue record for this book is available from the British Library.

5 4 3 2 1

ACKNOWLEDGEMENTS

With special thanks to Dr Linda Mulligan, Dr Ronan Kilbride, Dr Mark Coen, Mark Lynam, Ken Doyle and the staff of the libraries and databases consulted for the research for this book, particularly those at the National Archives of Ireland and Royal College of Surgeons in Ireland Heritage Collections.

AUTHOR'S NOTE

This book tells a true story, partly through reconstruction. Scenes and dialogue have been composed in some sections to provide narrative structure to the main events in the story, introduce elements of historical context, provide colour and set the scene. The important facts, people, dates and points of evidence depicted in these sections are based on real witness accounts and other documents surrounding the case. The events reported at trial have been condensed for length and readability; each witness is mentioned and the details of the evidence – as well as any exchanges that occurred between witnesses, lawyers, judges or jurors – are true to source.

The book is based on extensive research involving many archive documents including pamphlets, a lengthy brief for the prosecution, official reports and other sources as noted in-text. The material draws heavily, too, from contemporaneous reporting on the case from dozens of newspaper titles from Ireland and the UK. Some modern-day interviews inform part of the analysis of the evidence, as outlined in Part 5. This book is intended to be a detailed retelling of a truly tragic story and an attempt to honestly examine an extraordinary chapter in Ireland's criminal history.

Map of Ireland's Eye

Martello tower/
landing place

The Summit

Ruins: the Church of the
Three Sons of Nessan

Strand

The 'Long Hole'
(Body discovered)

Howth Harbour

100m

CONTENTS

Part 5

Part 6

PART 1

OUTSIDERS

Howth is a fishing village at the very top of Dublin Bay. It's there a long time, as are the names of many families that have weathered the centuries like the battered cliffs bordering the headland on which it sits. Besides fishing, the other economy keeping Howth afloat has long been the business associated with outsiders. The story you're about to read, tragic and quite true, begins – in one sense – in Howth Harbour, north of which is Ireland's Eye, a lonely island with dark rock faces, clean beaches and crumbling ruins casting shadows of former life. As the sun set on 6 September 1852, two Howth fishermen from one Howth family were preparing for their last job of the day – a trip to the island to collect a return fare.

Mick Nangle stood for a moment in the little boat with one eye closed. From his position, he could see the top of the island peeking over the harbour wall, seeming to regard him and his cousin as they prepared to depart.

'Is it nearly time?'

Pat was only half paying attention, busying himself. 'Nearly, Mick,' he replied with a hint of frustration. It was coming up on half past seven, the sun had been set for nearly an hour, and the Nangles were due at Ireland's Eye at 8 p.m. to collect two tourists.

The couple, the fishermen knew, were boarding up in the village with Margaret Campbell. By all indications, they were well-to-do. The man, William Burke Kirwan, worked in drawing disease and injuries for the hospitals, and

Dublin Libraries · South Dublin Libraries · www.southdublinlibraries.ie

liked to use his talents about the island, while his wife, Sarah Maria Louisa Kirwan – Maria – enjoyed swimming and walks about the nature of the place. The Nangles were getting on, but still made a living fishing, and ferrying outsiders to the island.

'Seagulls and rats,' said Mick decidedly after a moment, 'and spirits, too. The devil was on the island.' Pat looked over, preparing to hear a story he'd heard countless times before. 'He came upon St Nessan when he was in prayer,' Mick went on. 'St Nessan cast him back with holy water, and he soared through the air, right to Howth and struck the cliff with such force that he split the rock, and left the mark of his face forever. That's why they call it Devil's Rock.'

Pat stopped his busy hands for a moment. 'I thought he hit him with a bible?'

'Could well be,' Mick replied in deep thought. 'It must have been some belt.'

The harbour, and the boat, were lit by lamplight. A calm night. The peace was broken by two voices carrying onto the water from the pier. The remainder of the small crew, Tom Giles and Ned Kavanagh, came into view in the quickly fading light and boarded the little boat. With 30 minutes to go until pick-up, the men got to work at the oars and the vessel cut through the black waters with ease. The pale strand of the island's land-side shoreline was ignited by the light that remained. The ruins of an ancient church sat centrally on the main plain and some way up from the water. In the north-west corner of the island, the outline of the Martello tower, near the landing place, fought the dusk sky.

Minutes later, not far from land, Pat scanned the shoreline. 'Mr Kirwan?' No reply. Pat allowed the silence to fill his ears for another couple of seconds, then, in the dark, he bawled: 'Mr Kirwan!' Pat stood and looked to his feet, turning his head and pointing his ear to land, a palm held erect to keep silence. He called again. Nothing came back but the gentle lap of the water against the side of the boat and the distant breaking on the strand.

Mick was on his feet. 'Did you hear it?'

From the shore, a reply: 'Nangle?' The shape of a man appeared on the land and the men pulled closer. Pat climbed out of the boat and walked to greet his customer. The artist was alone on the rocks, just elevated from the landing place. At the man's request, Pat took the bags and made to return to the boat.

'Mr Kirwan, where is the mistress?' asked Mick, noting Maria's absence.

'I am this half hour looking for her over here,' said Mr Kirwan, pointing towards the rocks at the Howth side of the Martello tower. The artist explained that he and his wife had separated after a short shower of rain about an hour and a half beforehand. He thought perhaps she would be near the tower, given she'd gone off swimming on the beach, owing to a bad smell in the area. The last he'd seen her, she'd been walking east, over the hill.

The Martello tower. This image is reproduced courtesy of the National Library of Ireland [PD 2085 TX (149)].

At that, Mick instigated a search, setting off nimbly over the rocks in the direction of the main beach with Mr Kirwan walking behind. The two moved away from the boat, calling for Maria as they went. Meanwhile, Pat brought the bag and other items back to the vessel, joining Giles and Kavanagh.

Pat loaded the luggage into the boat. He sat down beside the items, eyeing what appeared to be Kirwan's sketchbook. The boatman brought his face close to the pages and let his eyes wander over Mr Kirwan's work for the day. Thirty minutes passed. With no sign of Mick and Mr Kirwan, Pat climbed out of the boat and walked to the strand. Facing south, all was still. Piercing the peace himself, he called for the men and set off walking after them. Looking towards the harbour, Pat noticed the last few vessels of the evening glide past him, and he heard men chattering on their decks.

Already, from their brief walk, Mick could see the lady was not on the strand, nor was she further up the hill or back at the ruins. 'It is a very extraordinary thing,' Mick eventually said, 'that you would be here at this hour of night without your mistress.' His comment was met by Mr Kirwan's silence. Mick continued: 'How is it that we cannot find her this dark night?'

Kirwan suggested they search further east, up the hill, towards the island's hidden part. The land-facing side of the island was that of an oil painting: browns, greens and a golden strand underlining its bulk. But the other side, a close view of which was reserved for seafarers and the most rugged swimmers, was all but a sheer drop. A jagged criss-cross of rock, sharp and slick. If the Nangles woke up some morning to find the island spun round and that steep, inhospitable cliff facing the shore, they might discover their lucrative side business of island ferrymen quickly dried up.

The one place where a person – though usually not women – could swim was a deep inlet at the south of the island, hidden from the harbour's view. The Long Hole did not tend to agree with the low and high waters of the surrounding shores, and when the two men reached the rocks facing down into its watery valley, they quickly saw that it was filled. A tall rock, central to the hole and standing some 22 feet high, split the little shore into two channels. The rocks flanking the deep, lengthy inlet were lethal and slippery, and the men were careful when retreating from the edge, deciding after a brief conference to try the boat again.

The Long Hole. Image from Sir Cusack Patrick Roney "How to Spend a Month in Ireland" via WikimediaCommons.

On the way back, the men encountered Pat, who himself had been calling for the pair. The three joined and, upon the realisation that none of them had encountered Maria, the situation became instantly more serious. 'I am afraid it is a bad job,' said Pat, as the realisation set in that something terrible may have happened. Kirwan wanted to keep searching, but Pat first returned to the boat, telling the other two men to stay put in case Maria showed up. When the fisherman came back, the trio resumed the search, heading back in the direction of the Long Hole. They split up. Mick took the strand right the way south, then east – a route that would bring him eventually to the destination, while Pat and Mr Kirwan took the more direct path past the old ruins of the church on grassier ground. Kirwan continued to call his wife's name, asking her aloud why she wouldn't respond, and telling her that she had the boatmen out looking for her.

Regrouping at the Long Hole, the three men peered down into the crevices. The tide had retreated beyond the craggy rocks guarding the inlet. Kirwan nearly stumbled, but Pat caught him. Pat was first to descend, reaching the bottom and peering again through the dark, scanning rocks that were now revealed after the retreating of the water. Pat saw the colour of her shift first, brilliantly white against the rock on which she lay, just yards from where he stood. By his later estimation, it was about 10 o'clock. Maria was dead; her arms, still warm, were spread out at her sides, and she was on her back. Her legs – feet clad in bathing shoes – were dipped some way below her knees into a small pool of water. About six feet away, the receding tide lapped gently into the Long Hole. The bathing shift she wore had slid up, leaving her lower half exposed. Pat pulled her up by the shoulders and worked frantically to restore some dignity by tugging her shift back down over her legs. The soft features Pat had set eyes upon in his boat the last few days were lifeless, and, he later said, bloodied. Pat called out that he'd found her, and Mr Kirwan scrambled from the darkness and threw himself across his wife's body, calling her name into the night, repeatedly shouting 'Oh, Maria!'

'Nangle, her clothes. Get her clothes,' managed Kirwan after a short while, pulling himself momentarily from the wave of grief that had washed over him. The boatmen at once searched around the nearby rocks. Mr Kirwan, on the men's empty-handed return, went off the way Pat had come. In a short time, he reappeared, holding a couple of fabric items in his hands, and asked the ferryman to fetch the rest before resuming his position, lying across his wife's body. Pat did as requested and found the elusive clothes on his second trip to the hole's tall, central rock. Maria's body, by then, had been wrapped in a sheet and a shawl. Pat and Mick could do no more for the man, and quickly decided that traversing the land in the dark with a body would be a heart-breaking task. Instead, they would round Ireland's Eye on their boat. They left the Kirwans lying as they were and marched quickly back towards the landing place. The Nangles reached their boat and their two fellow crewmen some minutes later, and immediately set out to reach the Long Hole by sea.

The ferrymen were an hour gone from Mr Kirwan. When they returned to the inlet, the boat's lantern revealed Kirwan's body, still slumped over Maria's. The boat, pulled into the Long Hole, was accessible by rocks above it, meaning it was only Giles who got his feet wet as he helped the Nangles to lift Maria's body into the vessel. The body was further wrapped in a sail and the men, at last, set out for Howth Harbour.

2

PROCESSION

Kirwan remained noticeably quiet during the solemn return journey. The boat had barely stopped when Thomas Giles became impatient in the face of the prolonged silence. 'Why would you not mind the lady and not let her go astray at such an hour?' he spat. Kirwan's reply – that he was too busy sketching – did not satisfy Giles. 'And how, Mr Kirwan, could you sketch Ireland's Eye and the Lord's Castle after night, and it so dark?' And then: 'Had you a sup in that bottle of yours? Did it make the lady tipsy?'

'No, my boy,' replied Kirwan. 'All I had was two bottles of ale, and all I gave her was three glasses.'

Not long after the boat landed, fisherman John Barrett had a knock at the door of his house beside the east pier. It was Pat Nangle, who relayed the sad story of the drowned tourist – he and his crew needed something to move the body. Barrett acted quickly, getting dressed and retrieving his dray, and the men hurried to where the body lay in the boat. Barrett didn't mention it to Pat then – the dots weren't fully connected – but he had felt something in the air that evening. Heard it, more specifically.

Hours before the grim visit, Barrett had taken tea with his wife and stood afterwards at the front of his home, facing the island. The location of John's house afforded him a full vista of the Eye. A rare, calm night kept him still for a couple of minutes before the first scream came. Loud. Heavy, as he would come to describe it. It came from his right; he couldn't be sure because of the distance, but it could have been from the Long Hole – certainly that end of the island – or the sea in between. Man or woman? He couldn't tell. More shouts – less loud – followed, and more again after Barrett walked to the pier for a better chance to hear. Returning home, Barrett shared his theory with his wife, that something was amiss at Ireland's Eye. Someone was adrift at the island, he concluded. Barrett kept these things to himself as he assisted the men in bringing the body ashore.

The people of a fishing village are no strangers to drownings. The death of a fisherman was a sad thing, and could mean destitution for his surviving family. Mrs Kirwan was not the first visitor to lose their life in the tides. The well-known surgeon, Richard Carmichael, had just three years beforehand died at Sutton, a couple of miles west of the harbour. It was a well-spun local yarn: the doctor, living at his summer residence in Sutton, rode his horse along the sandbar to the south of the peninsula, and parallel with the road. Depending on the tide, one could be separated from the land by high water, or very nearly none. At the top of the sandbar, a narrow channel of water separating it from Sutton would give the unfamiliar rider the idea it was shallow. This is the trap into which the doctor fell. Halfway across the stretch opposite the back of his residence, his horse plunged its front legs into the deep, hidden, high-walled cut in the centre of the channel. A strong current took the doctor, and the horse swam to shore. The surgeon's hat thereafter followed.

Local sergeant Joseph Sherwood was alerted to Maria's death and promptly exited the barracks at Howth to make his way to the body. Others, too, emerged from their houses as the news of the drowning spread. Father Hall, the local parish priest, was apparently not shy in sharing his suspicion of the artist; Kirwan, the Catholic clergyman happened to know, was a Protestant, while Maria was a Catholic. But the religious persuasion of tourists was perhaps not the most pressing of the sergeant's concerns as the procession came into view. Pat Nangle led the posse, and a white, wet bundle, about which the onlookers needed no explanation, sat on the level planks of the dray. The dray travelled the short distance to Margaret Campbell's house, where the Kirwans had been staying.

The cart's wheels came to a stop sometime after 11 o'clock. Maria's body was carried inside and Sherwood trained his eye on Kirwan.

Inside Mrs Campbell's house, Anne Lacy was calm. Forty years of being a nurse-tender in Howth prepared a woman for handling the drowned; it followed that she knew how to prepare and wrap a body as necessary. She and two other women – Catherine McGarr and Mary Robinson – were waiting in preparation for the body's arrival. Mrs Campbell's front door opened first into a hallway. To the right, a doorway led to the room where Mr and Mrs Kirwan had been staying. Across from that room was the kitchen, and Mrs Campbell lived in her quarters to the rear of the house, on the ground floor.

It was into the first room on the right that the men carried Maria's body. The sail was unwrapped, at Lacy's direction, by Pat Nangle. John Barrett stood for a moment and looked, for the first time, upon Mrs Kirwan's scratched face. Maria was wrapped in a bathing sheet, tied fast at the neck and knees with good knots. She wore a bathing dress, and a shawl was wrapped about her head. The room was quiet, but crowded. Barrett and Sherwood looked at the body. Pat Nangle looked at his sail. Mr Kirwan stood to the side. Two women stayed by the door; Mrs Campbell, in full knowledge that her poor sight would require a very close survey of the body, hung back, as did a second neighbour – a local woman named Anne Hannah.

The nurse-tender ushered the men out of the room. The body would have to be stripped and properly prepared. It would be Catherine McGarr who made a remark that elicited Kirwan's first outburst of the evening. 'We cannot yet prepare the lady,' said McGarr as the men filed through the door and into the hall, 'the police will not allow the body to be touched until an inquest is held.' McGarr's concern was valid, but the underlying insinuation proved to be not to the artist's liking.

'I do not care a damn for the police, or anybody else, the body must be washed,' declared Kirwan, and so it was done. The door was closed, and the rumble of indiscernible voices began to fade. The Nangles and Barrett left, and Sherwood accompanied Kirwan and the others to another room, where the fire was.

The bed clothes were soon drenched, and the sheets transformed under blotches of crimson. Anne Lacy cleaned the right side of the body, while

Catherine McGarr took charge of the left. It was Mary Robinson's job to hold the candle as close as she could. They weren't to know it, but the exact condition of Mrs Kirwan's body would have untold importance in the weeks and months to come. In statements they later made, the women detailed what they saw that night. 'There was a sheet tied round the neck and round the knees,' recalled Lacy. 'On opening the sheet I found a bathing shift on the body, right up across the chest under the arms. There was a plaid shawl round the head. The eyes were shut with clotted blood. There was a cut under each eye and on each of the eyelids. There were a large number of scratches on the face. The chin alone was unscratched. There was no scrape on the nose. The lip upper and under were greatly swelled. There were scratches all over the cheeks. There were a great many behind the ears from which the blood flowed. A large quantity of blood flowed from the ears. There was a ring in the right ear, I could not take it out.

'Catherine McGarr washed the left side. I did not mind whether there was a ring in the left ear or not. Blood was flowing from the lower parts of the body. I had a flannel petticoat put round the head to prevent the blood from soiling the place it flowed so freely from her ears. There was a quilt put under her body to catch the blood which was flowing from her body. Her belly was quite flat. There was not a drop of water in the body. I felt it and could not be deceived. If water had been in it, I must have known it.'

The nurse-tender noted a cut on the right breast, and scratches on the left. Maria's hair was loose, full of seaweed and sand. Running her hand over the body and feeling for the presence of water, Lacy was convinced there was none in the lady's stomach. She observed more scratches on Maria's cheek – the type, she thought, that could have been made by gravel or stones, or perhaps by nails. 'I opened the right eye; the white of that eye was as red as the blood. There were no marks on the ears of crabs or fish having cut them – neither on the surface or edges – nor was there any scratch on the forehead. If there was such it could not have escaped my observation as I washed the body from the top of the head to the feet. None of the teeth were broken. There was no bloody froth on either the mouth or nose. The side was black. There were no ulcers or sores of any kind on the body – it was clean and white.'

Catherine McGarr told a similar story. When the sail was removed, she could see that the body was tied in a sheet, with a knot at the neck and another on the legs, and the bathing shift was at the top of her person, under her head. 'I assisted to lay out the body,' said McGarr. 'The right eye was shut, the left was open. There was blood on both eyes with some scratches on the cheeks. There was a small scratch on the left temple – the lips were swelled – there were scratches on the right breast and a small one on the nipple of the left from which blood streamed as if suck was flowing from it.

'It was pure blood that flowed from it. The lips were swelled with white froth on them, sliming up. The teeth were closed, the body was limber, there was blood flowing from the ear – the side of the left ear was scratched. I saw the ring in the left ear. There was a flannel petticoat put round the head to catch the blood. A patched quilt doubled in four was put under the body, the blood having been coming from the body. I saw a scrape on each of the eye lids and under the eye. There was a scrape on the left cheek and a larger one on the right.'

One of Mary Robinson's first tasks, as candle-bearer, was to bring the light source close to the face, so Lacy could see whether or not Maria still had her eyes. 'I did so, and Mrs Lacy said she had her eyes, but that they were bloodshot,' Robinson later said. 'I held the candle while they washed the body. I was present when the sheet was untied. There was a shawl taken off the head. I saw a bathing dress in the room, but not on the corpse. I was present when the sail was opened. There was no bathing shift on as I recollect... I saw one of the breasts black – I could not say it was cut. Blood flowed from the ears. I did not see any flow from the breasts. I did not notice any other marks upon the body.

'There was no marks as if cut by a rat or a crab. I saw Mrs Lacy about to take the rings from the ears. She could not do so. The blood flowed so fast. I did not notice whether the lips were swelled or not or whether there was froth on them.'

There were some discrepancies, and a number of omissions which would later appear. One thing that all three women attested to was that Mr Kirwan's legs were wet. As they worked to prepare Mrs Kirwan's body, using blankets and clothes to stem a steady flow of blood, Sherwood had, in another room, noticed the very same aspect of Mr Kirwan's attire.

In the room across the hall, Sherwood stood next to a fireplace, watching the artist peel his boots, then his stockings, from his soaking feet. They were stubborn, but came away with strong tugs and spattered drops of water on the hearthstone. Jane, a daughter of Mrs Campbell, helped him change his stockings. Kirwan lay the wet ones to dry beside his boots, and rolled his trousers away from his shins. Steam rose from them. The policeman was curious. Here was Mr Kirwan, who hadn't, to his knowledge, waded in the ocean, soaked from the knees down – or perhaps further up; he couldn't be sure. Such was the saturation of his trousers that a small puddle formed beneath the chair as he sat beside the fire. He had them turned up, exposing his drawers to the heat.

Whatever suspicions the sergeant may have had then were not expressed. All that was left for him to do was notify the coroner of the death, mention the note of peculiarity and ask him to come quickly. Sherwood had a feeling, but nothing yet on which to base drastic action. He hoped he could trust Henry Davis to be as thorough as his reputation would predict.

3

THE WASHERWOMAN

Margaret Gillis stood quietly, wet to the elbows. Water dripped from her hands to the floor. She didn't move to position them over the washtub, letting the soapy water pool. The washerwoman's mouth hung open.

The window from where she'd received the news was open, too. Close to the ground, it allowed her to adjust the air in her dark home, which sometimes became stuffy with the starches and soaps. Margaret looked through the window. The passer-by who bore the information was gone, but she so clearly remembered Maria stepping through that very window just weeks beforehand. Dishevelled and scared. Margaret looked to an iron box in which sat a few coins, given to her by Maria before she went to Ireland's Eye, the day before.

When the Kirwans came, they were just tourists. The upper classes were typical – the train wasn't cheap – and an address like Merrion Street was nothing unusual. Howth had the joint distinctions of bustling fishing village and seaside retreat. The first sign normally came before summer, when the advertisements of the lodgings began to appear in the daily newspapers – promises of the escape of wilder, untouched life, with the comforts of finer lodgings one might see in the city. Letting the land for farming was common, and by the end of the decade, much was made about the letting of ground for building. Mr Harman stood at the railway station every Monday and Wednesday at 1 o'clock to catch crowds of well-attired speculators as they alighted; all the better to administer his presentation and offer of a 99-year lease. He, too, knew how to wax lyrical in the columns of newspapers: 'For its suitability, variety of scenery, purity of water, Howth stands unrivalled. The climate is highly recommended by the most eminent physicians, some of whom are permanent residents, and many respectable families reside there all year,' declared one of his ads. Margaret could attest to the odd doctor in the vicinity; at least one – Dr William Stokes – was a regular client.

The harbour had started the surge, but the railway opening made Howth more accessible than ever. When it first opened, in 1846, the trains stopped about a mile short of the town, but following a year of building work, the trains would come nearly as far as the water to reach the permanent station, right at the west pier. It opened on 30 May 1847, and that week – the first of June – had been like nothing the townspeople had seen previously. On the first Sunday, reporters lined up to document the crowds pouring out of the station, running like ants to the corners of the peninsula, clogging up the pier, roaming the headlands, cluttering the romantic bays and inlets. The newspapers predicted a new Dalkey or Killiney north of the Liffey. They laid it on thick: 'There the antiquarian finds the cromleach of the Magian priest, the ruined abbey of the pious monks, the feudal residence of the robber lords,' read one particularly effusive report in the *Freeman's Journal*, which continued:

> The naturalist revels in a perfect embarrassment of riches; upwards of five hundred distinct species of indigenous plants have been described in this habitat, some of them extreme rarity elsewhere, whilst the disposition of the geological strata, the curious minerals which exist within its area, the number and variety of marine animals visiting its coasts, offer never ending sources of occupation and amusement to those whose tendencies are that way inclined.

An opulent way to put it, but it had the desired effect. Tourists, in large numbers, came. Swimmers came, too. They always had. But tourism existed before that. The stage coach came each day from Nelson's Tavern, as far as O'Brien's in the village – but those people returned at 7 p.m. each night.

Long-term lodgings were common; year-round, in some cases. But the lingerers only distinguished themselves from the day trippers after some time, when they needed to visit a grocer, or have clothes washed.

One day in July, a young woman who introduced herself as Maria Kirwan had appeared at Gillis's door. For 10 weeks after that, Maria stopped by with clothes to wash. Through those visits and the slow loosening of the binds of unfamiliarity, Gillis learned that Mr Kirwan spent a lot of time in the city. Many nights, it seemed. The washerwoman was in a similar boat. Her husband, Alexander, was a sailor aboard a government vessel. It brought something resembling a steady wage, but the hours were demanding; Monday through Friday, he stayed aboard the boat, only coming home for the weekends. In a town where people came and went, a familiar face was of great value.

The visits at the window kept up, but the washing loads were less and less. It came to the point where Gillis asked her straight – where's the washing? The answer was simple – money was scarce. Mr Kirwan had told Maria that business was down and, in her own words, she couldn't afford to soil as many clothes as formerly. Gillis stopped asking for more washing, and did whatever she was asked to do.

That went on for some time, until the incident – the morning that stuck in Gillis's mind, and which had frozen her to the spot when she heard of Maria's death on Tuesday 7 September 1852. It happened two weeks beforehand. Alexander saw her first, walking in the street in the direction of his own home on a rare weekday on dry land. It was about 5 o'clock on a Thursday, and a bout of illness had rendered the seaman on sick leave. The lady seemed out of sorts.

In the house, Gillis was ironing clothes for Dr Stokes when Maria's voice carried through the two-inch opening at the window.

'Oh, will you let me in?' asked Maria in a hushed voice, throwing frequent glances behind.

'I will, Mrs Kirwan' replied Gillis, abandoning her station and lifting the window. Its ledge was quite low, and Maria was able to fold her body into the house with ease. Maria stood upright and tried to settle her garments, sticking her head once more back into the street, her eyes darting and her breathing heavy. Gillis strode to the window and put her own head out. Seeing nobody on the road, she shut the window firmly and turned to look at Maria, who was pacing about in front of the washtub.

'Your life is in my hands, Mrs Gillis,' said Maria, who stopped her nervous walk to look deeply into Margaret's eyes. She was panicked. The fabric of her clothes hung loosely about her frame, and Gillis realised she had dressed in a hurry. The clothes, too, were nothing like she had seen Maria wear in public. The lady's dress was normally impeccable, but as the washerwoman noted the brown frock, the silk mantilla and a hastily arranged bonnet barely covering her loose hair, she realised the woman was fleeing something. Or someone.

With the visage of propriety and perfection withdrawn, Maria opened up to Gillis. Her fears about Mr Kirwan were more than business being down. She was scared for her life. For two hours, the women talked. Maria told a story of a man leading a woman on a bad life, of altered appearances, of a man terrorising his wife because she did not give him children. At one point, Gillis offered a line of condolence: 'Even the best would have words.'

Maria Kirwan. This image is reproduced courtesy of the National Library of Ireland [PD 2085 TX (16)].

'They are not words,' Maria replied, 'but words and words.'

Maria did not go as far as to confide in any physical abuse to the washerwoman, but she did tell her a fact that stuck with Gillis for weeks afterwards, until she repeated it for investigators. Since moving to Howth, Maria said she had not slept a single night in the rented room with her husband without having the door wide open. At 7 a.m., Maria left the washerwoman's house.

By the time Gillis heard the news of the drowning, most of the village had, too. She had missed the rush to the quay, the talks of screams. But she knew where the body would be.

'I'll not have everyone in the village come in to look at the body, Mrs Gillis,' said Mrs Campbell as she blocked the washerwoman from entering her home a short time later. 'The inquest is about to begin, the coroner will soon arrive.' Gillis, standing at the doorway, was not about to beg. Not yet. She lifted a still-wet hand to her face and turned away from the door. It closed with a thud behind her.

More time passed. She stayed in the street long enough to watch a stream of men enter the house from which she'd been refused. When she was sure the inquest was over and the gentlemen had left, she again knocked the door.

'Mrs Gillis, I have told you,' began Campbell at the door, leaning in for the second part as not to arouse the attention of the people inside. 'Mr Kirwan has said nobody can see the body.'

'Can't you ask his permission?' The washerwoman was determined.

'I will not. Do you expect me to?'

Gillis had run out of patience, and she walked into the hallway, past a shocked Mrs Campbell and under a hail of hushed protestations. As she reached for the door handle to the Kirwans' room, a man's hand made it to the key first. In a heavy clunk, the door was locked. Gillis kept her eyes on the hand. Mr Kirwan said no words as he stared at the washerwoman, who slowly pulled her own hand back from the door handle. For the second time, she left Mrs Campbell's. This time, she went home.

Gillis never saw Maria's body, though she would play a part in the process.

The next day, a daughter of Mrs Campbell arrived to her door. She had a bag of washing – Maria's. A soiled sheet and the clothes Maria wore when she died were covered in blood. Gillis washed a large quantity of blood from where the lady's head lay, and even more at the seat – black in colour, she later swore, and congealed; similar to what would be found after a woman's confinement.

∿

On the morning Margaret Gillis was prevented from seeing Maria's body, Pat Nangle collected his sail at Mrs Campbell's. As it happens, before her marriage to Alexander Gillis in 1835, the washerwoman was, herself, a Nangle. Pat, going by his later accounts, quickly found that he had some washing of his own to do.

Pat's sail, like the items given to the washerwoman, was covered in blood. At least, that's what he would come to claim. Mick would say he saw the sail at his own home – but not until after it had been thoroughly scoured of any damning blood stains, let alone the pint of blood that his cousin said covered the fabric where Maria's head had been.

Pat and Mick, unlike Gillis, were admitted to Mrs Campbell's house when they arrived for the inquest on 7 September 1852. There would be no mention of blood flow that morning – from anyone.

4

THE INQUEST

Some are black, others grey, but all are green by name. They scuttle with an attitude bigger than their small frame at the sands around Howth, their home. Some braver people have been known to eat them in soup, but most curse them. *Carcinus maenas* is native to the waters of Europe's western edges and North Africa, but can be found much further afield. As such, it carries a number of names: European green crab; European shore crab; shore crab; or, most commonly, green crab. Its mud-coloured back is well known by those who live near the shoreline, and more so by those who fish. It's small – no bigger than three and a half inches across at maximum – but it breeds in huge numbers by way of compensation. In shallow waters, invasive green crab can quickly decimate a shellfish population. Forty half-inch clams in a day is easy work for a hungry green crab, but its tastes are not confined to seafood. The corpses of people drowned near the shoreline often wash up with the evidence of its voracious appetite. Cuts, scrapes – often at the eyes. Such was Henry Davis's understanding. In his role as coroner, he'd seen drowning victims up close. Maria Kirwan, at least on the point of the shallow cuts on her eyes and face, appeared no different.

Davis noted a tone of urgency in Sherwood's report that morning. It wouldn't be the coroner's first case of drowning that year. Twenty-odd, at least. The beginning of the sergeant's dispatch was unfortunately typical. A young woman had drowned while bathing – in this instance, during a day trip with her husband to Ireland's Eye. It was within the report's last few sentences that Davis caught wind of suspicion on the part of the Howth constable. 'This case appears strange, as there was a sheet about the woman when found,' read the end of the short report. 'Please come as soon as you can.' The coroner did what he could to prepare himself quickly and leave his Donnycarney residence and take the seven-mile journey to the fishing village north of the bay.

Once past the nearsighted widow, who gave him a close survey at her door on Howth's main street, Davis met Sherwood and Craddock – the sub-inspector in charge. After receiving a quick brief, the coroner found himself lacking both a jury and a medical man. The first would be easily assembled with a pro forma order of his own writing, but the latter proved more difficult to procure on such short notice. No physicians lived in Howth, as far as the coroner knew, and the only one nearby that came to mind had left his Baldoyle residence for the city for the day, according to the policeman who was dispatched to undergo the two-mile journey. Outside of that, the only medical men resided in either Clontarf or Malahide – both out of the question owing to their distance and the time pressure. One prominent physician did have a holiday home in nearby Sutton – but he had, alas, died three years beforehand. A drowning. The best the coroner could do was to procure the services of a medical man who was purportedly staying in the town – a Mr Hamilton.

Maria was laid on the bed in the room next to the room where the proceedings would be held. She was covered in a sheet, and quite clean. Henry Davis was a coroner and solicitor of some renown, but he was not a pathologist – a fact that did little to dent his confidence in his own ability to examine the dead. He pulled back the sheet. The various scratches flecked across the lady's eyes, face and body did little by way of surprising Davis, who, in a moment, attributed them to those blights of the shore with which he was so well acquainted – the green crab. By his own account, he had met with cases in which bodies showed evidence of the pests' work within an hour of being in the water. They went for the eyes first. Davis would go as far as to say that in some cases, the crabs had devoured the entirety of a skull's flesh, leaving it as though it had been recovered from underground. Sherwood, in the report which Davis received that morning, mentioned marks of violence – on the face, specifically. The coroner couldn't agree. And he had experience.

Another man with little pathological experience to speak of was James Alexander Hamilton, the medical man sent for by the police. After being sequestered from the stream of men who entered the home of Mrs Campbell – jurors, reporters, two lost-looking fishermen – the recruit was introduced to Davis and shown to the room where Maria Kirwan lay, to perform his own examination. The body was wrapped and ready for the coffin. He removed her cap first. Her hair was clean, no seaweed. A quick glance told him there were no depressions in her skull. There were cuts on her face and on her eyes in particular – they stood out against her pale flesh. A froth gathered at her mouth. An earring remained attached to one of her damaged earlobes, where it just about clung to a piece of integument. The cuts were curious. Cuts, or perhaps bite marks, he thought. Hamilton rigidly undressed the body and looked at the darkened flank and swollen abdomen. Strictly speaking, he'd never seen a drowned person before.

Hamilton brought his brief review to a close. Members of the jury were then shown the body, before attendees moved next door and began to hear from the witnesses. Patrick Nangle was first to give his information. 'I am a fisherman, living at Howth,' he began, before going into the particulars of the previous day, as far as the men's 8 p.m. landing at Ireland's Eye.

'Mr Kirwan was by himself, I did not ask him anything about Mrs Kirwan. Michael Nangle went off to look with Mr Kirwan for Mrs Kirwan,' recalled Pat. 'I remained a short time behind them and then followed them; Michael Nangle and myself, accompanied by Mr Kirwan, searched for her and continued our search along the east side of Ireland's Eye. When at low water mark, we found her lying on her back with her bathing shift on her, about her waist. A sheet was beside her partly under her.'

Pat's testimony came to an abrupt stop. He was interrupted by a voice, or voices. 'No, Pat, there was no sheet under her when we found her,' spouted Mick, half shouting. 'It was the gentleman who brought the sheet down.' The boatman finished his sentence with a finger pointing at Mr Kirwan, to whom all eyes in the room briefly shot. A murmur of voices grew in the room.

'That man is wrong,' declared Kirwan excitedly, pointing at Pat. 'The other man tells the truth.'

If you'll pardon me, reader, I'd like to note something important here. At this point in the real-life proceedings, Pat Nangle was, in fact, interrupted. That is not reflected in the transcribed depositions from the inquest, nor in any of the following day's newspaper reports – including a lengthy article in the *Freeman's Journal* of 8 September 1852. Pat would later apparently say that it was Kirwan who directed the coroner to stop him from continuing once he reached the topic of the sheet. The coroner later denied that he would take direction from a civilian in this way; Davis, much later, said it was in fact Mick who interrupted Pat, and that Kirwan chimed in, which could explain the mismatch in recollection. This is the version presented here. But, with the pressure the coroner would come to face, it would very much have been in his best interest to circulate this version of events. Back to the story.

The coroner directed his attention at Mick. 'When it comes to your turn to speak, I will have your account of it.' Mick, annoyed, muttered something and folded his arms. Pat, taking a nod from Davis, continued. 'She had also bathing boots on her. The body was on the rocks just out of the water and I believe it was the rock prevented the body being floated out to sea. Her clothes were ten or fifteen yards from where the body was found on a rock about six feet above the water's edge. It was close to where ladies bathe when they go on the island. I brought Mr and Mrs Kirwan over to the island the two days before. Mrs Kirwan wanted to stay as late as 8 o'clock, but we went over rather sooner.' When he'd finished, Davis asked if there was anything he'd like to add. Pat, for reasons that will never be totally clear, said there was not. His information was read back to him and he again confirmed it was the truth.

Mick Nangle then had his turn: 'I was in the boat with Patrick Nangle leaving Mr and Mrs Kirwan on the island as also in the boat returning for them, and with whose account of the matter up to the time of landing for them I agree. When we landed for them and he called up Patrick Nangle and gave him the bag and cloak to take down to the boat, I went up to him and asked him – where is the mistress? He said she went down to bathe a little after the shower (about six o'clock) and said he was in trouble, that he had gone along the strand to look for her and could not find her or hear her voice. He and I went along the strand at the east side, we did not see her. It was not low water then. We continued the search and returned along the same ground at low water mark when we found her wedged in between two rocks partly on her back with her feet in the water. I observed nothing on her but her bathing shift. Mr Kirwan brought down a sheet and a shawl and covered her with them till we brought her to the boat. We searched for the clothes and could not find them when Mr Kirwan went higher up in the rocks and found them. It was about ten o'clock when we found the body; Mr Kirwan appeared in very great trouble when the body was found.'

Kirwan, next, stood on cue. 'I am an artist, residing at No. 11 Upper Merrion Street, Dublin,' began his brief testimony. 'The deceased lady was my wife. I was married to her about nine or ten years. I have been living with Mrs Kirwan in Howth for five or six weeks and I was in the habit of going over to Ireland's Eye as an artist – Mrs Kirwan used to accompany me. She was very fond of bathing, and while I would be sketching, she would amuse herself roaming about or bathing.'

The day before had been a typical day, he said. Mrs Kirwan bathed at the Martello tower when they arrived, but she had to move because another party was due to land nearby. 'She left me in the latter part of the day about six o'clock, to bathe again,' recalled Kirwan. 'She told me she would walk round the hill after bathing, and meet me at the boat. I did not see her alive afterwards, and only found the body as described by the sailors.' The jury asked to see his sketches from that evening, and Kirwan readily produced his book. The men pored over pages, including a sketch of the Dublin Mountains, taken from the Martello tower on Ireland's Eye. The scene was lightly coloured with the hue of an evening's sky.

Arthur Brew of Howth followed Kirwan. Having spent some time on the island himself that day, it was he who spoke with Maria at about 4 o'clock, when his party was returning to the island. She had politely declined – the boatmen, she told him, were coming for 8 p.m. Finally, the medical man stood to state his name and testimony.

'I am a medical student,' began Hamilton. That short statement likely quickly grasped Davis's attention above anyone. 'I have examined the body of the deceased lady,' continued the pupil, who had been six years in the study of medicine. 'There are no marks of violence. A few scratches as if from the rocks. The body presents all the appearance of a person being drowned.'

And so ended the inquest and, as it appeared, the sad case of the drowning at Ireland's Eye. The jury reached a verdict of accidental drowning while bathing. A 'melancholy accident' was the label attached by some news reports – though there was a general failure to note the difference in the Nangles' recollection of where the sheet came from. Mick said, clearly, that Kirwan had brought down the sheet, while Pat said it was underneath her.

Apparently happy to skate over the gritty details of the contradiction was the coroner, Henry Davis, who left the fishing village with his business complete that afternoon. Whether or not there was some bother with the sheet was not of his concern; in his duty, he could only work with the evidence with which he was presented. True, he had not known that Hamilton was a medical student at the time he enlisted his services, but such was the lack of suspicion that a post-mortem exam would hardly have been called for. A superficial exam was surely all that was necessary. But there was one other detail to which he was not privy: the body had been thoroughly washed the night before. All traces of blood were disposed of, leaving only a coin-sized spot on the cap placed on Maria's head. It was just above the ear, from where much more had allegedly flowed just hours beforehand. When the formalities were over, Mrs Campbell bade her many visitors – witnesses, policemen, officials, jurors, reporters and two ageing fishermen bickering over a sheet – farewell. After they'd left, Margaret Gillis knocked at the door.

Sometime after the inquest, Mick was again summoned to Mrs Campbell's house – this time, by William Kirwan himself. The boatman did as he was asked. 'Nangle,' began Kirwan, apparently acknowledging the debt he owed, 'I have no money now, but I'll pay you at eight o'clock tomorrow morning.' The fishermen would indeed receive the payment they were promised – though not without incident. Before Mick left the house after speaking with Kirwan, he went into the room where Maria's body lay.

Kirwan stood at the door as Mick raised a cloth placed over Maria's face, gazing upon the scratches on her cheeks, nose and lips that had been noted by others. Her lips were swelled, and he swore her eyes were black and blue. 'It's a sad thing to see her there,' said the boatman.

5

SCREAMS IN THE HARBOUR

Anne Lacy stayed a day or so in Campbell's. Kirwan stayed only until the body was removed, and then left, but there would be one more unpleasant scene. When the hearse arrived in the village, the Nangles were said to have stopped it in the street, demanding extra payment. The new amount was two pounds, split between the four boatmen; considerably more than the three shillings initially agreed for the trip. When the issue was settled, the Kirwans finally departed Howth, gone as quick as they'd come, the excitement reduced to a simmer of chat and rumour.

That's where Sherwood found himself dwelling, in a hot pot of talk. There was little he could do about his suspicion, bar his attempts to separate the credible from the eager to impress, but his suspicion had its foundation. The signs were there from the night the body came ashore at the pier. And it wasn't the old cleric's supposed rantings; it was the wet clothes. The demeanour. A bathing sheet apparently being found beneath Maria was suspicious enough for Sherwood to mention it in his letter alerting the coroner. There was nothing to be said for hearsay, but then came stories of bawls and screeches heard from the island on the night of Maria's death that at least gave him remit to ask questions.

As Sherwood spoke with villagers, the action of talking itself multiplied the reports he received. Exact words, some heard. Others apparently reported the screams so loud as to be heard from impossible points on Howth's huge head. One story, the testimony of John Barrett, had only reached him during a follow-up conversation. Barrett's wasn't the only story about screams on the wind, though; there were five in total – five that merited official recording, at least.

⌁

Thomas Larkin knew the bay well. The sky, even better. It was the time between day and dusk, and the fisherman didn't need a watch to tell him to make for the harbour. The water was calm. No sea to speak of. The wind, light, was about west or north west. The fisherman made easy work, on his own, of rounding Ireland's Eye at the west, just near the Martello tower. Lightly, he sat atop the companion head, one hand on the hooker's tiller. Eyes on the harbour and the lighthouse, he checked back over his shoulder again to glimpse the last cut of sky beneath the clouds. Howth's harbour was generally quieter than it had been in decades past; constructed at great expense from 1807, it was originally the landing point for the King's mail packet boats, beginning in 1818.

It was, at the time, considered the most direct point of communication between England and Ireland. More than a thousand men worked on the harbour's construction every day at the peak of building activity. Challenges quickly arose. One mail ship, during the harbour's opening year, ran aground at Ireland's Eye. Another, carrying passengers, hit the lighthouse in fog. The channels between the island and Howth required care to be navigated, and were not helped by the constant build-up of sand at the harbour's mouth, which prevented vessels of a deeper draught from entering. This was an oversight. The currents were not properly surveyed and, unhelpfully, the sand built up at the same rate it was removed. The packet steamers outgrew Howth, and the Crown's mail deliveries moved to Kingstown, on the south side of the bay, in the 1830s. Howth, however, remained a haven for lighter vessels and fishing boats. Pleasure yachts, too. The size made it more than suitable for Larkin's 36-ton hooker on the night of 6 September 1852. Larkin spotted a handful of yawls as he stared through the jaws of the pier. Shortly, he'd have to rouse the crew to help.

A human screech leapt jaggedly from the calmness. Larkin's head swivelled left, back towards the strand on the island. His eyes, dry from tiredness but alert, darted from side to side, covering the beach in the dimming light, but it was too far, and too late, to see anything. Larkin ran to the lee-side helm and held his breath. He listened. The noise – definitely from the island and not the lighthouse or quay wall – was an odd one. Man? Woman? He couldn't be certain. He pulled back his hand to rap on the freezing hardwood for the men – there were seven and a boy below deck – but caught himself. Rap and say what? There's someone on the island? He couldn't be sure. Would he turn the vessel round at this hour to investigate a shout on Ireland's Eye, depriving the men of rest? They were setting out again at four o'clock the following morning, more than an hour before sunrise.

Larkin collected himself. A look told him he was about 20 perches from the Martello tower, and still needed a few minutes of concentration to get him and the crew to the harbour. He resumed his position. The second scream came a short time later. Less volume than before. A third howl. Lower again. So low it might not have been heard. Larkin banged frigid knuckles hard against the cabin door and out climbed a stream of fishermen. 'Take in the sails,' Larkin said, his eyes still facing the island as the hooker came into the harbour. The story he told – of mysterious screams from the darkened island – only elicited jokes from his crewmates. 'It must have been the *fear dubh*,' said one, evoking a local legend featuring a sort of spectre inhabiting the island, catching those who dared trespass. The men finished their work and bid him goodnight until the morning. It was Larkin's habit to stay on the boat Monday to Friday, sleeping atop the sway of the harbour. The next morning, the crew arrived to find Larkin up ahead of them. It was 4 a.m., as planned, but the sun would not be fully up for another hour and a half. They had a busy day ahead; September was the tail end of herring season. Of the hundreds of boats in Howth Harbour in September, a large proportion would be seeking the same bounty. The weather was to take a turn, but that day, conditions were fine, and Larkin passed by Ireland's Eye via the same passage without hesitation.

News at the pier, however, brought back the previous night's events. Arriving, as they had done the night before, at about 8 o'clock, the men had missed the bulk of one of the most terrible dramas Howth had ever seen. Larkin, of course, recounted his story about the screams to those who stood listening. The days passed and Larkin kept his routine. Fish in the bay, sleep in the boat. On Saturday, he ventured into Howth town, as far as the churchyard, where those congregated spoke of little else besides the drowning. Howth is an old place, filled with fairies and spirits, if the locals are to be believed. The shadows of the dead call from every ancient lane, each crag with a face. Before long, Mrs Kirwan had her own ghost story.

Larkin, with an interested audience, relayed his own story that, depending on who you believe, multiplied and morphed, mixing with the excitement and producing any number of fantastical versions. And perhaps it's true, that some were eager to be part of an event. Sergeant Sherwood, having caught wind of Larkin's story the day before the chattering at the churchyard, obviously thought there was something to it, and he paid the fisherman a visit that same Saturday.

———

Alicia Abernethy was nervous. Thomas was still a boy, but a keen and skilled sailor. Still, the light was going, and he'd yet to return home. There was a gang of them who spent any well-stretched evening they could at sea. But the setting sun and the fact she could no longer spot his yawl out around Ireland's Eye was causing Abernethy some bother. The labourer's wife went next door, as she did nightly, to ask the time. Five past seven.

Abernethy returned to her small house and walked into the garden, which was east of the pier, just yards from the strand where the ladies bathed. She leaned on the short wall. The sun was down, but some light remained, flecked on the rocks and the whiter parts of the breaking waves. There she had whiled away many evenings and watched the women swim, sheltered from the main thoroughfare of the town and the jangling business of the boats in the harbour.

That's why she could so easily recall the beautiful woman who appeared over the summer. The young lady wore a dark bathing cap, and appeared to get on well with the other women below. In the water, nobody came close. The lady's swimming was incredible. One evening in July, Abernethy herself saw the woman swim to the stake, a distance of some 30 or 40 perches, in high wind.

At her garden wall, Abernethy waited. It was between lights, and the silhouette of the island provided a reference by which she could try to identify the long sail of her son's boat. It was then, with her eye trained on the south-eastern part of the island, that she heard the first screech. It was an awful scream. Someone in pain – undoubtedly a woman. It came, she was sure, from the island. Two minutes later, another. Then another again, weaker each time. It was not until the following morning that Alicia was informed that she, and her husband, and her children, had missed the dreadful procession of the boatmen and the body on the pier. It was the woman – the swimmer – drowned. The Long Hole, where Maria was found and where Abernethy had never heard of a woman swimming before, was directly opposite. It was framed, perfectly, from within the only window out of which she cared to look. Abernethy thought maybe she would go to the sergeant. Or would she be one of a hundred gossipers and whisperers lining up to inject themselves into the lore of the old place? The decision was made for her: crossing her door, likely on his way to the inquest, was Sherwood, the sergeant.

<hr />

Catherine Flood was conscious of the time. The sun had set, it was getting dark and she'd still have to walk home after finishing her day's work at Mrs Singleton's. It wasn't far. Probably half a mile. Mrs Singleton lived at the railway station, and Flood near the ladies' bathing place. The station was west of the harbour and her house to the east. It was around 7 o'clock. The light would soon be gone.

The ladies living near that swimming spot would recognise a returning face. Flood and her neighbour of about 20 perches – Alicia Abernethy – knew most of them by sight. One, in particular, stood out that summer. Maria Kirwan, who came with her husband in June, was the most venturesome swimmer Flood had seen at that spot in more than 11 years living on its doorstep. The waves would be high, and it did not matter. When other ladies left the sea, she stayed in.

But Flood was not thinking about Mrs Kirwan's swimming abilities when she opened the hall door of Mrs Singleton's on 6 September 1852. That would come later. Instead, she was preparing to scrub the hall – and check how dark it was. A roar from the direction of Ireland's Eye caused her to stop. She stood quietly, scanning around the harbour. A short while later, she heard another yell. Then, she put her head down, and carried out the remainder of her work.

Flood returned home at 8 o'clock that night and didn't hear about the drowning until she arrived back at Mrs Singleton's to do it all again the following morning. The shouts then made sense, and Flood recounted what she'd heard. Abernethy, she would find out, had heard it, too.

Hugh Campbell was a fish driver. That wasn't all he was, and he'd turn his hand to many odd jobs before his time was out, but on the evening of 6 September 1852, he was in charge of a car and horse, waiting to be loaded with fish. The light was fast going and his car was still empty, so he kept doing what he usually did in those circumstances, and waited for the last of the boats to come in. It wasn't a bad night for it. Quiet, no swell, a light breeze – if even that. As he stood at the harbour wall, near the street opposite the lighthouse, he heard a shout that seemed to come from the island.

A man from the coast guard was walking behind Campbell; the fish driver figured that some poor devil had probably fallen asleep and missed his boat. Campbell had heard calls like that before. And that's how Campbell recalled, at first, what he'd heard – 'a call'. Though in later renditions of the story, there were more than one.

Campbell walked across the road to his house, with his back to the quay wall. As he reached for his door, another shout caught his attention. To his ear the bawl wasn't panicked, and he couldn't tell if it was a man or a woman. A slow, feeble sort of shout – maybe for assistance. He walked back to the quay wall and waited again, ear to the island. From what he'd heard, and what he could see of the sparsely populated piers, it surely came from Ireland's Eye, east of the lighthouse from where he stood. The broad patch? The Long Hole? Was that a third cry? This time, weaker – if it had happened at all. Like someone waking from a sleep.

The few boats that were still moving in the harbour were coming to rest, bar one. Pat and Mick Nangle, accompanied by two other men, began to row against the evening traffic flow and departed the harbour. Campbell watched their boat make tiny wavelets in the dead-calm water. Hours later, at midnight, he would hear the terrible news, but said nothing about what he heard. Perhaps he would never have spoken about those shouts. But when the police came knocking a few days later, he had no real choice.

6

BEHIND CLOSED DOORS

Death seemed to follow Margaret Campbell. As a sextoness, she was required to be well acquainted with it. Chapel and graveyard upkeep were in her duties by title. Mrs Campbell was also a mother and a widow. Another of her occupations, that of landlady, gave her manageable income owing to the attractiveness of Howth to people from the city seeking refuge and amusement. Mrs Campbell lived with three of her children. Financial strains, according to some sources, apparently meant weekly payment for lodgings was requested and, in the case of the Kirwans, readily accepted when they'd arrived on her doorstep one bright June morning. They took the room to the front of the house, opposite the kitchen. In idle chat with Mrs Kirwan, the lady had mentioned that their city house was being painted, and that they may stop until November. Mrs Campbell wasn't complaining about that.

In time, Mrs Kirwan endeared herself to the locality through her rambles and daring feats in the water. More than once, Mrs Campbell had heard Maria's mother ask her to take care during those adventurous swims. Maria's mother, Mrs Crowe, came to Howth sometimes. Good, too, because otherwise Maria was often alone in her room. The young woman could walk around the back of the headland to the Baily Lighthouse at the south of Howth, facing Kingstown, or sometimes more directly over rocks and between thick ferns around the Ben. On longer ambles, a walker could go as far as Red Rock, and face Dublin across the bay, or skirt nearer the castle grounds, which gave the very best views of the tombolo at Sutton and Baldoyle, as far as you'd like over

Dublin to the west, all the way to Wicklow to the south and, on the clearest days, you'd even catch the purple peaks of the Mourne Mountains to the north.

William had business in Dublin and went most days by train. It seemed he slept away from Howth for half the week. Mrs Campbell didn't think much of that – he had work in the city. On the days he came back to Howth, he came by the 5 o'clock train, other days the 6 o'clock train. The odd time, by the last train. Another routine Mrs Campbell became regrettably acquainted with was the couple's fighting. In the weeks she'd lived with the Kirwans, she'd seen them go word for word. Other times, she heard William berate Maria. They could go a whole day without conversing, save for the necessary transactions involved in the asking of some essential question.

One evening in July, it started again, but it seemed different. More turbulent. As she sat in her room listening to the uneven grumble and booming of raised voices, there came a rap at the door. She was thankful for the distraction, and the company. 'Is he in?' Anne Hannah's eyes flitted behind Mrs Campbell as she stood in the doorway. She was another who had done some washing for Maria – the first, in fact. By virtue of that arrangement, Hannah probably saw Mrs Kirwan three times a week. Hannah lived two doors down and, like many Howth women, her husband worked on a merchant vessel, leaving her in the company of her mother most days. She would frequently pop in to talk.

Hannah also had dealings with William. Less pleasant ones. Mrs Campbell was well acquainted with the story: Mr Kirwan had passed Hannah's on his way home to Mrs Campbell's one evening, and Hannah had the door open, looking out with the dog at the step. The dog barked at Mr Kirwan, who kicked up something of a fuss, at the peak of which, Hannah was threatened with a summons unless she got rid of the dog. It seemed so cruel a threat as to be empty, but Mr Kirwan appeared to be a number of things in that moment, and litigious was one of them. They got rid of the dog.

'He is, come in.' Mrs Campbell stood out of the way to let her neighbour in. 'Oh, Anne – I think he's beating her.'

Hannah responded in disbelief, but the women's conversation was cut short. The same angry rumble arose from the Kirwans' room. As the two women sat in silence listening to the noise, they deciphered, a couple of times, a singular phrase: 'I'll end you.' Kirwan proceeded to call his wife a strumpet, among a string of abuse. A loud rattle and what sounded like a chair being thrown across the room caused Mrs Campbell to jump up and run to the door, but there was little she could have done. It was locked from the inside. The women listened intently, and were later able to recall some other shards of the abuse; he accused her of robbing the shirt off his back. She asked, in return, that he let her alone. The noises did eventually die down, and Hannah went home. The couple later left the house but appeared to walk separately, because Mr Kirwan returned home 30 minutes before Mrs Kirwan.

The house was small. Kirwan, it seems, felt it appropriate to address Mrs Campbell on his return. Something about an offer in Australia. Something about how Maria should live her life better. Something about it being a pity – because she'd seemed like such a proper, sober woman. Mrs Campbell just listened. There was no other noise that night. In the morning, Mrs Kirwan was complaining about her thighs, which she said were blackened. The incident remained in Mrs Campbell's memory for the apparent cruelty underlying the ominous threats heard through the door. Yet the widow declined to include the story when she was first asked about the couple in the weeks after Maria's death.

***

Catherine Kelly recognised her face, but couldn't place her at first. The rain was so dense, it was a wonder she'd made out any features at all. Then she had it: the Marlborough Street Chapel. It had been four or five years, but Kelly remembered Maria's face – they had known each other well enough for a salute as they crossed paths on the way in or out of the church, but not enough to speak in any meaningful way.

The rain was bad that day, for the summer months. It came suddenly, as it often did, and Kelly beckoned Maria into her house. The more formal introductions began, and the chat drifted easily. Maria, Kelly ascertained, was some way away from Campbell's – about a mile. Mr Wall, the butcher, had been her destination. Kelly lived on the south side, or 'the back', of the hill. That side of the cliffs was punctuated by the Baily Lighthouse, which was nice to look at, but was widely viewed to be of questionable utility. Locals would have remembered 1846 when a packet steamer sat itself up violently on the rocks below. Everyone agreed the Baily needed a fog bell.

When the conversation finished and the rain stopped, the lady left. At that point, she had been living in the town three weeks, without Kelly's noticing. And so it continued that their paths crossed infrequently, but Kelly would not soon forget the next time Maria came to her. It was five or six weeks before the news of her death rattled the village that she once again spotted the lady walking near her house. This time, Kelly stopped her arm as it shot to give a wave; the lady was fretted. Nervous. And as the visitor approached, Kelly could see she walked with a limp.

The conversation that day was different from their first. Upon seeing Kelly's face, Maria burst into tears. Inside the house, Kelly quickly produced a stool and Maria told her what she already knew. A story about doors being locked and windows shut fast. A story about brutality and a savage beating with a walking stick. Maria asked if Kelly had anything to rub on her wounds, to ease them. Upon lifting her clothes and exposing her blackened thighs, Kelly retrieved a bottle of hartshorn and oil and told her to keep the bottle.

In the wild, a couple of days later, Kelly encountered Maria briefly again. The update was fleeting and worrying, yet better; Kirwan was still treating her badly, but perhaps not as poorly as previously. Kelly saw Maria Kirwan one other time after that. The setting was Kelly's house. Maria, this time, was eager to take action. Mr Kirwan had dealt her more heavy blows, and she was ready to tell someone. Then she mentioned Alderman Egan, and asked if Kelly knew him. And of course she, like anyone who lived in Howth, knew about Cornelius Egan. A merchant by trade who later became an Alderman of the Dublin Corporation, he would have been a neighbour in the geographical sense of the word, but Earlscliffe – a large house facing the sea on the south side of the head and just one of the properties the Alderman owned in those years – was likely not the type of place you could simply approach and rap the door. No, Kelly put a stop to that plan. There would be no help at the Alderman's door. 'I advised her to go home and to tell the sergeant of police about it,' Kelly later recalled, 'but at the same time I advised her not to tell anyone till she told the sergeant.'

That day, Kelly walked most of the way back to Maria's lodgings. Somewhere on the road, Maria agreed Kelly's way was best. She would go to the sergeant. Then she told Kelly a part of the story she had only previously heard rumblings about: secret lives, impossible feats of deception. And yet more cruelty. In Kelly's words, 'She had said to her husband if he would give her a little way of living by the week or year she would give up the name of Kirwan, and never go near him or look at his side of the street, that Kirwan said no he would not give her anything the old barren brute, what use would be giving away to the like of you. I'd see you damned and very well hanged fast. I advised her to bear it patiently.'

Maria never went to the sergeant. Three weeks later, her body was on John Barrett's dray.

7

ONE MONTH LATER

6 October 1852

George William Hatchell leaned his head out of the car and looked up. The sky, grey, was the threatening type. Nervously, he pulled his gaze from the heavens and returned it to his newspaper: 'The weather has become remarkably wet and cold. Yesterday it rained the entire day; the consequences have been the stoppage of outdoor work, and, we fear, will seriously interfere with Ballinasloe fair.' The doctor did not share the *Freeman's Journal's* concern for the Ballinasloe fair. It was his own work that troubled him.

'Tell me again,' John Tighe began, himself immersed in a bundle of notes on his lap, swaying gently to the rhythm of the car. 'When was the deceased interred, Dr Hatchell?'

The doctor didn't need to check his books. 'More than three weeks ago, Dr Tighe.' The two sat in silence, the noise of wheel crunching earth filling the small space between them.

Hatchell and Tighe were of the well-respected doctor subdivision of Dublin's gentleman class, the former the surgeon to the household of the Lord Lieutenant and the constabulary, and the latter of Steeven's Hospital and also registrar and resident apothecary at the Protestant Hospital and Adelaide Institution. Hatchell would have a glittering career, becoming inspector general of lunatic asylums and serving many Lord Lieutenants; but on the morning of 6 October 1852, decades before his death at his home – like Kirwan's, on Upper Merrion Street – he was a pathologist, and Tighe his assistant. Their task for the day was an unpleasant one. A post-mortem done so late was sure to yield patchy results, at best. Exhumation was an entirely different prospect.

'If I may,' Tighe began again, his eyebrows furrowed as he ran through his notes. 'What's this about a sword cane?'

'I'm not entirely sure,' Hatchell answered, truthfully. He had followed the case in the newspapers closely, but the apparent use of such a secret weapon had not yet been entered into the public realm. 'It appears that came from one of the boatmen who ferried the pair to the island,' he said, glancing at his own notes.

Hatchell and Tighe were greeted by a small party of police and two gravediggers as they stepped off the car and faced the main entrance of Glasnevin Cemetery. The men walked to the burial site, sometimes tramping over uneven, sodden turf. The gravediggers at the plot confirmed the wetness with their appearance. Hatchell peered into the disturbed grave, seeing the coffin lid and a good deal of water surrounding it – two to three feet, he guessed.

The men raised the coffin. Water poured from its joints and out from beneath its lid when it was pried open at the graveside, overwhelming the grass and creating small pools within the darkened mounds of excavated soil. The water had, evidently, penetrated the protective shell. A second coffin, sitting within the first, was removed, and opened. Any hopes that the inner guard had kept the body from the water were quickly dashed. Maria's clothes, wet, were removed. The body, Hatchell noted, was quite decomposed. The maceration of the skin further complicated matters. The doctor got to work, making notes as he went, with Mr Tighe assisting.

'I opened the head,' the doctor later reported, continuing, 'there was no fracture. The brain was in a semi-fluid state which rendered it impossible to trace whether any disease existed in it or not. The upper lip appeared as if swelled. It might have been produced by the state the body was then in.

'The body was then opened. After having examined whether any dislocation or fracture of the neck existed which did not appear; on opening the body found the lungs collapsed with the minute vessels gorged with blood. The internal portions of the body were comparatively free from decomposition. The heart was in appearance healthy, fluid, perfectly empty, both at the right and left side. The stomach was contracted and empty. The small and large intestines were greatly distended with air or gas.

'The uterus was small and contracted, having a small ulcer in it. The body had no appearance whatever of having had ulcers or sores on it. On the contrary, I would say from the appearances it was the body of a fine healthy woman.'

With the day completed, the surgeons were none the wiser. 'The appearance of the lungs and heart exhibited those appearances which are quite compatible with death produced by drowning or strangulation,' said the doctor, in a statement sworn on 15 October. What was clear was that the state of congestion in the body led the doctor to believe that Maria had asphyxiated; whether by accident or at the hands of a murderer, he was too unsure to say, though there were no apparent marks of violence. Deputy Inspector General of the police, Major Henry Brownrigg, who was overseeing the investigation, had requested Hatchell's attendance at Ireland's Eye. As the doctor left Glasnevin to return to the city on 6 October, he thought perhaps it was time he took him up on the offer.

Down the line, Hatchell would make more than one statement regarding the post-mortem examination, and in future accounts, some further details would be provided. But we will come to those. He concluded the first statement as written above – that the cause of death could not be definitively proven, but it was either by drowning or strangulation. In another statement included in the prosecution brief, the following paragraph appears:

From the state the body was in I found it impossible to come to any positive conclusion on the subject of the cause of death. Had I opened the body immediately after death and found the stomach and lungs in the same state as I found them on my examination I would have been inclined to think that the woman's death had been produced by strangulation or by having been forcibly immersed in water – but from the length of time which had elapsed from the time of death until I saw the body, the appearances might have so changed as to render it hazardous to form any opinion on the subject.

———～～———

On Merrion Street Upper, PC James Malone lay in wait. It was 7 October – the day after the post-mortem examination on Maria Kirwan's remains. The trap was set: a constable named Cleary stood in full uniform at the front of the house, visible from the target's front window. He knew what the target looked like; should he use his front door, the constable would have an easy job of it. Malone, meanwhile, was positioned at the rear of the opulent home, dressed in plain clothes, and accompanied by another officer in uniform. Both were out of sight from the house's inhabitants. It was about 6 a.m., and the operation to arrest William Kirwan for the suspected murder of his wife was under way.

It took a while, but at 7.30 a.m., Kirwan came out through the coach house and into Malone's path.

'Is your name Kirwan?' asked the policeman.

'What do you want to know for?' replied the man in the lane, not realising he was speaking with a constable. When Malone revealed his profession, he repeated the question: was he Mr Kirwan?

'I am one of them,' said the man.

'Are you the Mr Kirwan that buried the late Mrs Kirwan?' pressed the constable.

Kirwan confirmed that he was, and Malone made him his prisoner. It's reasonable to suggest that Sherwood felt satisfaction at the news, despite regrets bound in the delay in examining the body, and also the exercise in tongue-biting he endured while he watched Kirwan's soaked clothes drip on the floor at Margaret Campbell's house. Sherwood's time had been taken up talking to locals, and visiting the Eye with surveyors and policemen in Pat and Mick Nangle's boat. One of those visits yielded a clue: Sherwood spotted it – Mrs Kirwan's bathing cap, sitting at the high-water mark, crumpled and barely visible, and with its two strings pulled into a hard knot. Mrs Campbell had identified it when they reached the harbour once again. A good find.

After Kirwan's arrest, Sherwood wondered what he might find at Merrion Street. All was quiet when he arrived with his companion, Mortimer Redmond, who was thankfully just as silent. The action on that affluent thoroughfare, what little of it there had been in the end, was over by then. Sherwood checked his watch – not yet noon. The next-door neighbour let the policemen through to the back yard, through which they could access Kirwan's over the wall. The back door was open. The men proceeded quietly into the home and peered into rooms as they went. This went on for two floors, until they reached the top of the second flight. On the landing, they were surprised to encounter a woman.

'Who are you?' Sherwood tried not to alarm her as he asked the only question he could. The answer, he could never have expected.

'Mrs Kirwan,' replied the woman.

Sherwood walked past the woman and into a bedroom, which contained the only bed in the house. In the large bed, far too small for it, was a child, no more than a couple of years old, quite still. Boy or girl, Sherwood couldn't quite tell. A boy of about ten stood at the bedside. Elsewhere, Sherwood found a table. Upon it, tea and bread and butter. A teapot sat, still warm, beside the fire. It didn't take a sergeant of police to decipher that they had interrupted breakfast. The children, the woman said, were Mr Kirwan's.

PART 2

8

THE STORY SO FAR

That's the story, insofar as there is one version of the 'story'. After Maria's death, an enquiry took place in September, her body was exhumed a month after death and just under four weeks following the burial, after which Kirwan was arrested and another enquiry took place. Kirwan was then sent forward for trial. Much of the story you've read so far, and some of what you will read, is pieced together from witness statements, not then made public, contained in a large file comprising a brief on behalf of the Crown, among other documents.

The genesis of real suspicion, Kirwan's wet legs notwithstanding, appears to have occurred very shortly after the inquest on 7 September. The morning after, the first reports hit the papers. The next day again, Henry Davis, the coroner, had a visitor. He later said that the caller had reason to believe that Kirwan murdered his wife – 'grounded not on anything that occurred on Ireland's Eye, not on anything that occurred at Howth, but on acts of Kirwan's, alleged to have been committed by him years before'.

Davis told the sub-inspector about the new information that evening. On 15 September, at Howth, depositions were taken before Norbury Furnace. Also in attendance were Cornelius Egan, the aforementioned Alderman, and the Earl of Howth. The enquiry was overseen by Major Brownrigg. On that day, Margaret Campbell was questioned. The story you've read about the trouble between Mr and Mrs Kirwan would come from information she later swore, because on the first day, she seemed to consider it unworthy of mention. In fact, she said 'no couple could have lived more united'.

Also on that date, Catherine Kelly was interviewed. Kelly told police about the apparent beating and recounted a similar story when she was again interviewed in October, the amalgam of which you've already heard in the last section. At this point, Pat and Mick had given their testimony at the inquest, but would again be called upon. The other people interviewed on the 15th were Thomas Larkin and Hugh Campbell, who said they heard the screams. Police had spoken with others by this point, as evidenced by comments by Sherwood at later dates, but in terms of sworn testimony, that's what investigators had.

Why, then, the exhumation in early October? There was one other statement, sworn on 21 September, this time in front of Cornelius Egan. Keeping in mind that the person who came before Henry Davis the day after the inquest, bearing stories of an evil man's hidden past, was never identified – perhaps the following would tend to dispel that mystery. It was a Merrion Street neighbour who came forward after reading about the 'drowning' in the newspapers.

Below is the full record of the statement:

Police district of Dublin Metropolis, to wit – The information of Maria Byrne of No. 1 Lower Merrion Street in said district, taken before me Cornelius Egan one of the Magistrates of the county of Dublin. Informant being duly sworn upon oath deposeth and saith:

Saith that informant was intimately acquainted with a lady named Sarah Maria L. Kirwan, wife of William Kirwan, artist of No. 11 Upper Merrion Street in the city of Dublin and about six years ago the said Mrs Kirwan told informant that she had lived a very unnatural life with her husband by his not stopping at home at night and she had good reason to believe he had a family elsewhere and sometime after she told informant that she had also good reason to believe that her said husband put poison in broth that had been prepared for her use for the purpose of taking away her life and when she upbraided him with the offence he threw it out and informed her that it was only alum he put into it and discharged the servant girl for apprising her mistress of the transaction and in some time after she told informant that her husband directed her to take a quantity of tincture of henbane. She consented and took all that was in the house.

He then desired her to send out for more that she might take half a pint of it without doing her any injury. She accordingly sent the servant girl for some to a shop in Sackville Street. The servant having informed the shopman of the quantity her mistress had previously taken who informed the servant that her mistress had taken a sufficient quantity to kill her or drive her mad and the said shopman was about to give the servant in charge to the police when she ran away.

The said Mrs Kirwan remained in a dangerous state for a period of six weeks from the effects of the said tincture of henbane, during which time she was attended by Doctor Rynd and when supposed to be dying and visited by the Rev. Mr Mulhall of Westland Row Chapel, during which time informant also visited her and was told by the said Mrs Kirwan that she would leave her death on her husband whose intention she had no doubt was to poison her. Informant saw at the same time in the house Mrs Kirwan's mother, Mrs Crowe, who now resides at No. 88 Lower Gardiner Street, who told information that she would have her son-in-law tried for his life – if her daughter would die.

She then had a conversation with Sergeant McCarty of the B Division of police on the subject and also to Doctor Quin of Westland Row Chapel and also to Mr Nicholls of No. 1 Lower Merrion Street. Informant ascertained that the said Mr and Mrs Kirwan had left their residence No. 11 Upper Merrion Street about five weeks ago. Informant immediately suspected that said Mr Kirwan had taken his wife to some strange place to destroy her and she made enquiry from a porter in the Fitzwilliam Estate Office as to where the parties had gone to and to said porter informant spoke concerning her suspicions and also to Mr Nicholls aforesaid, and on the 8th instant Mr Nicholls drew informant's attention to a paragraph in the newspaper detailing the death and inquest on Mrs Kirwan at or near Howth, and informant has no doubt on her mind that the said Mrs Kirwan was wilfully drowned by her husband who informant has strong reason to believe made away with other members of his family under very suspicious and mysterious circumstances.

The information was signed at the bottom by Egan and Maria Byrne. An explosive statement, and not the first time the 'secret family' was mentioned; Catherine Kelly had reported Maria saying something similar: 'Informant also states that deceased told her that her husband said he had sent Anne Kenny and her seven children to Australia and now they would lead a happy life.' Another part of Catherine's first statement echoed Byrne's closely: 'The deceased told her that about five years back she was sick when she was ordered stewed oysters but that her servant girl advised her not to eat them as she, the servant, was afraid the master had put something into them.'

Byrne's statement introduces the medication henbane, which goes by many names. The source plant's true name – *Hyoscyamus niger* – is less memorable than its other monikers, like 'stinking nightshade' or 'black henbane', nor does it immediately conjure its most celebrated use. It is supposed to be the poison of choice of Hamlet's uncle Claudius, but it's older than Shakespeare; it sat atop the heads of the dead of Hades on the banks of the Styx. Painkilling, sleep – it did it all. But, most importantly for this part of the story, it is highly toxic. In smaller doses, its leaves, seeds and liquids can produce a sort of drunken stupor. Beyond that, hallucinations. Beyond that, death.

On 6 October, 31 days after Maria's death, and just under four weeks after burial, her remains were taken out of the ground at Glasnevin and examined. The next day, Mr Kirwan was arrested, as you've read. Newspaper reports in the early days of the investigation reveal much about the narrative – and how attitudes undoubtedly shifted as stories filtered through to the public. The *Liverpool Mercury* reported Maria's death on 10 September in a 23-word report: 'Mrs Maria Kirwan, wife of Mr William Kirwan, an artist, was accidentally drowned while bathing in the sea at Ireland's Eye, on Monday.' The simplicity of the story would change dramatically. You could argue, by then, that it already had.

The capacity for the development of potential rumours connected with the case was detected early. In fact, the government enquiry set up initially at the police station in Howth on 5 October (subsequently resumed on the 8th and 15th) – commenced by Major Brownrigg – was held in private. Brownrigg 'expressed strong dissatisfaction at the ex parte statements on the subject that had already got abroad in the Dublin papers,' according to quotes reported in many newspapers following the case at the time. After the last day of those proceedings, Kirwan was committed to trial at the next commission.

The *Freeman's Journal* was notably disturbed by the privacy surrounding the enquiry. In a leader in the days following Kirwan's committal for trial – the thrust of which was published in many other papers in Ireland and England – was pointed in that regard:

> There may be many cogent reasons shown for carrying on an investigation privately through even several adjournments, but we can admit none for the conclusion of a secret examination and the committal of a prisoner for trial without publication of the grounds on which he has been committed. Were such a course tolerated by the public, or slurred over by the press, it would lead us back to the dark ages of the Star Chamber, the black dungeon, and the torturer.

In the *Freeman's Journal* of 22 October, Charles Fitzgerald – identifying himself as an agent for Mr Kirwan – had the following published in the letters section:

> In consequence of the evidence taken by Major Brownrigg on the investigation relative to the above lamentable event, being private, and, of course, not published, reports most injurious to Mr Kirwan have been put into circulation and which, from the medical evidence given on the said investigation, as well as on the inquest, are completely negatived; I would,

therefore (through your columns), request of the public to suspend their judgement on the matter until after the trial, which is to take place at the next Commission on the 25th instant, when I have no doubt of his being fully and honourably acquitted.

There are some examples of prejudgement of the case within the newspapers at the time – enough to warrant caution on the part of officials, at least. One such report, in the *Newcastle Courant* of Friday 22 October 1852 – which, incidentally, also ran the *Freeman's Journal*'s comments on the debacle – recapped and overstated the progress of the case as follows: '[S] uspicion afterwards fell upon her husband, who married a second time within a few days of her death; and the body being exhumed, there was a medical examination, which ended, it is said, in the discovery that the deceased had been strangled. Mr Kirwan was then arrested.'

The *Cornish Telegraph*, *Dublin Evening Packet and Correspondent*, *Manchester Times*, *London Evening Standard* and *Stirling Observer* – to name a few – also repeated the claims that the post-mortem unequivocally found that Maria had been strangled and that Kirwan had married a concubine of sorts a day or two later. Wrapped up in much of the reportage, too, was the unmistakable hue of titillation on the point of the class of people involved in the mystery. Reports were quick to mention that Kirwan was wealthy – a man of prominence and 'considerable' means. The scandal was all the more readable owing to its emergence from behind the doors of a Merrion Street 'fine mansion', as one early report characterised the house.

Some papers came down harder on one side than others did. Headlines and other pieces of print-layout information – the 'furniture' – were not then quite as developed as on-page communicators as they are now, yet it is curious to note that many of the headlines atop early reports in British and Irish newspapers concerning the Kirwan case told their own stories. Below is a quick selection of five headlines around the time of the conclusion of the government investigation.

- The Late Case of Drowning at Ireland's Eye (*Dublin Evening Packet and Correspondent*, 12 October)
- Mysterious Death of a Lady at Ireland's Eye (*Morning Chronicle*, 14 October)
- Murder of a Wife by Her Husband (*Bradford Observer*, 14 October)
- The Tale of Mystery (*Saint James's Chronicle*, 19 October)
- The Case of Drowning at Ireland's Eye (*The Advocate – Irish Industrial Journal*, 20 October)

Even when there was no sworn information being made public between 12 and 20 October, the event was being interpreted as everything from a simple drowning, to a mystery death, to a murder. Inconsistency and speculation grew in the vacuum caused by Brownrigg's caution on the matter. Kirwan also had the misfortune of being shot into the public eye at the same time as another quite gruesome murder case. Patrick and Margaret Smith – brother and sister, both elderly – were robbed and brutally murdered, the weapon being the bar that held closed the door of their small cabin near Swords, Co. Dublin. A 'sanguinary' crime by the estimation of the *Cork Examiner*, which ran the two stories in tandem. In *Lady's Own Paper*, the story of the Smiths ran alongside their 23 October report on the Kirwan investigation; in *The Atlas*, the Smiths ran immediately after the Kirwan case on the same day. The *Bradford Observer* ran short reports on both stories on 21 October – Kirwan first, the Swords murder second. Kirwan's case was headlined 'The Murder at Ireland's Eye' and the brutal killing of the Smiths followed, topped with the headline 'Another murder.'

The sum of these parts would likely not determine the outcome of the trial that followed – the real newspaper war was yet to begin. On Tuesday 25 October, a true bill was found against William Burke Kirwan, meaning he could be sent forward for trial. The next day, at a sitting of the Commissions Court, he was arraigned and pleaded not guilty. On the orders of the Attorney General, Mr Plunkett for the prosecution successfully applied for a postponement of the trial until the next commission. Kirwan, who bowed to the bench upon being notified his trial would take place at a later date, would get his day in court, but not until December.

9

TWO LIVES

William Burke Kirwan (spelled 'Bourke' in some source materials) led two lives. In both, he was an artist. In both, his partner was referred to as 'Mrs Kirwan'. In only one, he was legally married – to Maria. In the other, he had eight children – with a woman named Teresa Kenny. Two separate, full lives – both in Dublin, only miles apart. In most newspaper commentary, the situation was outwardly criticised for the perceived inbuilt debauchery. For the case of *The Queen* v. *William Burke Kirwan*, it would prove to be significant – while the jury were told repeatedly to disregard their preconceived suspicions about the man, the situation was equally relied upon to provide motive for the alleged murder. No matter the interpretation, the Kirwans' lives prior to Howth were central to any discussion about the trial that eventually took place.

William and Maria had been married for about 12 years at the time of her death. He was a Protestant and she a Catholic. William, an artist of some renown and talent, made a healthy income from – among other things – anatomical illustration, painting portraits and landscapes, and via the ownership of a number of properties. He was the son of Patrick Kirwan, a picture dealer from Co. Fermanagh who operated in Dublin. Maria, also from Dublin, came from more modest means – her father, James Crowe, was a lieutenant in the 2nd West India Regiment of the British army, according to Walter G. Strickland's *A Dictionary of Irish Artists*. At first, the couple lived at Parnell Place, William's family home, and he kept an office on South King's Street. Later, the couple moved into a property on D'Olier Street, and then to No. 6 Merrion Street Lower in 1845. Roughly five years after this, they moved for a final time, to No. 11 Merrion Street Upper. Patrick, William's father, lived with them on Merrion Street.

Throughout virtually that entire time, William was effectively married to Teresa Kenny, who, by her own account, was 31 around the time of Maria's death. There is evidence to indicate that Teresa presented as Mrs Kirwan. They had seven children together, having lost an eighth, according to Teresa. By the time of Maria Kirwan's death, Teresa was renting at Richmond Parade in Summerhill. Before that, they had been located at Sandymount Avenue, and before that again at Jervis Street. For these various properties, William Kirwan hired servants. Authorities were able to reach servants who had worked for the Kirwans, across both family units so to speak, at the different addresses across Dublin. A number of them were examined by the Crown solicitor.

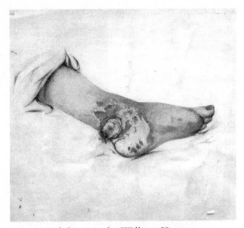

Anatomical drawings by William Kirwan, courtesy of the Royal College of Surgeons Ireland.

The staff servicing the two Kirwan houses would have no reason to meet. Yet their stories leave similar impressions. His work provided the perfect excuse for a man who needed to disappear – sometimes for a night at a time, sometimes half a week. That's how Catherine Toole remembered it. For half a decade she served the Kirwans – William and the woman who she believed to be Mrs Kirwan. The lady paid her wages, and answered to the name. In her time employed, five years, the couple had moved from No. 27 Jervis Street to a different home on Sandymount Avenue and added three children to their existing four. And for the last 18 months of her employment, up until the summer of 1852, Toole worked alongside another servant, named Kate Byrne.

'Mr Kirwan generally slept in the house with the lady whom I always considered to be his wife,' recalled Toole. 'Mr and Mrs Kirwan appeared to live on the most affectionate terms and appeared to be very fond of their children. Mr Kirwan slept some odd nights abroad. On them occasions Mrs Kirwan used to say he was in the country, he generally slept in Sandymount Avenue. On some occasions Mr Kirwan used to be absent for several days together when Mrs Kirwan has told me that he had gone to England.' For the majority of the time Toole spent with the Kirwans, there was no other woman to whom Toole attributed the title of 'Mrs Kirwan'. There was, however, the incident at the gate.

A collision of Kirwan's two worlds had occurred some time before his wife wound up on Barrett's dray, but exactly when the first crossover took place would be a matter of contention. Toole remembered a lady approaching the house, around six months before she was interviewed in October. As Byrne looked through the window, Toole left the house and went to the gate to address the lady who had arrived. 'She wanted to know who lived there. I said Mr Kirwan,' recalled Toole. On Toole's return to the house, her mistress asked who was at the gate and what they wanted. The servant replied and said it was a woman asking who lived in the house. Mrs Kirwan – or rather, Kenny – then went to speak to the woman at the gate, and Toole went about her work. Byrne never asked her colleague what happened, and that, it would appear, was the end of the lady at the gate. But further witness accounts held in the case files shed more light on what had occurred on that March day at the end of the garden in Sandymount Avenue.

One woman who said she knew what had happened at the gate was Maria Crowe, mother of (the real) Mrs Kirwan. In fact, though neither Toole nor

Byrne mention a second person, Mrs Crowe said that when her daughter travelled to Sandymount, she went along. By the time she gave her statement to the Crown, Mrs Crowe was living at No. 88 Lower Gardiner Street and James, her husband, was dead. The revelation that William was living with another woman in Sandymount apparently came as a surprise to Mrs Crowe, if you go by her initial statement to the Crown. The two, she considered, lived in harmony, except for one incident in Howth in the short space of time that the couple stayed in the fishing village.

On that occasion, during one of her weekly visits about two months before her daughter's death, Mrs Crowe found Maria angry with her husband. That was partly due to the fact that he had been gone for a number of days, but also because he had been working to 'oppose her', as she put it. The younger Maria revealed to her mother that William had beat her with his cane, but over her clothing, so there would be no mark. She accused him of being with the woman from the cottages in Sandymount. The statement provided by the widow revealed not only the interaction between Teresa and Maria in March, but an additional detail not picked up on by the servants who had been there on the day: that she had visited the house twice.

On the first occasion, Teresa had been more amenable, by Mrs Crowe's account. 'I accompanied the late Mrs Kirwan to Springfield Cottages Sandymount Avenue where I saw a woman who called herself Mrs Kirwan. She said her husband was a clerk,' recalled Mrs Crowe. Extending her hand to show Teresa her wedding ring, Maria had said: 'Pardon the liberty, but I would like to see your husband.'

'That's an odd thing,' the mother of Mr Kirwan's children had replied. 'It would appear that you are throwing a suspicion on my character.' Maria denied the charge, but the pair arranged to return some days later so that the 'real' Mrs Kirwan might meet this clerk husband. When they arrived, they were headed off at the gate and Teresa wouldn't let them through, according to Mrs Crowe.

For someone so involved in the case, there is little input from Kenny in the documentation. There is some, however: 'I know Mr Kirwan. I have known him since I was seven years of age,' begins one of the few records of Kenny's direct experience that still exists – her sworn statement included in the brief for the prosecution counsel. 'I am now 31 years of age – I have a family of seven children. I lost another – Mr Kirwan is the father of those children. I went to live with Mr Kirwan about 14 years since. I cannot tell at what time he was married to the late woman. I did not hear of the circumstance until within the last six months. I had a house in which I lived. Mr Kirwan had another in which he lived. He visited and sometimes slept at my house.

'My residence was in the outlets, his in the city. I was never married to him. I cannot recollect whether he promised to marry me or not. Mrs Kirwan called on me about March last. After that I made up my mind to go to Australia. That visit was the first intimation I had of Mr Kirwan's having been married.

'I would have gone to Australia but that a son of mine had an attack of inflammation of the lungs and I wanted to have him, who is about 3 years old, cured before I'd go. I mentioned to Mr Kirwan of Mrs Kirwan having called on me. When I next saw him I asked him. I cannot recollect what he said on the occasion. My youngest child is nine months old. I did not hear of the death of Mrs Kirwan until about 5 days since. About that time I brought my son Walter William Kirwan who was ill, to get advice, to Mr Kirwan's in Merrion Street. The child could not be removed and I remained there with it. It is not now expected that the child will live.'

A fascinating statement. It necessitates a number of questions. For one: why did Kenny lie about her husband's occupation? By Mrs Crowe's recollection, she said he was a clerk. Frances Clare Finlay, who had rented Kirwan and Kenny a house on Richmond Parade in Summerhill, recalled the lady saying her husband was an engineer who would be away for long spells in the country. That took place during the summer of the Howth getaway. Kenny also said she didn't know about Maria until around the time of the incident at the gate. Yet Kenny's brother's statement – contained within the same cache of documents – indicated that he knew about Maria Kirwan's existence years beforehand. Nicholas Kenny, who had been on poor terms with his sisters following a bereavement in the family, also said a wedding took place between Kirwan and Kenny.

'She was married to Mr Kirwan in 1839,' said Nicholas of his sister. 'I was not present at the ceremony. My late brother Mr Edward Kenny wrote to me when in England that my sister Mary Teresa had been married to Mr William Kirwan. My brother Edward died of brain fever. I was not apprised of the circumstance for 30 hours after the death in consequence of which I have not since been on terms with my sisters. Mr Kirwan is of the Church of England. My sister Mrs Kirwan was a Roman Catholic. She changed her religion with him which was another reason I did not speak to him.' About whether or not the two were actually married, Nicholas left no doubt as to his own understanding of events: 'I heard that Mr Kirwan was married to another woman, his late wife, about three years since but I can't tell how long or at what time he was married. Mr Kirwan and my sister were recognised by all their friends as man and wife. I have not spoken to Mr Kirwan for ten years past.' Of course, this is the testimony of an estranged family member – one who didn't attend the ceremony he mentioned. And the man who told him about it was dead. Another acquaintance of the Kirwans, Maria Mac Mahon, who had lived with them for a number of years at No. 27 Jervis Street, said she knew Kenny as Mrs Kirwan, and that Mr Kirwan was often away. Mac Mahon had little else to add, other than to say they lived on very good terms, and that William was a 'silent, dogged man'.

Between the lines of Kenny's statement is the dire situation she found herself in after the case broke. The reason she was in the city at all was owing to the ill health of her son, and with her provider facing a murder charge, her situation was deteriorating. The landlord at the place she rented on Richmond Parade, Charles Frederick Finlay, encountered Kenny on the street around the time all of the above statements were taken. The mother of several children had asked if she could stay three more months owing to the ill health of one of them. 'The woman calling herself Mrs Kirwan and her children are still in my house,' said Finlay at the time of his statement. Her situation, she would later say, became worse when she was forced to leave those lodgings.

Laudanum was popular in the 19th century, partly because of its ease of procurement. As a substance, it's a staple of the various reckless Victorian-era elixirs pasted across the front pages of newspapers then, and which are now considered quite effective death potions. It came, classically, in a small dropper bottle, and was used to treat a variety of conditions – anything from a tickly throat to a sleepless spell, and especially pain relief. Its addictive nature was granted by its key ingredient, opium, which was mixed with alcohol, saffron and cinnamon to produce a bitter liquid that devastated the poor and well-off alike.

After the dawn of the 20th century, its status as a freely available cure-all came slowly to an end; headlines around that time concerning the drug, often termed 'deadly laudanum', usually feature death. Among the many fatal stories, there's the lady who took an ounce per night to fall asleep – eventually dying (*Leitrim Observer*, 16 November 1912); the Welsh minister who succumbed to his own slumber-seeking remedies (*Belfast News Letter*, 27 December 1905); and the man named Edward Lloyd Price, who was found at Blackrock, Dublin after having taken enough to kill 19 men (*Irish Independent*, 27 January 1908). In the latter case, the coroner told the inquest he believed 'laudanum should not be sold except on an order from a doctor'.

Although regulations were looser in 1852, the sight of the bottle was still enough to make Mary Byrne concerned about the safety of her mistress. Mrs Kirwan had introduced the dark little vessel after complaining to Byrne that she couldn't sleep. Mr Kirwan had told her to take it, she said. Byrne, at the risk of exceeding her needlework remit, told her not to drink the laudanum. Byrne's time living with the Kirwans was short, just three months, but it offers an insight into the earliest section of the marriage, pre-Merrion Street. Despite her brief spell with the couple, Byrne had experienced quite enough to interest investigators. To find the first time William struck his wife, or at least the first that was witnessed in some capacity, one has to travel back to 1844, when the couple lived on D'Olier Street.

It was the same old story, even as early as 1844. Mr Kirwan was missing for chunks of time. Sometimes, he would go out at 8 p.m. in the evening and return at 5 a.m. the following morning, using a personal latch key. Once, Byrne heard a loud crash upstairs in the sitting room. She quickly ascended the stairs, but stopped short of opening the door. Through the timber she heard Maria's muffled cries. The needleworker was sure that Mr Kirwan and his father were in the room at the time. Later, in the safety of their solitude, Maria told Byrne that William had, indeed, struck her in the midst of an argument. It was at D'Olier Street, eight years before her death, that Byrne said she was first told by Maria that she had heard her husband was with another woman, and that she was in 'great trouble'.

Though Byrne ceased to live with the Kirwans, she kept up contact and frequently visited Maria when the Kirwans moved to Merrion Street Lower, not long after the incident in the room. It was in that second dwelling that Maria revealed her husband's attempts to coerce her into taking laudanum for her sleeplessness. After the second move, to the bigger house on Merrion Street, Byrne lost touch with Maria – though not by complacency on the needleworker's part. She frequently tried to see her former employer but was headed off at the door by the new servant. That move was nearly 18 months before Maria's death – in that time, she saw her former friend, 'a quite mild, inoffensive woman' just twice, on the street, by chance.

Anne Molloy was permitted to go where Mary Byrne was not. When she was hired as a servant, the couple lived on Merrion Street Lower, and Molloy was kept on following the upgrade to No. 11. Judging by her observations, Mr Kirwan kept his habits up to near-identical rhythms – a latchkey for ease of movement and a spectre-like presence in his own home. Molloy witnessed the couple largely on good terms, but for one occasion. It's a depressingly familiar story: Molloy heard screaming in the parlour. Hurrying up the kitchen stairs to investigate, she met Mrs Kirwan coming out of the room, then her husband, who told her in no uncertain terms that family affairs were not the business of a servant. As for the secret family, Molloy heard whispers. Once, she was given the impossible task of tracking William when he left on one of his evening departures. Following him into a dark Merrion Street, she quickly found herself looking up and down the road at nothing. Kirwan, purposefully or not, had slipped her, and her task – to see if anybody awaited him on the road – went unfulfilled. By the time she was given a discharge and left in September 1850, the only secret between the two that she could verify underscored a different manner of distrust between the two: Maria took confession, but would never tell her husband.

The last verifiable servant to document Kirwan's behaviour in the house was Anne Maher. By the time of her year-long stint serving the Kirwans at No. 11, things seem to have quietened down somewhat. Kirwan kept up his nocturnal absconding, his father died and there were no beatings. At least, none she disclosed to the Crown. When Maher left, about 12 months before the trip to Ireland's Eye, Kirwan had begun attributing his wife's behaviour to her supposed emotional disposition: 'I often heard Mr Kirwan charge Mrs Kirwan with being passionate, and have heard him say she was a passionate woman.' Maher noted that Kirwan also had a back-door key for No. 11, which he took to using the odd time for his various comings and goings. It would be the decision to take that back-door route that led him into the path of James Molloy.

—⁓—

It's been mentioned briefly in this chapter, but William's work, in many ways, defined him. In the literal sense, he was frequently referred to by his profession in newspaper reports: an artist. The same could probably be said of the book you're now reading. The occupation granted him status and, as newspaper reports constantly reminded readers, considerable means. William's most notable job was as an anatomical draftsman for surgeons, sketching various parts of the human anatomy, maladies and conditions for use in medical settings. Some of his work still exists in collections in the National Library of Ireland and the Royal College of Surgeons. Walter G. Strickland notes Kirwan was a pupil of the portrait painter Richard Downes Bowyer and, from 1836 to 1846, exhibited watercolour miniatures and domestic subjects in the Royal Hibernian Academy. Kirwan also worked for the engraver Henry Gonne, and for Hodges and Smith on Grafton Street, and was employed as a painting cleaner.

The hard line between his professional career and his two domestic situations appeared to provide a convenient cover. Arthur Kelly was a man who dwelt on the professional side of that curtain. For about fourteen years, he worked in close quarters with Mr Kirwan – for the first seven as his assistant, and for another seven as his employee. When Kelly first met Kirwan, he kept his office at South King Street and lived at Parnell Place. Kelly's professional relationship with Kirwan predated even his employer's marriage to Maria. Yet Kirwan's employee did not attend the wedding, and wasn't even sure where the ceremony took place. After Parnell Place, the Kirwans moved to D'Olier Street and William operated his business from home. This meant Kelly began to work closer to Kirwan's personal life; at the house, he would see Mrs Kirwan often. Yet Kelly's association was still not close enough to gather an opinion about the terms on which they lived. That lasted for four or five years. It was the same case when the couple, and Kirwan's business, moved to the two locations on Merrion Street.

'I had no intercourse while at Upper Merrion Street more than before,' said Kelly. 'I am not aware of any person living with him as Mrs Kirwan, but the lady who lived in Merrion Street with him.' Kelly did mention that it was odd for Mr Kirwan to go to the country in the summer. In that respect, his decampment to Howth was unusual. While the couple were there, Kelly still attended Merrion Street for work, until the time of Maria's death. During that time, Mr Kirwan's attendance was patchy. There were no servants left at that point – they had been discharged when William and Maria took up residence in Mrs Campbell's. The closest Kelly appeared to get to Kirwan's personal life, besides working from his employer's home, was his attendance at Maria's funeral.

Kirwan's employee had been to the house between the time of Maria's death and William's arrest, but he didn't know who else was living in the house, besides Mr Kirwan. Kelly, like many others, had heard that 'there was a

Miss Kenny in the house at the time of his arrest, by whom he had a family of children' – but he couldn't clarify when exactly that person arrived. If she was living there beforehand, he didn't know about it. Kelly said he never spoke to Mr Kirwan about his wife after they went to Howth. Nor did he ever speak to Mrs Kirwan about Mr Kirwan. If there were complaints – or otherwise – about Mr Kirwan's treatment of his legal wife, then Arthur Kelly never heard them. Despite working alongside William Kirwan for 14 years, Kelly knew precious little about the man's personal life. William Kirwan's carefully maintained cloak of mystery, opaque and used to its fullest potential, appears to have worked both ways.

10

SKELETONS

Charles Frederick Finlay had rented the room in good faith. Charles' wife, Frances Clare, handed the key over to Mrs Kirwan – at least, that's who she said she was when she took the house at Richmond Parade in June 1852. So far, Finlay had been paid in rent and excuses for her husband's frequent absences. Mr Kenny, of Mabbott Street, had given a good reference, upon which Finlay had based the decision to let the house – without meeting the man.

Then came the information. A caller told him all about 'Mr and Mrs Kirwan'. She was not his wife at all, and he had a reputation for not paying his debts. During a conversation in August, after much fuss trying to catch him, Finlay told him as much. 'I heard you are a man that never pays anyone, and that the lady is not your wife,' he had told the artist, point blank. Mr Kirwan, however, explained himself well, and Finlay was satisfied enough to let them stay. In fact, coming away from the interaction, he later said he felt that the person who had given him the information had constructed a slight on Mr Kirwan's character. For what reason, he was not sure. The next he spoke to his tenant was in August, when Mr Kirwan said he would be leaving owing to the health of one of his children. The date for their departure, then, would have been 2 October, but Kirwan asked for a couple days' grace. Finlay was happy to grant them, at that point satisfied that the man could be trusted to pay his debts.

The story of Mr Finlay's encounter with Mr Kirwan around the end of summer 1852 is a small window that reveals a reality about the artist that by now should be clear: rightly or wrongly, there were curious stories in circulation about his character. Depending on what you read, William Kirwan was anything from a sober, industrious and level-headed professional who loved his wife, to a licentious, devious, cruel bigamist who had perpetrated multiple murders. Perhaps the stories were all true. Others implied they were rumours that tended to poison the minds of the public and damage his character.

In the dining room, supper was ready. Maria Byrne sat with her husband and their host. The food was prepared but there was a place setting missing. The conversation ebbed and the men prepared to eat. When it appeared that Kirwan's wife was not going to appear and they were about to eat in her absence, Mrs Byrne eventually spoke, asking where the lady of the house was. Mr Kirwan, she was sure, had a wife – she'd heard it a number of times. And yet she had never seen the woman. Byrne's husband was on close terms with Kirwan – both men worked for Hodges and Smith, the publishers on Grafton Street.

'Mrs Byrne, I am afraid you are misinformed,' replied Kirwan. 'I have no wife, I'm not married.'

'I'm afraid I must insist,' she replied. Mr Kirwan stared for a second longer than was comfortable, before abruptly rising and marching from the room. A few minutes later, he returned with a young woman who he introduced to the table.

And that, Mrs Byrne later swore, was how she came to meet Maria Kirwan. The incident at the dinner was just one of a number of damning stories told by Mrs Byrne, who was a neighbour and, the lady said, a close acquaintance of Mrs Kirwan for nearly 10 years. But the concealment of marriage was not the only story of suspicion surrounding Mr Kirwan's character which emanated from Mrs Byrne. Another much more serious claim was that he had, some years previously, been connected with the disappearance of his brother-in-law. In the statement she gave to the Crown solicitor, by which time her own husband had been dead nine months, Mrs Byrne said Mr Crowe (brother to Maria Kirwan) and Mr Kirwan left the house 'one day after dinner'. Kirwan returned three weeks later, but Crowe had not been heard from since. The latter had about him a large sum of money, with which he intended to travel to America. It seems that this was not the first time Mrs Byrne had made the connection between some wrongdoing by Mr Kirwan and the supposed disappearance of Crowe. That much is indicated by the following line from her statement: 'Mr Kirwan complained to Mrs Kirwan of my having circulated the report that he, Kirwan, had murdered his brother-in-law Crowe.' Further down the line, Mrs Byrne would also reportedly blame Mr Kirwan of doing away with her own husband.

There was, incredibly, another allegation that rendered William Kirwan a three-time suspected murderer – one which had endured for more than a decade before his trial, but which would emerge more notably in January 1853. Anne Bowyer, wife to Kirwan's former employer and teacher Richard Downes Bowyer, accounted for her husband's disappearance in 1837 by claiming that Kirwan had murdered him. On top of that, she also claimed he had stolen various valuable papers and books belonging to Mr Bowyer – the supposed widow was quite dogged in those allegations, upholding them for years.

We will return to the Bowyer case and Maria Byrne's claims a little later. But, suffice to say – there was ample suspicion surrounding the wicked life of William Burke Kirwan. And that's to say nothing of the seduction debacle from the late 1830s.

———∾∾∾———

In the streets of Dublin, fliers appeared. In large letters at the top was the word 'STOP'. The object of the posting was a call-out of sorts, broadcasting allegations about its target – one who had, as one report relayed, 'grossly and infamously inflicted an irreparable injury upon the writer and his family, and had acted as a thoroughbred paltroon [sic]. That in consequence of his not acting even as a bold villain would have done, the writer felt it a duty to God and to man to exhibit to the world an arrant coward, whom hell had vomited forth to infest humanity with his pestilential breath.'

The year was 1839, the 'arrant coward' was William Burke Kirwan and the allegation was seduction. William Collins Jones, the brother of the alleged victim, had posted the charges in a bid to force Kirwan into one of two actions: marry 'the victim of his demoniacal possession' or risk his life in a duel. The timing of the episode is interesting – of course it's not the most interesting part, but it's close, because one must deduce that around late 1839 is close to the beginning point of his other confirmed relationships. The basics of the story, as Victorian a yarn as there could ever be, were outlined in a report in *Saunders's News-Letter* on 16 August that year. Billed as an 'affair of honour', the report detailed a hearing of a suit by Kirwan against the alleged flier writers and distributors: Messrs Jones and Fausset. The latter was present, the former – the writer – was not.

Seduction was quite a serious charge in the 19th century. It was both a way to protect the dignity of the women involved and a facility to compensate the men associated with those women. The father of the woman in question often took the suit to win monetary damages, and the crime was based around the luring of a woman into having sex under false pretences – promises of marriage, for instance. Newspaper archives from the 19th century have many examples. One, *Cavanagh* v. *Jameson*, was covered in the *Belfast News Letter* on 30 April 1819. The defendant in that case was a farmer's son, who had met the plaintiff's daughter ('a plain-looking girl, about 20 years of age, and who had the appearance of a decent servant maid') in a field 'by appointment', where he promised to take her to America as his wife. In the field, there took place an incident described within the report as both 'unfortunate business' and 'criminal intercourse', but no marriage afterwards came. The father sought compensation for the loss of his daughter's services. The jury awarded him 100 pounds.

But Kirwan, in the report from 1839, was not formally charged with seduction – he was the one taking action against Jones. In any case, Kirwan denied the allegations made on the placard. 'He is not a deliberate seducer who had formed and matured a plan to withdraw innocence from the path of virtue, and his acquaintance with the girl arose from an accidental interview at the theatre,' said his lawyer at the time. 'So far back as the 30th of December, Mr Kirwan was in the pit of the Abbey-street Theatre, when a respectably dressed female came in, unaccompanied, and sat on the seat before him. She shortly changed her position and sat on the same line of seats with him.'

That's the extent of the play-by-play of the night in question. Of course, neither of the two fates – a duel or marriage to Ms Jones – transpired. A later report in the *Belfast News Letter* from January 1853 sheds further light on what happened. Mr Kirwan's relationship with Mrs Jones had been more than a meeting at the Abbey Theatre; he had lived with her for some time, beginning in 1837, according to that report. When he left, she became destitute in Holyhead and later returned to Dublin, where she thereafter died in a 'wretched' state. The later report says that Mr Jones – the brother – tried to meet Kirwan to demand an explanation. That failed. Nor would Kirwan agree to a 'hostile meeting'. Jones resorted to the placards only when he felt he had no other option. Kirwan tore down the posters with the help of a few recruits, including his father and sisters. The problem did not go away; Jones severely horsewhipped Kirwan. The artist prosecuted his assailant, but the court, according to the report, only punished the horsewhipper nominally: '[S]uch was the impression on the court that it considered the law was fully satisfied by the verdict, merely sentenced the defendant to be imprisoned until the rising of the court. It is as well to remark that the sessions were adjourned before half an hour had expired.'

The episode, at least, goes as far as demonstrating the less-than-pristine reputation of Mr Kirwan when it came to the conduct of what could be labelled his romantic affairs and, more broadly, his treatment of women.

PART 3

11

THE TRIAL OPENS

The court at Green Street was sometimes packed. Other times, the pageantry of the law escaped the gaze of the public and proceedings went on nearly in private. But the trial of William Burke Kirwan for the murder of his wife was an undoubted sensation in the capital, the country and abroad. Long lines of hopeful spectators filled the avenues leading to the courthouse from the early morning of Wednesday 8 December 1852, and many frustrated gentlemen – their class highlighted in reports denoting their unusual rejection – were turned away, resigned to hearing the second-hand scraps of information that bled onto the street via unofficial messengers.

The story of the trial is well-documented, both in contemporary newspapers and in an 1853 report by the barrister John Simpson Armstrong, produced by collating two sets of notes taken by shorthand writers and the notes taken by the judges. Using those sources, a vivid picture of the evidence and events can be established.

The judges on the day, Justice Philip Cecil Crampton and Hon. Richard Wilson Greene, took their seats at about 10 o'clock. Minutes later, a pulse of energy flowed through the packed assemblage, from the bar to the press paddocks and high up on the overhanging galleries, as the Clerk of the Crown summoned Kirwan. Necks crooned, benches creaked and the more eager shifted out of their seats to observe the disgraced artist, under the close watch of a jailer, enter the door at the lower section of the dock and walk up to the bar at the front of the court. Reporters' heads dipped and pencils scribbled furiously on paper; those acquainting themselves with the proceedings via the following morning's papers would likely correctly guess that they each first wrote the word 'respectable' before detailing his disposition.

Kirwan was calm. If he was anxious, he did not seem so. Aged 36, official records say he had grey eyes, offset by darker brown hair and eyebrows. His dress was neat. A close-fitting, black paletot covered his stout frame, and a tall stock collar of black satin sat beneath his chin. He wore black kid-skin gloves, to match the rest. His orderly dress was a reflection of his demeanour. Collected. Together. While the press detailed Kirwan's wardrobe, the jury was empanelled, with the prisoner challenging three. The following 12 men were sworn: John Dennis, David Drummond, Edward Evans, Edward J. Figgis, Christopher Flanagan, Maurice Flanagan, Charles F. Goodwin, James Halpin, Charles B. Johnson, Richard Johnson, James Kerr and Patrick Langan.

Kirwan was then placed in the hands of the jury on the following indictment: 'The jurors for our Lady, the Queen, upon their oath do say and present that William Burke Kirwan late of Howth in the county of Dublin gentleman not having the fear of God before his eyes but being moved and seduced by the instigation of the devil on the sixth day of September in the sixteenth year of the reign of our Sovereign Lady Queen Victoria with force and arms at Ireland's Eye in the county of Dublin aforesaid did wilfully feloniously and of his malice prepensed kill and murder one Maria Louisa Kirwan against the peace of our said Lady the Queen, her crown and dignity.'

Kirwan had pleaded not guilty. The Clerk of the Crown put a simple question to the prisoner: 'Are you ready for your trial?'

'I am,' he replied.

In his corner, Kirwan had considerable firepower. Walter Burke, William Brereton and John Curran were able practitioners, but Isaac Butt – Trinity College lecturer and recently elected MP – was a barrister of powerful reputation. 'Genius' was a word often accompanying his name in newsprint. *The Standard* (some four years before Butt heard anything of William Kirwan, knew the tides at Ireland's Eye so closely or indeed associated the date of 6 September with anything other than the date of his own birth) had this to say: 'Mr Butt is not merely the most powerful advocate at the Irish bar, in addition to being a learned and acute lawyer, he is beyond comparison the first of living advocates, probably the greatest master of forensic eloquence that the bar of either country has seen since the retirement of Brougham or Erskine. He is besides a man of the purest character in public or in private life.' Those who remained until the second and third days of the trial would get a chance to see these plaudits play out.

Portrait of Isaac Butt by John Butler Yeats, via National Portrait Gallery/Wikimedia-Commons.

The task of opening the trial fell to John George Smyly, coincidentally a neighbour of Kirwan's on Merrion Street Upper, who was acting as prosecution counsel alongside Edmund Hayes and John Pennefather. To the differences between direct and circumstantial evidence, Smyly devoted his opening gambit. 'Gentlemen of the jury, you of course fully recognise the distinction between these two species of evidence; you are of course aware, that what is called "direct evidence" is, from its very designation, the evidence of parties who have themselves witnessed the perpetration of the act – who have been present when the crime was committed – who have heard the shot fired – who have seen the blow struck or other injury inflicted, by which the death of the victim was caused, and the murder effected.

'But, gentlemen, the other description of evidence is that wherein witnesses are brought forward, each and every one of whom gives a relation of certain circumstances coming within his or her own cognizance and observation and relates a series of facts thus stated, when collected and compared, constitute an aggregate assemblage of circumstances which tend naturally and forcibly to impress the mind with a conviction of the guilt of the accused party – then you have a case sustained upon what is properly termed "circumstantial evidence".'

Smyly next addressed the point of curiosity which had so tightly grabbed the public's attention. 'I much fear,' said Smyly, 'that in this sad case, affection and kind regard, on the part of the husband, have not gone hand in hand with duty. I say this, because I believe there can be no doubt thrown on one portion of the case which will, I think, be proved to your satisfaction in the course of this trial, namely, that the prisoner, although he was married during a period of 12 years to the unfortunate lady who has met an untimely death (as alleged) at his hands, had been, during nearly the whole of that period, living and cohabiting with another woman, by whom he had a numerous family of children; and it should be observed, that this double connexion of the prisoner – the one with his lawful married wife, and the other of an illicit and immoral character with another woman – went on through this long period of years undiscovered by the prisoner's wife, and, what is more strange undetected (as it would appear) by the woman with whom he kept up this private and illicit intercourse.' The deception, Smyly said, was only discovered months beforehand. With those circumstances in place, Smyly danced through the story as many in the room knew it.

The first witness was a man of maps and numbers. Alfred Jones, the Rathgar draftsman, went through a description of the island's geography for the uninitiated, and the measurements he procured over a couple of days with the Nangles on the Eye were produced. Jones pointed out the key locations. The following table shows Jones's calculations, based on the almanac, of the height of the water above the 'Body Rock', deemed to be about a foot high where Maria's head and shoulders lay.

Time	Water's distance above the Body Rock
3.30 p.m. (high tide at Dublin bar)	7ft above
6.30 p.m.	2ft 6in above
7 p.m.	1ft 9in above
7.15 p.m.	1ft 4.5in above
7.30 p.m.	1ft above
8 p.m.	3in above
9.30 p.m.	2ft below

Kirwan, Jones calculated, was 792 yards from the Long Hole when the Nangles arrived to ferry the couple back to Howth. That's 43 yards from the Martello tower, which itself is 835 yards from the Long Hole. The ruins of the church were about 280 yards from the entrance to the inlet. Jones noted another key feature at the Long Hole: a rock which, due to its placement, meant a person could travel – and remain dry – from where Maria was discovered to the mouth of the hole, where the boat had pulled up when the men rowed around the island.

The clothes, too, were somewhat easily accessible: 'A person could walk from the strand to where the clothes were without climbing during any portion of the way,' Jones said in an answer to Crampton who, like Butt, tried to make practical sense of the data. All of that went to indicate that the clothes, where they were discovered on the rock that sat centrally in the inlet, could be accessed from the land, or 'strand' side of the hole, which was south-west and inland, without climbing.

For the remainder of the first day, the packed crowd watched as a string of Howth villagers took the stand, describing in detail the fateful night. Margaret Campbell went first. She began by stating for the court her occupation and the various comings and goings of the Kirwans, including Kirwan's trips to town, the couple's trips to Ireland's Eye and their day-to-day relationship.

Through Mrs Campbell's recollection of events, the jury had its first taste of Kirwan's mistreatment of his wife prior to her death. 'During the first month or six weeks they lodged with me I observed quarrelling between them more than once; I heard angry words from Mr Kirwan to his wife,' Mrs Campbell told the court. 'I heard him say "he would make her stop there". I heard him miscall her – I heard him call her a strumpet. I heard him say "I'll finish you": I do not think they had been a month with me at that time... the next morning I heard her say to him she was black from the usage she had got the preceding night; across her thighs I think she said it was.'

Mrs Campbell went on to say that her neighbour Anne Hannah arrived before the episode was complete – you, the reader, have seen the particulars of this story already. The problem for Mrs Campbell when she relayed the evidence at trial was that she had made a number of sworn statements that tended to contradict the latter, harsher version of the Kirwans' time at her home. Mrs Campbell finished the particulars of their trip – the black travel bag they brought, how it was their third trip to the island in a week, and how she recognised Mrs Kirwan's bathing cap when she saw it in the possession of Joseph Sherwood, after it was plucked from the rocks. The court heard about how Mrs Kirwan was brought to the house and placed first on the floor, where the sail was unwrapped. The widow described Kirwan's wet stockings, and how Maria – as far as she could tell – had been in good health.

Mrs Campbell was cross-examined by Mr Burke. 'It did not appear strange to me that a gentleman having rooms in town should sometimes remain away. I heard them quarrelling more than once. The first difference was shortly after they came. There was a second, and I could not say when there was a third. They had quarrelled at different times,' she said. 'I could not say when they had a fourth, it was in the first quarrel that he used the language to Mrs Kirwan which I have mentioned; it was about a fortnight after they came to live with me. Subsequently they had an odd word now and again. He never used violence but the once.'

At this point, Mr Burke asked about the previous statements she made – the much less damning ones. Mrs Campbell was asked if she knew Major

Brownrigg – in front of whom she would have given information previously. She looked closely at him before confirming that she had, she thought, seen him at Howth before. While she was present at the inquest, she did not contribute. 'I did not offer myself as witness, I did not then tell anything of what I have told today,' she said. The widow was sketchy on the details, but recalled being brought before Norbury Furnace, and giving information. But she said, without question, that the information was not given under sworn oath. In court, she acknowledged that she had merely signed the information. The Clerk of the Crown then read her first statement taken before Mr Furnace, from 15 September – the top of which clearly stated that it had been given under sworn oath by Mrs Campbell.

'Saith that the late Maria Kirwan, who was drowned at Ireland's Eye, lodged in her house for near three months, with her husband, Mr William Kirwan. For the first fortnight they did not live happily together, but during the remaining time, up to her death, informant considers no couple could have lived more united. Informant has heard Mrs Kirwan's mother, Mrs Maria Crowe, caution her daughter frequently to not be too venturesome swimming.'

Mrs Campbell, when the statement was read out, said: 'The information was taken at Howth, and my name and handwriting is to it. I did not consider I was sworn in making it. I was sworn, but not before Captain Furnace, there was no book put into my hand.' Turning to the judges, she reiterated: 'There was no book in my hand, none whatever.' The cross-examination continued, and Mrs Campbell was again shown another statement, this time from 8 October before Major Brownrigg. The information, again, was read out: 'Saith that I know Mr Kirwan who is now present. I did know his wife; she is dead. Mr and Mrs Kirwan lodged in my house for about three months before her death; they came to my house in June and continued to live in my house from that until the time of her death. I never knew Mr and Mrs Kirwan to disagree but on one occasion while at my house, which was shortly after they came. I don't know what the quarrel was about, but I heard high words. They lived, while in my house, as happily as any couple could do.'

Mr Burke was first to speak after the information was read; he asked the widow why, in the latter statement, she said they only quarrelled once – yet, just minutes beforehand, she had told the court that they quarrelled a number of times.

'I meant that he only beat her once. I answered all the questions I was asked – I did not think of any more,' replied Mrs Campbell, saying that when she was asked originally, she had not recalled the episode she heard from behind the door. The witness finished her testimony by recalling that she heard Mrs Crowe – Maria's mother – caution her about her venturesome bathing.

Patrick Nangle introduced himself to the Green Street Courthouse as a fisherman and sailor. He'd lived at Howth all his life and knew the tides. The boatman described for the jury the 'stout, handsome woman' of about 28 or 29 who he, along with Mick Nangle, Giles and Kavanagh, ferried to Ireland's Eye on 6 September 1852 with her husband, William – and not for the first time. On the day, they brought with them a bag and two bottles of water. 'The lady had a little reticule basked in her hand,' said Nangle. 'Mr Kirwan had a stick of the kind called a tuck stick.'

You, the reader might be wondering – what is a tuck stick? Nangle was asked to elaborate. 'I mean a stick like a sword cane,' said the fisherman, presenting the first official mention of a weapon with the potential to cause extensive bleeding. Nangle was allowed to move on at that point, and he described the day's events. He brought the Kirwans over at 10 a.m. Then he brought the Brew family over at noon – and then back at about 4 o'clock. He saw Doyle's boat out that day, too. While bringing the Brew family back, the men encountered Maria, who told them to return at 8 o'clock, passing up Mr Brew's offer of an earlier departure.

At about 7.30 p.m. or 7.40 p.m., depending on the report, the crew undertook the roughly 15-minute journey to Ireland's Eye, getting there at about 8 o'clock, or shortly before. Reaching the island, Kirwan handed Patrick the bags and Mick asked after the lady, instigating the search, the movements of which Nangle detailed minutely for the court. Mr Kirwan, at one point, nearly fell. The point where he nearly fell was directly above the rock upon which they later found Maria and, had he indeed slipped, he would surely have died. Pat, at trial, said he discovered the body at about 9.30 p.m., crying out to the rest of the search party when he did so.

Patrick described the body and how he found it. For the benefit of the court, he acted out the posture: the *Freeman's Journal* wrote 'here witness stretched himself out, with his arms by his sides'. Maria was on her back, with her bathing shift high up on her breast, 'leaving the rest of her person exposed'. Pat, as he had done at inquest, swore that she was laying upon a sheet, which was then wrapped around the body. Her head dangled back off the rock, but was also between two rocks. Maria's feet were in a small pool of water. 'Blood was coming from the ears or down the head, there was a good deal of blood on her face, there was also blood coming from her side and from her private parts. There was a cut on her side. I covered her with the dress and tied the sheet about her neck and across her legs before Mr Kirwan and Michael came up,' Nangle told the court. The body was pliant and not cold, though Nangle also said her arms were stiff. Later, he clarified again saying the arms were 'not stiff'.

Questioned at this point, counsel sought to clarify the statement about the vaginal bleeding. Nangle swore the blood was not natural.

'No, it was from a cut,' he said.

'From a cut?'

'Yes, from a sword cut.'

'How do you know?'

'I saw it.'

That exchange escaped Armstrong's report of the trial, and was contained in the *Freeman's Journal*. It appears in an account of the trial presented later in a pamphlet published in Dublin. But within all accounts, the fisherman next recalled finding the clothes. Or, not finding them. At Kirwan's direction, the Nangles had fruitlessly searched the area for Maria's clothes, but Kirwan had afterwards found them quickly, telling Pat to retrace his steps and fetch the rest. The fisherman swore that he had already searched the place where he later found the garments. 'I went and found them,' Pat told the trial. 'I had searched the very same place before and did not find them.'

The fisherman said he and his cousin then went back to the boat, bringing it around to the landing place and wrapping the body in a sail – which, the next day, was bloody on collection at Mrs Campbell's house, requiring a good scrubbing with a broom. They brought it, then, back to shore, and Pat said he went to get the dray. Brereton commented to Pat: 'This case did not prove a good haul for you.'

'No, to my grief,' said Pat. 'I wish I had never seen it – it was a very bad haul.'

Brereton asked more about the wounds: 'Upon your oath, did you see a single wound upon her body?'

Pat swore to seeing scratches – pin like – and said 'the private part of her body was greatly cut. The blood would have not flowed if otherwise.' The fisherman insisted the scratches could not have been caused by crabs. He couldn't swear that there were no crabs in the Long Hole, but he was sure the crabs would not have had enough time to do their work on the body.

It was during the cross-examination that some of Nangle's inconsistencies were interrogated. For example, why had the fisherman not mentioned the suspicion surrounding the finding of Maria's clothes at inquest? His testimony from 7 September was read back to him – it excluded much of the detail he had so far revealed in the witness box. 'I said nothing about Mr Kirwan having found the clothes when giving my information, because I was ordered to draw back,' replied Pat. 'When Mr Kirwan went up the rock to look for the clothes he did not go higher up than I did. Will swear that I searched the rock well. I do not care how dark it was, I searched the rocks and could find nothing. But afterwards, Mr Kirwan went up and after being a few minutes away came down and told me to go up again and I would find them. I then went up and found them. I will swear that the clothes were not on the rock where I found them. They had not been there for me to find.'

The sword cane came up again. Another aspect missing from Nangle's early testimony. How could he be sure Kirwan had a sword cane? It's a reasonable question: a cane that's secretly a sword is, by design, quite a lot like a regular cane. To be so obvious a concealed weapon as to illicit the suspicions of a ferryman would defeat its purpose. 'I cannot swear it was a sword cane which Mr Kirwan had with him,' conceded the fisherman towards the end of his testimony. 'It looked like one. Mr Kirwan used to carry the same cane before.'

Nangle finished his testimony, in part, by repeating his description of Kirwan laying his body over his wife's dead one, exclaiming 'Oh, Maria!' In his closing lines, he highlighted the fact that the whole episode was most inconvenient: 'I was not paid well enough for the assistance I gave. I got three shillings for the use of the boat. I demanded £2 for my trouble that night, and got it. Mr Kirwan left £1, the police sergeant passed his word for another. I caught the horse's head and would not let the dray go until I was paid.'

Michael, Pat's cousin, was next in the witness box. The fishermen told stories with many similarities. Unfortunately for those who try to piece together what happened on 6 September 1852, their stories also harboured many key differences. Mick put the time of their departure for the island at 7.30 p.m. and confirmed it was he, and not Kirwan, who first mentioned the absence of Mrs Kirwan. 'When I went up I said to Mr Kirwan "Where is the mistress?" – before I spoke had made two or three steps towards the bank to go down.'

Mick said he and Kirwan searched without success, Pat later joined the search, and on their return to the Long Hole, Pat spotted Maria. About 30 minutes elapsed between their first and second search to the Long Hole, the first limited by the higher tide. Mick mentioned how he and Kirwan went 'through the weeds' while traversing the island – the land was thick with vegetation, and there had been a shower. Mick expressed that he was not confident of finding Maria at the Long Hole – it was odd for women to swim there.

The big difference between the cousins had not changed from the inquest, or the multiple interviews in between: when Kirwan went to get the clothes after the Nangles came back empty-handed from their search, he carried two items, according to Mick. 'Mr Kirwan then went up the rock, and I followed him. He said "Here they are." I then saw Mr Kirwan come down, bringing something white in his hand like a sheet and also a shawl. He slipped coming down the rock. Pat Nangle and Mr Kirwan were putting the things on her.' Mick, he said, asked Kirwan to accompany the men to the boat, but he would not leave the body. Giles had been the only man to get wet, by his recollection, while they were moving the body into the boat. Around Maria's body were wrapped the shawl – around her neck – the sheet, and finally the sail.

Mick was cross-examined by Butt. 'Mr Kirwan called out for the lady whilst he and I were looking for her together, but not as loud as I did,' said the fisherman. 'When we met him on our arrival at the island he never made mention of his wife until he was spoken to about her. It was I proposed to search the Long Hole and remarked that if anything happened the lady we would be apt to find her at low water. Mr Kirwan said he was afraid there was. He seemed uneasy while searching for Mrs Kirwan.'

After Mick Nangle, Thomas Giles was briefly interviewed and not cross-examined. In helping to place Mrs Kirwan in the boat, Giles said he got wet to the knee. William told Giles that he had given Mrs Kirwan three glasses of porter – in other statements, he had said ale. Arthur Brew confirmed he was on the island and had seen the Kirwans – she was walking and reading, he was sketching near the church ruins.

The seventh witness was Hugh Campbell – the first of five to give evidence on the screams. Campbell, the fish driver, said he was waiting at the harbour wall when he heard a call coming from east of the lighthouse – placing it in the vicinity of the Long Hole. 'The voice was very weak,' he said. 'The cry was calling for assistance.' Campbell told the court he heard three cries. According to Armstrong's version of the trial, he said: 'I heard more than three cries. In three minutes after I heard the first cry, I heard another cry, and shortly afterwards I heard the third.' Other accounts said he left it at 'three'. The cries were weak – on that point he stood fast. Voices from the island were nothing new, he'd heard them before. A half hour after the cries, he saw the Nangles depart the harbour for the island.

Mr Hayes examined Campbell. At the point where he asked what kind of cries they were, and if there was any difference between them, Butt objected to the questioning. Campbell said he heard no words and could not tell whether it was a man or woman. On cross-examination by Butt, Campbell said he didn't mention the cries until the police called, and he then swore information before Captain Furnace. It was not quite dark when he heard the cries – but somewhere between day and dark – 'about half past seven o'clock', according to reports.

Thomas Larkin, the sailor, was the next to tell his story about screams of distress. Where Butt caught Larkin was on his estimation of the intervals between the first and second scream. At trial, Larkin said 'there could not have been eight minutes between the first and second cry'. In a response that became something of a trend for the defence, Larkin was read the information he swore before Brownrigg the previous October. On that occasion, under cross-examination by Mr Curran, Larkin had said: 'I suppose there was about eight minutes from the time I heard the first bawl, until I heard the other two.' Larkin's response to the mismatch at trial, was: 'I cannot speak as to minutes.'

Alicia Abernethy was the most specific with her details. The cries, she said, were those of a woman. Of the time she heard the screams, she was certain – 7.05 p.m. She knew because she went to a neighbour to check. She 'looked at the clock before she came out'.

'In order to hear the screams I suppose?' was the counsel's reply. Abernethy's answer of 'Yes', according to reports, elicited laughter. She said she was not fabricating the story.

Catherine Flood next recalled hearing the screams from Mrs Singleton's at about 7 o'clock, adding that she knew Mrs Kirwan to be an 'excellent' swimmer. John Barrett, who owned the dray upon which Maria was transported, swore to hearing 'two or three' screams from his front door near the east pier, and 'two or three more' shortly after. That was about 7 o'clock. He denied having had conversations with Catherine Flood about the screams. Barrett swore no statement at the inquest and neglected to tell the police sergeant about the screams – at first.

The first day of the trial concluded with the women who washed and prepared Maria's body. Maria's injuries, at this point, are well covered and will be discussed further. Scratched eyes, much blood. Bleeding from the nipples and vagina. From the ears, too – but 'none of her bones were broken'. Anne Lacy, like Nangle, said the scratches could not have been crab marks. The belly was flat to the backbone, said Lacy, and the blood voluminous; she swore to seeing some on the sail when it was taken off Maria's body. One eye was open and the other closed, and bloodshot. 'The body was clean and white, a beautiful creature,' she said. No major deviation there – minor ones, perhaps, but no new entries into the canon of medical evidence.

The same cannot be said for Catherine McGarr, who, on top of the observations generally in agreement with Lacy and her own previous accounts, added something new, that 'the mouth swelled and the nose was crooked on the face'. Previously, the egregious nose injury had escaped her sworn testimony. McGarr, at trial, gave the damning account of Kirwan's disregard for procedure when it came to washing the body: when the witness suggested they wait for the police to wash the body, Kirwan allegedly replied: 'I do not care a damn for the police, or anyone else – the body should be washed.' Mary Robinson, who held the candle, swore only a very short description of the body, corroborating the various scrapes and bleeding, and was not cross-examined. All three women concluded their evidence with commenting on the wetness of Mr Kirwan's trousers at Mrs Campbell's house.

It was past five o'clock when proceedings wound up for the day. Crampton told the jury it would be better if they did not separate. They would be provided with dinner, but not with any strong drink. 'Might we not be allowed a glass of wine?' asked one juror.

'It is better not, gentlemen,' replied the judge – to laughter in the court, and not for the first time that day. The jury were conveyed to the Northumberland Hotel.

12

THE VERDICT

The second day of the trial started in much the same way as the first: with a large, anxious crowd gathered at the doors of the Green Street Courthouse. The first witness, Joseph Sherwood, gave yet another account – less detailed, compared with others – of Maria's body, as he had remembered it before and at the inquest. The policeman next noted Kirwan's wet legs and stockings, describing the droplets forming on the ground and the steam rising from the damp. The constable proceeded uninterrupted until he came to the point of recalling the day he went to Merrion Street and found Ms Kenny with her two children at No. 11. Butt objected to the evidence, as Kirwan had been arrested at the time; Crampton agreed with the lawyer's point.

Mr Hayes, for the prosecution, then brought the testimony back to No. 11, and began a series of questions that sought to subtly paint a picture of something approaching a domestic scene. Hayes asked if the constable had seen a bed – and he had, but just the one. The prosecution then asked if he had seen 'any signs of breakfast'. Yes, he said despite Butt's objection, there was evidence of breakfast – tea, bread and butter arranged on a table.

Producing Maria's black bathing cap with its strings pulled tight in a knot, the constable moved on to his visits to Ireland's Eye since the night of the alleged murder – one of which had produced that piece of evidence. After 13 months stationed at Howth, the policeman was sure it was possible that a person on the mainland would be able to hear shouts on the island. He detailed the contents of the Kirwans' luggage, as he found it at Mrs Campbell's: 'I saw the bundle opened; I saw a flannel and a white petticoat, a gown, a shawl and a stays,' Sherwood told the court. 'I am sure there were two petticoats – I did not see any chemise. I did not see any marks of blood or dirt on these clothes.'

Anne Molloy was the 16th witness. The servant began by detailing her professional relationship with the Kirwans – that of cook and servant at their two Merrion Street homes, until her discharge in September 1850. Molloy, when she swore information previously, had been one of the handful of domestic employees to give insight into the daily life of the Kirwans – but on that day, in that court, the judge was not interested. 'I do not see what these things have to do with the question at issue,' he told Mr Smyly, whose reasoning – that the evidence was intended to 'show the prisoner's course of life' – was not sufficient. That was the end of Molloy's contribution.

At this point, the trial reached a pivotal moment. Teresa Kenny's evidence had the potential to address outstanding problems with the basis of the Crown's suggested motive, and shine light into the dark corners of what had been described as Kirwan's criminal engagement – the double life that gave this case its scandalous undercurrent. What was Kenny's relationship with Kirwan, exactly? How long – if at all – had she known about Maria, and vice versa? All in attendance at Green Street were, no doubt, keen to hear from the object of half of Kirwan's affections – the 'other woman', the mother of his many children.

Teresa Kenny's name was called, but she did not come forward. The trial moved on.

William Bridgeford – the landlord at Sandymount – was next brought up to give the dates of the four-year stint that William spent at his property with the woman he always considered to be Mrs Kirwan, but who was actually Teresa Kenny. Catherine Byrne, a former servant at Sandymount Avenue, described, briefly, the seven children the couple had, the fact they slept in the same bed and the 'strange lady' that called to the house once to make inquiries.

Next, the other witness to the disturbance at Mrs Campbell's in the summer of 1852 took the stand – recalling the noise behind a closed door, furniture tossed about and Mr Kirwan's ominous, angered repetition of 'I'll end you'. After some prompting by Isaac Butt, Anne Hannah also recalled the tiff she had with the artist about her barking dog – the one she sent away at Mr Kirwan's behest, though she maintained he never threatened to prosecute, and the little affray would not amount to 'a quarrel'.

With those brief sketches of Kirwan's various domestic situations in situ, the medical evidence was heard. James Alexander Hamilton – the medical student of famed little experience – was the 20th witness. Hamilton was a student of about six years, during which time, he told the court, he had attended all of his lectures and had experience with the appearance of dead bodies and dissection. 'I saw the face at first,' said Hamilton, after describing the situation of the body in Mrs Campbell's house, 'and I moved the cap and made a superficial examination of the head in order to see if there was any fracture or depression of the skull. I did not detect anything of the sort; there was a kind of mark or scratch on the right temple, such as would be caused by the rubbing of a body against a rock – it was only an abrasion of the skin.' He recalled the scratches around Maria's closed eyes, the lids of which 'presented a livid appearance, as if in a state of decomposition'.

'I did not open the eyes,' said Hamilton. 'I remarked that the lower edge of one of the ears was cut, as if something had been biting at it; the earring was held on by a slight strip of integument.' The student described the thin, light froth about Maria's mouth. Examining the body, he said he found the abdomen to be 'full and firm'. 'I could not ascertain whether there was any water in the body, but I thought at the time there might have been,' said Hamilton, in keeping with his earlier statements, adding: 'There were no marks on any part of the body that attracted my particular attention. I did not examine the body very closely – I did not examine the private parts. I did not see any blood where she was lying.' Hamilton went on to say that the skin around the eyes was quite abrased, and that he saw the breasts, but didn't see any major cut there – though, it was possible a shallow one could have escaped his notice.

'On looking over the body, I did not see any mark of violence,' said Hamilton. 'I never examined the body of a drowned person until I examined

Mrs Kirwan's, but I would recognise the marks usually exhibited by such bodies.' Besides a coin-sized stain of blood on Maria's cap, there was none to speak of. And with no immediately visible traces of blood mixed with the froth, no bruises and considering the full abdomen and pale skin – he figured, 'as a medical man', it had to be a case of drowning. Hamilton was then asked the question that ended his involvement in *The Queen* v. *William Kirwan*: did he think, 'as a medical man', that he had discharged his duty by the superficial examination which he made?

'I do not,' he replied. 'But I knew nothing at the time to excite my suspicion.'

The medical student was followed by a doctor. George Hatchell, whose post-mortem examination had apparently originally left him without a strong opinion, gave a much more detailed rendition of what he observed at Glasnevin Cemetery on 6 October – 31 days after Maria's death. And with it, a decidedly more formed view on what likely took place. With the wetness of the grave and the water in the coffin described for the benefit of the jury, Hatchell commenced with detailing the main strand of medical evidence for the prosecution.

'I examined the scalp carefully, but I could not find any mark of violence there,' the doctor began. 'Over the right eye there was an abrasion, or marks of scratches, and also on the prominent part of the right cheek, under the right eye. The right eye was rather protruded, and the left one particularly so; that I presume was rather the result of the decomposition. I partially opened the eyes and found that the white part of them was exceedingly vascular, or injected with blood. I examined the ears; there was an earring in the left ear, but the lobe of the right ear was wanting. There was nothing remarkable inside the ears; there were no injuries outside, inside or behind the ear, that I could observe, decomposition having set in too far. The upper lip was swollen, and the tongue protruded between the teeth; the inside of the lips was very vascular; the tongue was marked by the teeth, both above and below. There was a sort of soapy matter about the face and mouth, such as usually presents itself on bodies in an advanced state of decomposition. On opening the head,

I found the membrane containing the brain in a very flaccid state; on making an opening in it, the brain, being in a semi-fluid state, flowed out freely. The brain was of a light pinkish colour all over – the fluidity of the brain was owing to decomposition; the brain was a little more red than I expected.

'Having been informed that the blood flowed from the ears and knowing that such a symptom was often the result of a fracture at the base of the skull, I examined that part with great care, but I could not detect any fracture. I examined the trachea and the larynx, but there was nothing remarkable about them. I examined the vertebrae of the neck, but found nothing like dislocation there. I examined the right breast, and found a superficial cut or scratch under the right nipple; I saw nothing to account for blood flowing from the nipple; there was an extensive lividity on the right side, but that is not remarkable in a dead body; the lividness depends on gravitation, according to the position in which the body may be placed. I examined the fingers, but I found no marks on them; the cuticle of the hands and nails were coming off like a glove, but that was from decomposition.

'About the lower part of the body I observed some degree of swelling; the labia and anus were swollen, and the interior of the vagina was very vascular and injected with blood, much more than was usual; these appearances I would say were produced by congestion of the veins, arising from pressure, or by any thing that would impede the general circulation of the blood through the body. The body was that of an exceedingly well formed woman; on making an opening into the chest I found the lungs congested at the posterior, inferior and at the lower portion of the anterior parts; the interior parts of the body were fresh and healthy and completely untouched by decomposition; the congestion of the lungs was caused by the engorgement of the blood; their appearance was such as would result from a sudden stoppage of respiration.

'I examined the heart and found it perfectly healthy; it was empty both on the right and left sides; the large vessels leading from it were also empty.'

To this point, Hatchell's evidence remained virtually unchanged, if augmented, from his statements made during the investigations in October. Since he last swore information, however, he had visited Ireland's Eye on several occasions. 'I went to a place called the Long Hole,' said the doctor. 'Nangle the boatman pointed out to me the place where the body was found. The Long Hole is a deep creek running up into the island – the creek is divided by very large stones transversely. The stones are about midway, between high and low water mark.' Here, Hatchell pointed to a map, indicating the position of the stones and high and low water mark. Smyly then asked the question that was too much for Butt to tolerate: 'From your knowledge of the place, the observations you made at it, and from your observations upon the body, are you able to form an opinion as to how this lady came by her death?'

'I object to this question as illegal,' interjected Butt. 'The inference drawn by the witness from what he has seen at Ireland's Eye, and from what he has been told, ought not to be received in evidence. I do not object to the witness giving his opinion, founded upon his professional skill and knowledge.' A discussion unfolded. Crampton told Butt he was inclined to think the evidence was admissible, but would look into any authority on the point. 'There is a case cited in Roscoe,' responded the defence counsel, 'in which several of the judges doubted whether a medical witness could give his opinion on the very point the jury had to decide.'

Baron Greene said he thought the opinion of Dr Hatchell on the matter of science was so mixed up with fact that it could not be legally put. Smyly was told to put the question in some other form. This small battle would reverberate on a day of tense, technical, interpretive medical evidence. Mr Smyly rephrased: 'From the appearances you observed on the body, are you able, as a medical man, to form an opinion as to the cause of death, and what is that opinion?'

Hatchell replied: 'I am of the opinion that death was caused by asphyxia, or a sudden stopping of respiration; from the congestion in the vagina, from the engorgement of the lungs and other circumstances, I would say that in all probability the simple stoppage of respiration must have been combined with pressure of some kind, or constriction, which caused the sudden stoppage. I do not think that simple drowning would produce, to the same extent, the appearances I saw.' A change from his earlier position. One which did not go unnoticed by Butt. However, for the meantime, Smyly was happy to hammer home the point.

'Would simple drowning cause the appearances presented in this case?' asked the prosecution counsel.

'Not to the same extent,' replied Hatchell.

It was time for cross-examination. Isaac Butt asked again if the body presented appearances that death 'by drowning alone' would not cause. Hatchell repeated: 'Not to the same extent.' The doctor then clarified: 'I don't think I would have found the same amount of congestion in the vagina in a case of simple drowning.' That, combined with the congestion in the lungs, swelling of the upper lip and extreme congestion of the inside of the mouth, led him to believe it was likely that Maria's death was no accident.

'On your oath,' resumed Butt, 'when did you first form the opinion that death by drowning alone would not account for these appearances?'

'I formed it at the time I was making the post-mortem examination,' replied the doctor, prompting Mr Butt to read the statement made by the doctor in October, which said that 'the lungs and heart exhibited those appearances which are compatible with death produced by drowning or strangulation'.

Mr Butt resumed his examination. 'Will you say now, on your solemn oath, that the appearances of the lungs were not consistent with death by drowning?'

'I have seen a great many…' the doctor began, but Butt was seeking a simple response.

'I am not asking you, sir, what you saw; answer "yes" or "no" to my question, and remember the solemn oath you have taken.'

Hatchell repeated his opinion: 'I think the engorgement was more than I ever saw in cases of drowning before. This opinion is founded upon what I have seen.' Mr Butt was not finished, labouring the point written on the paper before him, sworn by the doctor who now appeared to be altering his opinion. 'Is it true that the lungs exhibited an appearance compatible with death produced by drowning?' asked the counsel.

'You have not finished the sentence,' replied Hatchell.

Butt again read aloud: 'The lungs and heart exhibited the appearances compatible with death produced by drowning or strangulation – is that true?'

'It is true.'

'Is it true they are compatible with death produced by drowning?'

'To a certain extent they are.'

'Do you swear, from their appearances, that death could not have been caused by drowning alone?' asked Butt.

'I have said that the engorgement I saw was to an extent I never saw produced by drowning before.'

'Was the engorgement compatible with death by drowning alone?'

'I don't think it was.'

'You say it was not compatible?'

'It depends altogether on how the drowning occurred: if the drowning occurred very suddenly, the engorgement would not be so great as where the drowned person struggled to save himself or herself.'

'Was that what you meant to convey on your direct examination?'

The doctor replied: 'I did not mean to say whether she might have struggled by herself or with another; the appearance presented by the body would be occasioned by a person drowning struggling with himself or herself. The appearance presented by the lungs must have been caused by struggling. I think it very likely that the appearance of the vagina would have been occasioned by struggling in the water for life; a struggle and compression amount to the same thing. I went down to Ireland's Eye, on several occasions, in company with Major Brownrigg. I am surgeon to the constabulary, and he is deputy inspector general of constabulary. He took a strong interest as a magistrate in the prosecution. I was asked by Major Brownrigg to go to Ireland's Eye; I thought it right, for the sake of the prisoner, and for every other reason, to make myself acquainted with all the facts.'

'Did you alter your opinion as to the cause of the death after you visited Ireland's Eye?' asked Butt.

'I did not,' replied Hatchell, confirming that he had indeed heard of the possibility of violence being used prior to making his examination. In fact, his examination was tailored precisely upon what he had heard; bleeding from the ears, the vagina and the rumoured prospect of a long, sharp instrument stabbed into the body. 'There was no injury of the ears internally,' said the doctor on these points. 'I did not examine the tympanum, but I did not see any marks of violence about the ears as far as I examined, having been told that instruments had been run up into the body, I examined to see if there were any traces of such having been done, but I did not find any whatever. There was no appearance of violence in the vessels of the vagina, such as having a sharp instrument thrust up.'

Butt next asked: 'Suppose a person went into the water with a full stomach, would that be likely to cause congestion?'

'It would, but not to any great extent. Going into cold water is likely to cause a fit, but it is not likely to cause a bleeding from the ears. I think a fatal result might follow from a person going into cold water with a full stomach,' replied Hatchell.

This went on, with the doctor parrying questions on the topic as Butt attempted to eke out minor, technical concessions in a bid to return the doctor to his previous opinion – that there was more than one possible cause for Maria's death. He asked: 'Have you ever heard of a fit of epilepsy being produced by a person going into cold water with a full stomach?'

Hatchell said it was possible. The doctor added at that point that the blackness he saw on Maria's body was due to the gravitation of blood, and not a bruise. To Mr Smyly, Hatchell said he had heard of people screaming at the outset of a fit of epilepsy – though never more than one scream.

Mr Butt again took the reins: 'Do you mean to say that a person in epilepsy will not give more than one scream?'

'I will not say that they will not give more than a single scream, but I never heard more than one.'

Butt's questioning here was designed to create room for alternative explanations. Hatchell resisted it well. 'Did you ever read in the newspapers of the defendant in a case in which I was engaged in the courthouse of Roscommon, being seized with a fit of epilepsy, and screaming so loudly and so frequently, that the court had to be adjourned?' asked Butt, concluding a rally of questioning and, ultimately, the doctor's testimony.

'I did not, but frequent screams are not impossible,' said the doctor, conceding, at least, that much.

Henry Davis, the experienced coroner whose work on this case would become perhaps more heavily scrutinised than even the inexperienced, self-professed 'medical man' whom he engaged to attend his inquest, took the stand as the 22nd, and final, witness for the Crown.

'I viewed the body of the deceased, Maria Kirwan, on that day, and the jury were with me at the time I did so,' he recalled. 'I afterwards, however ascertained that it had been washed, prepared and laid out in readiness for my arrival.' The coroner told the court that the marks of crab bites were common in cases like these. Green crabs were the specific creatures; 'I am well acquainted with the appearances produced by them. There were marks of those bites upon the eyes as well as upon the breasts of the deceased, Mrs Kirwan.' On this point, he was clear: a body did not need to be long in the water for crabs to begin feasting. On the proceedings themselves, Davis insisted he conducted them perfectly regularly. Kirwan, whom he had never previously met, was sworn in following a request by the jury – but he was not a prisoner at that time.

Statements, on the day, were sworn and read back to witnesses, and each was asked if they had anything to add, Davis said. To the best of his memory, all were signed, either in writing or by a mark. He recalled Mr Kirwan interfering with the deposition of one of the Nangles, and one of the Nangles interrupting the other. Here, Butt interjected. 'I think I ought to interpose,' said the defence counsel, 'if only for the purpose of reminding my learned friend that he is cross examining his own witness.'

Mr Hayes replied: 'I am endeavouring to elicit evidence from him to suit me, Mr Butt.'

'No,' said Butt, 'I think it unfair that the Crown should endeavour to throw discredit upon the testimony of their own witness.'

'I think Mr Hayes ought to treat him more gently than either Mr Butt or Mr Brereton have done,' said the judge.

'Come now, sir,' said Hayes, 'have you great experience in crab bites?' A ripple of laughter made its way around the crowded court room.

'No,' replied the coroner.

'How many bites have you seen on a body?' he asked, but the coroner could not give a number. They attacked the eyes first, he said – they needed less than an hour to have an effect on a body. He had heard of crabs attacking the ears – but not the inside of them. Davis confirmed to Butt that he had told Mr Kirwan at the inquest to ask the witnesses any questions he thought proper. Here, the statement taken by Kirwan at the inquest – the most bare-bones rendition of the day detectable in virtually any recorded account – was read out. The case for the prosecution closed.

It was impossible to exaggerate the solemnity of the duty before the jury. That statement – atop Isaac Butt's remarks to the jury, which came next – was undeniable. The lawyer reminded the jurors that his job was not to lead the jury astray; unquestionably, he was there to state the case as favourably as possible for the prisoner, but that fact did not extend to the misstatement of fact, or a will to mislead a juror's judgement. He made the plea which ran centrally through his and any subsequent defences of William Kirwan: to forget the stories and rumours – 'dismiss all those slanders' which had injured his client's reputation.

For the purposes of examining the prosecution's evidence, Butt divided the facts into three groups: the appearance of Maria's body; the screams from the island; and the so-called 'moral facts', which were, the lawyer suggested, impossible to now separate from the charge. At the outset, he reminded the jury that 'the law and Christianity presumes every man innocent till he is proved to be guilty. If that be the rule in a case where some person has done the fatal deed, it applies infinitely stronger to a case where the question is raised – was there a crime committed at all?'

Butt, firstly, addressed the evidence as to the cries, 'if they came from the deceased lady at all', which was never actually proven. Larkin's evidence, the defence counsel suggested, was more consistent with the cries being those of Kirwan and the Nangles searching for Maria on the island. Judging by the intervals he quoted – eight minutes between the first and second scream – and the condition of the light, it would be nearly impossible to infer that Kirwan had murdered Maria, arranged the body and made it back to the Martello tower in time for the arrival of the boat. In fact, Butt said it would be better for the prisoner if the jury did believe that the screams were the dying cries of Mrs Kirwan, 'for the time must have been very short from the hearing of the cries until the Nangles landed; and if they were her dying screams, it is clear, beyond all doubt, that she had not come to her death by the hands of her husband'.

On the screams, the boatman Larkin was the only reliable narrator, as far as Butt was concerned. He had not much time for Alicia Abernethy, whose account of hearing the screams from one of the furthest distances of any earwitness was a little too perfectly aligned. 'She was a mile further from the island,' said Butt, 'and appeared to have prepared everything to hear the screams.' If the jury believed Larkin – and they had no reason not to – then they might also remember that Mr Kirwan said he had been looking for Mrs Kirwan prior to the arrival of the boatmen. Was that the cry the fisherman heard? Was it enough to supply reasonable doubt on the point? Maria was a strong woman, and Butt thought it not unreasonable to think she would be capable of screaming when meeting her death. 'It is impossible to take them on reliable evidence as dying cries,' said Butt, 'but even if they were dying cries, there was nothing to fix the prisoner with guilt.'

The defence counsel reminded the jury that no definite mode of death had been clearly identified. 'Dr Hatchell talked of compression,' he said, 'which was a convenient phrase. But I ask you, as rational men, to fix in your minds any one way in which, consistently with the evidence, he could have murdered her? Did he strangle her? Did he go into the water and drown her? It would not do to say that they were alone on the island, and that he must have killed her in some way, for you must have distinct grounds for arriving at such a conclusion.' Eight minutes was a long time to elapse between two death cries. 'What would a strong woman be doing in the meantime?' One natural supposition was an attack of epilepsy.

Next, Butt addressed Kirwan's extramarital affair. His behaviours were widely known and had been trotted out as a motive by the prosecution lawyers. 'It is undeniable that he had formed an unfortunate connexion; but surely that is a long way from coming to the conclusion that he therefore murdered his wife,' said Butt, who doubted the inbuilt motive. Both women, he said, knew about the situation – one which 'no man could justify'. To conflate that undoubted, ongoing offence which his wife had to endure with the guilt of her murder, 'would be monstrous'.

In his long and powerful defence of Kirwan, Butt mentioned the prisoner had been confined to bed for a considerable time, such were the effects of Maria's 'melancholy death'. That very death, he stressed, was not proven to have been caused by violence – according to the appearances on the body. Butt asked the jury to remember how the prosecution never asked whether, from the medical appearances alone, Dr Hatchell would be able to identify a cause of death. Instead, they wanted an opinion from him formed via the medical evidence, mixed with details gleaned from his day trips to the scene, or, as Butt put it, 'an opinion, combined with the officious zeal and suggestions of the constabulary officers and the agents of the crown solicitors, who brought him down to Ireland's Eye to tutor and instruct him.' Dr Hatchell had proven, through his own examination, that strangulation did not take place; yet he introduced the word in evidence. There was no violence, but 'compression', according to the doctor: 'What in the name of common sense, did he mean by compression?' asked Butt.

Bleeding caused by physical compression would surely leave the signs of violence – and internal organ injury – that were specifically missing from the post-mortem. Butt pointed to the froth at Maria's mouth and the swelling of the lips as evidence of drowning or a fit following dinner on the island. On the scratches, Butt reminded the jury of Henry Davis's long career, during which time he surely had gained the necessary experience to identify a crab bite. And if not a crab bite, surely then falling against the rocks would produce a scratch. Butt also reminded the jury that it was not his duty to fully account for those scratches – it was the prosecution's. This was a case, said Butt, in which only an innocent man would not be able to fully explain what happened at the Long Hole. Nevertheless, the scratches from crabs and the seaweed in Maria's hair did incline Butt to believe that she fell in the water, struggling, and there remained.

On Kirwan's appearance, Butt reminded the jury that he had no defensive wounds. If it was demonstrated that she died by drowning – as opposed to strangulation – the only mode would have been submersion: 'If you do believe the prisoner to be the murderer,' said Butt, 'I see no other possible way for him to have done the deed, except by following her into the water, when she went to bathe, and holding her under it until she was drowned. To make out, and sustain that extraordinary supposition, evidence is brought before you to show that his boots and trousers were wet. Why, if the prisoner did commit the dreadful deed in that way, it would not be his boots and trousers, but his coat and arms that would be wet.' There was no doubt in Maria's swimming abilities. 'But good swimming, gentlemen, is no protection against drowning, if a person be seized with a fit.' Swimmers, he said, often die by drowning.

Butt then disregarded the sword cane theory – Nangle's claim – as another rumour that was undone by Dr Hatchell's examination. He threw further doubt over the doctor's impartiality when he wondered why the prosecution had not called Dr Tighe, the other doctor present at the post-mortem, who perhaps was not brought to Ireland's Eye in advance of the trial to alter his opinion. The Crown had not brought forward key evidence, though Butt added that he relied upon the high characters of those men in concluding that they did not intentionally withhold it. The post-mortem examination, he thought, was satisfactory, and showed the lack of violence marks, to which Butt frequently returned.

Butt remarked on Kirwan's behaviour. Would a murderer have opted to stay with the body of his victim in the darkness of the Long Hole while the men went to fetch the boat? Could his feet have become wet in the pool of water at Maria's feet – as described by the boatmen? Butt did not put much weight in the testimony of Patrick Nangle, favouring that of Michael; his recollection of Kirwan coming down from the rock with clothes and something like a sheet in hand made more sense to him. He rubbished claims by Pat about the mystery of the hidden clothes. Parsing these and other circumstances at considerable length, Butt pleaded with the jurors to arrive at the only possible verdict, as he saw it: acquittal. Witnesses were then called for the defence.

The two experts called by the defence on the second day of the trial were designed to topple the prosecution's case at its root – the medical facts – and emphasise the question: was it proven that a murder took place?

Butt's first witness was Francis Rynd. An Irish physician of some prominence, Rynd's legacy following his death in 1861 would, primarily, be the invention of the hypodermic needle. But on the second day of *The Queen* v. *Kirwan* in December 1852, from the very first question, it was clear that his testimony would be as fraught with technical challenges as Dr Hatchell's. In his opening gambit, Rynd said he had heard the evidence given by Dr Hatchell, regarding the state of the body post-mortem.

Butt asked: 'Judging from all these appearances, which you state you have heard described, what cause would you assign for the death of the party upon whom they were found?'

'My Lord, I must really object to that question,' interjected Smyly. 'Here is a medical gentleman produced, who was not present at the post-mortem examination, and who, for all we know to the contrary, may never have seen the deceased, and yet is examined for the purpose of proving the cause of her death.'

Butt was instructed to ask the question again, but to keep it rooted in general scientific appearances, rather than specifically about the cause of Mrs

Kirwan's death. The latter was 'evidence too home to the jury box', Crampton said. Butt tried again, multiple times, reaching an acceptable formulation on his fifth attempt.

'All those appearances which you have just described, would produce asphyxia, and the person should die; in other words, it would cause a stoppage of the breath, and of the circulation of the blood, which would end in death,' replied Rynd to essentially the same question from the defence counsel.

Butt next asked: 'In your judgement, as a medical man, do you think those appearances could be caused by external violence, supposing there to be no external marks of violence upon the body?'

'There should be manifest marks of external violence to produce them,' replied the doctor – and more than the scratches as described.

Butt asked if those appearances could be produced by a fit of epilepsy. 'They would,' replied Rynd, adding, 'without any concurring cause' when asked by Judge Crampton to clarify. Rynd said an epileptic patient might scream several times during a fit, and that bathing in cold water on a full stomach might contribute to produce such a fit. The surgeon said an episode like that could explain the state of the body as earlier noted. 'If the brain were more than naturally pink,' said Rynd, 'a month after death, it would be a proof that there was a greater quantity of blood present in the minute vessels of the head, than perhaps was natural, which would tend to cause apoplexy.' The surgeon said the flow of blood could have been accounted for without internal injury being present, but added that 'the blood might have oozed from the tympanum, or if the congestion were very great, it might have been the result of external oozing'.

Butt again asked if the appearances, including the blood flow, could be explained by an epileptic fit after a meal. 'I think it very probable that such might be the case; general congestion would produce a flow of blood from the vagina, and that general congestion would very probably be produced by sudden immersion in the water with a full stomach,' replied Rynd, adding that froth on the mouth could be the product of an epileptic fit. Congestion, he said, could cause bleeding from the skin. If someone had a fit and suffered a bout of apoplexy, the doctor thought the various blood flows could be accounted for.

However, asked if that level of congestion and ear-bleeding could be produced without causing internal injury or without leaving a mark, Rynd hesitated for some time, before answering: 'Apoplexy might be produced by a blow upon the head that would not leave a mark, and yet the congestion would be so great that an exudation might take place; the blow might leave a very slight mark upon the scalp, but the abrasion would be so slight that it might not be perceived.' In the event of strangulation, he said, the effects of decomposition would highlight the markings – not obscure them.

Mr Smyly asked what the doctor would expect to find during a post-mortem examination on a person who drowned. Rynd listed congestion of the lungs and brain and possibly of the vagina. Bleeding from the ears, he said, could be possible, though he had not before encountered it. Addressing a question from Mr Butt at this point, Rynd said blood could continue to flow from the body of a drowning victim as late as the day after death. The doctor said there were no real discernible differences between the froth produced in epilepsy versus drowning, save for the possibility of blood in the epileptic froth, if the tongue was bitten. The surgeon had also seen the lips of a victim of 'simple drowning' grow large and swell.

Smyly moved on to the theory that the lack of marks of violence could possibly be produced by an assailant holding a wet cloth over the nose and mouth. Rynd conceded that could be possible. In answers to Crampton, Rynd said a person having a seizure could possibly scream a number of times, for two to three minutes after 'the moment of falling'. The first scream, he told Smyly, would be the worst. Towards the end of Rynd's cross-examination, the only official mention of familial epilepsy was entered into evidence – and in curious circumstances. Rynd revealed that he had attended Mrs Kirwan six years beforehand, when he treated her for a fever. He was not aware at the time if she suffered from epilepsy. Rynd said he was recently told 'that her father died of a fit of that nature'.

'May I ask if it was a person who has taken an anxious part in this trial who gave you that information?' replied Smyly.

'It was indeed,' replied Rynd. 'It was a person deeply interested therein.'

Next up, another physician, Robert Adams, was examined by Mr Brereton. 'Congestion of the lungs might arise from a variety of causes, from drowning, from suffocation or from an epileptic fit,' said the doctor. As for bleeding, any cause that produced congestion of the whole muscular system could trigger it. Adams agreed with Rynd that an epileptic fit could be caused by a person going into the water after a meal, and the blood of a drowned person generally continues in a liquid state for some time. On the issue of screams, he was certain that a loud scream announced an epileptic fit, but it would be unusual for further screams to occur.

In response to cross-examination, Adams said that the wet-cloth suffocation would produce effects akin to drowning or hanging, and possibly bleeding from the ears. Pressure on the chest (such as a person kneeling on another person), he thought, would not produce extensive congestion – but pressure on a windpipe would. 'Suppose I put you into the water and put my foot on your breast,' said Smyly, 'would that produce congestion?'

'If my mouth were under water, it would,' replied Adams.

After a short back-and-forth, Smyly continued: 'Now, suppose we add this ingredient – that while the individual was in the water, there was an extreme struggle, what effect would that have upon the bodily symptoms?'

Adams: 'I suppose it would cause a great deal of air and water to get into the windpipe, and produce congestion.'

Smyly: 'Would a protracted struggle increase those effects, think you, Mr Adams?'

'The longer the struggle the greater the congestion would be,' replied the doctor.

Smyly turned to the matter of the froth, which Adams described as air in the windpipe mixing with water and mucus. Smyly wondered if there would be more air in the body of a person who was drowned by force, compared with one who had accidentally drowned. Adams couldn't say, but on further questioning, offered his opinion that there would be more froth on the mouth of a person who had been forcibly drowned. As for bleeding from the ears and vagina, the doctor had never personally heard of a case of either epilepsy or accidental drowning where those two things occurred. Brereton then re-examined his witness on the point of the supposed extreme pressure on the chest, which Adams said he thought would not be able to produce the effects seen without leaving some mark of violence.

'In the case a wet sheet was put over the mouth and nose of a person, would it produce three loud and terrible screams?' asked Brereton, teeing up an answer from Adams that caused further murmurs of laughter in the court room. 'That is not a medical question,' said the doctor.

Judge Crampton had the last question: 'Supposing death to have taken place by forcible submersion, or from accidental drowning, would you be able, from the appearances described, to state which species of death they were attributable?'

'My Lord,' said Adams, 'in my opinion, no man living could do so.'

Adams was the last defence witness. Mr Hayes replied on the part of the Crown. On the point of forgetting rumours and favouring facts sworn in court, Hayes said he agreed with Mr Butt. From the outset of his reply, Hayes had some repair work to do. Butt had, in various ways, suggested poor practices in the way the investigation was carried out, from the possible withholding of evidence, to coaching witnesses. Hayes denied the lot.

'Dr Hatchell's testimony, I will admit, did not come up to what the Crown had been led to believe and expect, but I see no ground, whatever, for the assertion, that he did not state the truth,' he said. 'His evidence, which was given fairly, candidly and impartially, amounted to this: that the symptoms and appearances presented by the body of the deceased were consistent with death produced otherwise than by violence. That testimony, in its general aspect, was favourable to the prisoner; and yet the gentleman who gave it has fallen under the lash of Mr Butt's indignant eloquence.' Hayes continued outlining the evidence, and only when Hayes stated that Kirwan 'shamelessly' presented Kenny as his wife, did Butt interject.

'I wish to correct my learned friend,' said Butt. 'There is no evidence that the prisoner had introduced this woman to the public as his wife.' Smyly insisted Teresa Kenny had presented as Mrs Kirwan; it was how Mr Bridgeford and the servant at Sandymount addressed her. He moved on, and asked that Mr Butt only interrupt if he misstated a fact, and not for 'word-catching'. The prosecution counsel went on to remind the jury of the disturbance at Mrs Campbell's and ask: 'Are these facts consistent with the kind and genuine affection that ought to exist between the husband and wife? Are they not the very antipodes of affection?'

As for the idea of epilepsy, Hayes wondered why there was no real evidence to speak of. 'As the prisoner has forborne to produce such testimony, it is not too much to infer that there was none such to produce; and we must take it as proved that the deceased was a perfectly healthy woman,' he told the jury. On the screams, Hayes said that Hugh Campbell's testimony – that he saw the Nangles' boat depart a half hour after he heard the screeches – debunked Butt's theory that Larkin had been listening to the fishermen shouting on the island, as they swore they left at about 7.30 p.m., and the other witnesses heard the screeches at about 7 o'clock. Hayes also thought that a point raised by Butt – that the acoustics of the island may have allowed a person on the shore, but not on the island, to hear a call from the Long Hole – was not a substantial excuse for Mr Kirwan having not heard the cries.

The jury was reminded that it had been Mick, and not Kirwan, who suggested they look for Maria. Hayes favoured Pat's version of the search, as opposed to Mick's; the infamous sheet should have been 'high and dry', and not on the rock. A narrative was offered. At 7 p.m., William Kirwan approached Maria in the water, taking the sheet with him. 'Let us suppose she saw his dreadful purpose, can you not conceive and account then for the dreadful shrieks that were heard, when the horrid reality burst upon her mind, that on that desolate, lonely island, without a living soul but themselves upon it, he was coming into that Long Hole to perpetrate his dreadful offence.' If he succeeded in putting her under the water, might not she have struggled violently and shrieked again – 'fearful, agonising and fainter'? Hayes said this was not mere imagination but a rational deduction from the evidence.

The fact that Pat Nangle could not discover the clothes on his first scale of the rock he knew so well was 'passing strange', but exactly how the clothes came to be there was for the jury to decide. He highlighted Kirwan's insistence that the body be washed. Offering a new excuse for the scratches on her face, Hayes excluded the concept of green crab bites and instead favoured the idea that Maria scratched her own face while trying to pull the 'terrible sheet' from her mouth and nose.

'Consider all the facts; combine and compare them; bring your knowledge of human nature and of human affairs to them and try if you can, in Heaven's name, to come to the conclusion that the prisoner is not guilty of the crime laid to his charge,' said Hayes, wrapping up.

'If, without a rational doubt, you are conscientiously convinced that this woman came by her death by the hands of him who ought to have been her protector, come well or ill, come weal or woe, it is your duty, painful though it be, to bring in the dreadful verdict of guilty, and leave the rest to God.'

***

Judge Crampton began his charge to the jury, telling them to put away all prejudice, and disregard anything they may have heard about the case outside the confines of the courtroom. 'Gentlemen of the jury, you have been apprised that in this case there is no direct positive testimony against the prisoner,' said the judge, according to Armstrong's report. 'If, gentlemen, in such a case of circumstantial evidence, you cannot, in your consciences, reconcile the innocence of the prisoner with the facts that are laid before you, and the circumstances relied upon in the evidence against him, it will be your bounden duty, upon that circumstantial evidence, to find the prisoner guilty. If, on the other hand, gentlemen, you can reconcile the facts and circumstances that are relied upon as affording a chain of evidence against the accused, with his innocence, you are bound to find him not guilty.' If the minds of the jury were in a 'state of honest doubt on the subject', it was their duty to acquit.

Judge Crampton made clear to the jury that the previous character of Mr Kirwan, on its own, was not proof of a murder having been committed. 'The evidence before the 6th of September has not a necessary connexion with either the guilt or innocence of the accused. You have heard a good deal with respect to the character and immoral habits in which it appeared the prisoner indulged previous to the 6th of September. There is no necessary connexion between the character and conduct of the prisoner previous to that date – with, perhaps one exception – and his liability to the charge which is the subject of this indictment. They may furnish you with a motive, unquestionably; but you will recollect how very difficult it is to connect a single motive with the subsequent act.'

Crampton put the time of the discovery of the body at 9 o'clock. This is at odds with other statements throughout the prosecution brief, which variously put that time at 9.30 p.m. and 10 p.m. The sheet was mentioned, as was the corresponding disagreement between the Nangles. The threatening words heard on that occasion recounted by Mrs Campbell were 'evidence of treatment unbecoming by any man, but especially a husband'. Whatever about the terms the pair lived on, it was 'beyond all doubt' that the prisoner did not entertain a 'single and entire devotion of heart and affection to his wife'. On Maria's body, there were external marks, certainly, but none that could cause death. On the whole, Crampton said, there was not much disagreement between Hatchell, Rynd and Adams. All three said the cause of death could not be external injuries. Suicide was ruled out. There were no marks of 'violence' – though Crampton excluded the Crown's theory of a wet cloth over the face from that definition.

Crampton said 'all the medical gentlemen, Drs Hatchell, Rynd and Adams, are agreed that the symptoms and appearances of external and internal injuries would all be consistent with a person being drowned either by simple drowning, or by what he might call forcible immersion – being kept under water. Dr Hatchell went a little further then the other two in stating, that his conception was, that appearances of congestion would be to a greater extent developed where the drowning was forcible, than they would be where the drowning was merely simple drowning. Dr Adams was decidedly of opinion that from the appearances that were suggested to him, no conclusion could be arrived at as to whether death had been by forcible means or by simple drowning. Therefore, on the subject of the cause of death, you are left even by the doctors in a state of great uncertainty and mystery.'

Crampton referred to the scratches. They were made either by crabs, or during a struggle, or 'there may have been precipitation from a height', which caused them. 'You cannot find any man guilty of the most trivial crime upon suspicion or conjecture,' he told the jury. 'Your verdict should be found on a firm, stable basis; and that should be either direct testimony which you believe, or facts and circumstances which you believe and cannot reconcile with the innocence of the prisoner.'

It was up to the jury to decide if Kirwan's cries upon finding Maria were truly sorrowful, or an act designed to fool the fishermen and everybody else. The Nangles disagreed on the finding of the clothes. 'Michael Nangle swore that after Mr Kirwan came down from the rock, on which the clothes were found, that he had in his hand a shawl, and something white. Whether it might have been a chemise or a sheet was not stated,' said the judge, summing up his view of that part of the evidence. There was no stain of blood on the clothes that were in the bundle, the judge reminded the jury. While Pat said he did not see a shawl until it was already wrapped around the body, Michael said the items that Kirwan carried (the shawl and something that was possibly the sheet) were wrapped around the body, which would imply it was the sheet and the shawl that he carried, as they were later identified as being wrapped on the body.

It's a convoluted point of evidence, and one which rested on the jury believing one Nangle over the other. One of the men was mistaken, Crampton said, though he didn't think either was lying. Pat Nangle's difference of account between the inquest and trial, on the blood and sheet, were also highlighted for the jury's consideration, though the judge said that a more detailed account would generally be expected in a criminal trial. Whether or not Nangle was stopped from continuing was not completely clear: while there was some evidence of an interruption, Henry Davis also swore that each man was given a chance to add anything at the end.

The judge entertained the defence counsel's position on the screams, that they could have been those of the Nangles when on the island. 'It is an important circumstance to have regard to, that the cries of the boatmen might have been more numerous than the screams.' It's important to note, the judge said, that all sides agreed that cries were heard 'coming from Ireland's Eye' a little after 7 o'clock on the evening of 6 September. 'It will be for you to say if the screams undoubtedly came from the Long Hole, and if they did, they undoubtedly came from the deceased lady. Were they the cries of a drowning person requiring help, or of a person suffering from violence? What caused them? Undoubtedly pressing and imminent danger of some kind. Were they the screams of a person suddenly seized with epilepsy, or were they caused by pain, or fear occasioned by another person?' It would be for the jury to decide how Maria came upon the 'Body Rock' and there remained. The jury were to consider whether she – an experienced swimmer – fell on the rock after a fit, or whether the tide threw her onto the rock. The judge ruled out the theory that she may have fallen from where Kirwan nearly stumbled, as a fall of that height would produce bruising.

'Let me now implore of you, not to confound suspicion with evidence,' said Crampton, concluding the charge. 'If you cannot account for these facts and circumstances to which I have called your attention; if you cannot reconcile them with the prisoner's innocence, you cannot go beside them. If you cannot satisfy yourselves that Mrs Kirwan's death was the result of violence by any other person, you must give the prisoner the benefit of any rational, well founded doubt you may entertain and acquit him.'

The jury retired a little before 7 o'clock. Forty minutes later, they returned under direction from the judges – but they informed the Clerk of the Crown that they had not yet reached a verdict.

'Gentlemen, is there any likelihood of your agreeing?' asked Crampton. The jurors having said no, the judge replied: 'Then, gentlemen, it will be my duty to direct you to retire to your room for the night.'

The foreman asked Crampton if he would take a verdict that night, should they be able to arrive at one. The alternative would be the night spent in the jury room.

'Yes, gentlemen, but you can scarcely expect me to sit here waiting for you,' replied Crampton, approaching the edge of his patience after 10 hours of proceedings.

'Certainly not, my Lord,' replied the foreman, 'but what is the latest hour tonight that you would receive a verdict?'

Midnight was the answer, and the court adjourned until 11 o'clock. When the judge resumed his seat, the anticipation was great, with the pressure of the crowds in the hallway having led police to close the doors to the courtroom early. No agreement, and no probability of one.

'If I thought you would agree to a verdict within any reasonable time,' said the judge, 'I would think it my duty to remain, but if you are not likely to agree, all I can do is to let you remain together for the night and adjourn the court till tomorrow. Consult together again for some time, and let me know if you can agree.'

The move elicited two responses from the jury: the first was a request for more chairs, as they were lacking in the jury room. One can assume the room was also cold, judging by Crampton's remark that he hoped they had their 'great coats' with them for the night ahead. The jury also asked if 9 a.m. the following morning would be an appropriate time to deliver the verdict. Crampton said he would return then if they had a decision, but if they had no further questions, they'd better retire. The judge rose to leave.

'My Lord, there are several of the jury who would wish to hear the testimony of Surgeon Adams again, if possible,' said the foreman.

The judge was sorry to hear that, because he had left his notebook with his evidence behind him when the court last adjourned. However, the judge offered to recall the evidence from memory. A juror asked: 'In Surgeon Adams's opinion, could the appearances on the body have been produced by drowning alone?' The judge replied that the doctor's opinion was that the congestion in the lungs 'and other parts' could have been caused by simple drowning or forcible immersion.

'Then those appearances might have been the result of simple drowning?' asked an unnamed juror.

'They might,' replied the judge.

The jurors huddled for a couple of seconds. The foreman then asked the judge what his opinion was as to that evidence, and the weight they may attach to it. Crampton said the evidence was the same as Rynd's and substantially the same as Dr Hatchell's; the appearances on the body could have resulted from simple drowning, strangulation or suffocation. None, he reminded the jury, saw the body in its original state. The judge was asked to wait a bit longer, and at 11.30 p.m., word reached the crowds: there was a decision.

The courtroom hummed as the jury filed in. The apparent feeling in the room – that Kirwan was heading for acquittal – echoed in the prisoner's demeanour, whose coolness in the face of proceedings did not falter as the moment approached. That self-possession did momentarily crack – a wobble noticed by most reporters in the room – when the Clerk of the Crown asked the question: 'Gentlemen, have you agreed to your verdict?'

'We have, my Lord.'

The situation, for a moment, painted itself onto Kirwan's face as the turnkey put forward the prisoner to face the decision. The clerk took the paper and read to the bottom.

'Gentlemen,' he said, 'you say that the prisoner, William Burke Kirwan, is guilty.'

The reality hit Kirwan like a thunderbolt, as the room erupted in noise. Newspaper reporters peered closely as the man they watched crumpled. 'An awful lividness overspread his face; his limbs seemed to grow weak under him;

and, opening his hands which had clenched the iron bar on front of the dock, he threw himself – or rather let himself fall – into the seat behind him' read the *Catholic Telegraph*'s report of the trial's dying moments.

The prisoner was removed, and the court adjourned until 10.30 a.m. the following day. The courtroom emptied of spectators, each deeply affected by the scenes at Green Street.

13

THE SENTENCING

The doors to the courthouse were thrown open shortly after 10 o'clock. Day three – a sentencing, and much anticipation, in the offing. The noise, bustling and confusion stopped abruptly as Judge Crampton took his seat alongside Baron Greene. Kirwan was brought to the bar, dressed in black and carrying his familiar cool manner. He bowed.

Isaac Butt rose, stating his intention to make an application on behalf of his client, and to raise a number of points. The first referred to the evidence heard about Kirwan's situation at Sandymount. Was that evidence – that he had resided there and that Ms Kenny has passed as his wife – properly received or not? The evidence to which he referred, specifically, was that Kirwan had lived with another woman at Sandymount, who called herself Mrs Kirwan; that a lady called to inquire for the prisoner, and was received by the woman as Mrs Kirwan. Butt considered the evidence inadmissible, and calculated to give rise to a motive. The second point, Butt said, was that the verdict of the jury was founded on Dr Adams's testimony, to which Crampton replied: 'It may have been.'

'There was no doubt of it,' said Butt, who went on to recall that Mr Brereton had proposed to ask Mr Adams whether he had heard, and concurred with, Dr Hatchell's interpretation of the cause of death – yet he had not been allowed. That decision by the court may have caused a prejudice in the minds of the jury. Crampton did not think the points merited a respite of the day's judgement in order to consider them. Mr Curran weighed in, questioning whether depositions made by the prisoner could be raised against him. The judge replied that at the time the depositions in question were taken, Kirwan was not a prisoner.

The Clerk of the Crown addressed Kirwan and asked why the sentence of death should not be passed. Kirwan's voice, in reply, was firm. 'My lords, might I claim the indulgence of the court for a few moments, for the purpose of stating some matters connected with this unfortunate affair, that have not been brought out on the trial,' he began.

Kirwan then told his story. His bid to evade the scaffold began by outlining the particulars of the bag in which the provisions were held. Food, and the accoutrement for dining, were among them, as was the lady's bathing dress. They brought a basket. On the order of Mrs Kirwan, the luggage for their day out was given to Michael Nangle's daughter by Mrs Campbell. The bags were then given to Michael, who put them in the boat. On the morning of his wife's death, he told the court, they did not sail straight for the island, instead taking some time to collect other passengers.

The prisoner earnestly described the comings and goings of the Nangles, and the quick clip at which their boat approached during the afternoon when they were ferrying another party, owing to the direction of the wind. He said that he sketched, while Mrs Kirwan spent her time swimming, walking and reading. He recalled a dinner shared under the shelter of an outcropping of rocks among the components of what appeared to be a normal day out. The couple spoke with the Nangles when they arrived with another party, and declined the early return at 4 p.m. The shower came. They walked to the Martello tower/landing place, where Kirwan began a detailed sketch facing Howth. Maria left him from there, and it was the last time, he said, that he saw her alive.

'I continued at the sketch for more than a couple of hours, till it was getting duskish, which was a common thing with me. I then washed my brush and colours, and put them into my bag. I came to the landing place and deposited it there,' the prisoner told the court. 'I then saw Mrs Kirwan had not come according to appointment. I walked towards the high ground to see if she was coming along the hill. I called out her name, saying the boat was coming. I then turned to the bank for the purpose of seeing if the boat was coming.' Kirwan said he then walked towards the strand, turning back to see the rowboat advancing, and calling out to its crew. As the boat advanced further, Kirwan asked them why they were late, and told them to make haste.

After they landed, Pat took his things from their position on the bank. Michael – as he now knew him, though he did not know their first names at the time – came straight up and asked where the lady was, and immediately, Kirwan said he could not find her. Then they searched through the thick grass, which was sopping after a shower and quickly soaked his light trousers. As they searched, Kirwan said perhaps Maria had fallen. He and Michael then walked the island, shouting for the missing woman. They reached the church, then passed upon the flat land and their view of Howth was obscured, until they reached the Long Hole, searching as far as the water would permit. Pat's own cries reached them then from the bank. 'I told Michael Nangle to answer, and expressed my gratification that Mrs Kirwan, I was sure, had returned to the boat—'

Here, the prisoner was stopped.

Kirwan's address to the court, at this point, far surpasses your average plea for mercy following a guilty verdict. 'I am sorry to interrupt you at this painful moment,' Crampton said, putting a stop to it, 'and you must be well aware that your counsel entered into all these subjects. It is impossible for me now to go into the evidence.'

'I beg your pardon, my Lord, for the interruption,' replied Kirwan, hope, platform and his life fading away before him. 'I consider myself a doomed person, from the trial that has taken place, and the sentence about to be passed; and I state these matters as well out of regard for my own memory as for the sake of those friends who have been with me, who know my character from childhood, who know my innocence, and who feel it yet as I do. If your lordship be willing, I will proceed – if not, I will stop.'

Crampon granted him a final word. Kirwan said: 'I have only to state with regard to the provisions being found, there was no evidence on the subject. Sergeant Sherwood was one who had charge of the bag, and he was not asked about it. The coroner also knew of it but he was not asked about it, and therefore he did not state what he knew. My sketchbook was examined by the jury – it was produced for them.'

Crampton entered into a long, damning address, some of which would arise in the future discussion of the evidence, but we'll come to that. The judge delivered his speech with a solemnity that impressed the attending reporters, and he concluded by donning the black cap, and issuing the direction of execution. 'It now remains for me to pronounce upon you the last awful and solemn words of the sentence of the law – namely that you, William Burke Kirwan, be taken from the place where you now stand to the place from which you came – the prison – and that from thence you be taken to the place of execution – the gallows – and that you be there hanged by the neck until you be dead, and that your body be buried within the precincts of the gaol and, oh! may the Lord have mercy on your soul.'

Kirwan had trained his gaze on the judge during those final words, leaning on the bar in front of the dock. Upon the words that prescribed the undignified fate of his mortal remains, emotion, at last, won out. His head dropped between his hands and a low, suppressed moan of anguish escaped from deep within his body.

Kirwan composed himself and was once again allowed to address the court. 'Convinced as I am that my hopes in this world are at an end, I do most solemnly declare in the presence of this court, and of that God before whom I expect soon to stand, that I had neither hand, act, nor part in, or knowledge of, my late wife's death; and, I will state further, that I never treated her unkindly, as her own mother can testify.'

The prisoner was removed from the dock.

～

Kilmainham Gaol, shortly after noon on the same day, welcomed its newest condemned soul. Kirwan arrived in a covered car from Green Street Courthouse, and accompanied by a party of mounted police.

When he arrived at the prison, he was first escorted to the room he occupied prior to his conviction at the juvenile class yard, and was later transferred to the capital yard, where it was intended he would remain until his execution, which was set for 18 January 1853. The downtime was customary, and usually allowed for a convict's transformation from self-proclaimed innocent to a repentant, religious drafter of confession. Even if the confession never reached the eyes of the public, they may be issued to the ear of a conscientious hangman as legs and arms were pinioned prior to the dark march to the scaffold. Kirwan did not confess, though he did ask for a cup of tea and some dry bread. The appetite for this story was surely on the minds of editors as they detailed his first hours behind bars. Kirwan, allowed to wear the same fine clothes he sported at trial, did little but lie down or pace on the day of his conviction, complaining of feeling languid and taking only a little nourishment. Deemed a risk for suicide, he was constantly supervised, and at least one jailer slept in the spacious apartment with him. The room had a fireplace, a bed and at least two items of reading material: a prayer book and a bible. He was allowed visitors.

Kirwan slept just three hours on his first night in prison, asking for a wake-up call so he could do some writing. At 5.30 a.m. on Saturday, he began to write using the materials provided, but a confession was not forthcoming. On the contrary. As the weekend wore on, authorities confiscated his property to the Crown. Between writing, visits from clergymen and a notable uptick in mood, Kirwan maintained his innocence.

PART 4

14

LETTERS TO THE EDITOR

When it came to the aftermath of *The Queen* v. *Kirwan*, it's difficult to know exactly where the war between the Irish press and certain sections of the English press began. A good bet would be the following sentence, printed by *The Times* in one of the first reports following the verdict: 'The case of Mrs Kirwan will retain a painful notoriety even in the dismal annals of Irish crime.' It seems like an innocuous comment, and in fact it's not an uncommon construction in crime reporting at the time. Read around any murder in the 19th century and odds on you will discover a newspaper leader proclaiming the crime to be the worst in memory, or in the country's history, and so on. This was different. An English paper commenting upon the 'dismal annals of Irish crime' – as though those depths knew a darkness and barbarity unrecognisable by civilised nations – was intolerable.

'*The Times* omits no opportunity of slandering the Irish people, whether or not the text of the attack be germane on the occasion,' declared the *Dublin Evening Packet* on 14 December. 'What have "the dismal annals of Irish crime", we ask, to do with an act so unparalleled in Ireland before? Perhaps the worthy Cockney who penned the sentence had in his mind's eye the Messrs Manning, Rush, Greenacre, those amiable partners, Burke and Hare, and the other respectable Saxon gentlemen who have appalled the world with their murders…'. Much the same from the *Cork Examiner* of 15 December: '*The Times* knew well that in giving such a description, it was pandering to the grossest and most outrageous prejudice and ignorance, and that the event to which it referred had no affinity to the atrocities, which it has been in the habit of gloating over as Irish.' In the grand scheme of the coverage, it's a small spat – but it belies a bigger point of conflict among the press: a palpable Anglo-Irish tension running through the back-and-forth in newsprint.

More generally, a large portion of the initial drama played out on the letters pages. The evidence was attacked, much to the chagrin of the defenders of the verdict. 'Sir, when I was a boy and playing with some companions on a hill near a fordable mountain stream, a young woman passed us on her road across,' wrote 'An Observer' in *The Times* of 16 December.

> We saw her on the bank taking off her shoes and stockings and entering the water. The stream was broad and shallow at that particular spot and it was a usual thing to cross it in that manner. After a while we were startled by a loud scream, and, on looking in the direction of the river, we saw the young woman, at a place which was certainly not two feet deep, overthrown, carried down by the water, and vainly struggling to regain a footing.

You may well guess where the story goes: the lady died, and the writer used this instance to illustrate the point that a person may drown in shallow water. Without witnesses, the death of the young woman may well have been deemed a murder.

One prolific contributor on the topic, alias Jehu, attacked different parts of the evidence with gusto in the pages of *The Standard*. The contributor – who was, the paper assured its readers, a 'ripe' lawyer – went about discrediting several of the witnesses, from the boatman to the landlady. Dismissing the cries as the screams of seabirds, he posited his own theory: that Maria, a capable swimmer, struck a rock chest-first while traversing unfamiliar waters. Or, he thought, perhaps she fell from the point at which Kirwan himself nearly tumbled during the search. The supposed lawyer also gave a shout-out to 'Humanitas', a writer in *The Times* the previous day who claimed familiarity with Ireland's Eye and theorised that it was perfectly possible that someone else could have landed on the island and committed the murder. This would then explain why Maria's body was left the way it was, 'where it would be found, and thus [designed to] prevent a further search among the rocks, which might have detected the real culprit or his boat'. It's worth noting that Humanitas was also responding to the previously mentioned letter from 'An Observer'; and thus the web of verdict deniers grew.

Another letter writer in *The Standard*, 'An Attentive Reader', weighed in on 16 December. There was little evidence, but because Kirwan 'was a man of immoral character and connected with another woman, the doubt (and if there was a doubt the prisoner was entitled to the benefit of such) was decided against him, and he sentenced to die as a murderer!' This view – the man with the non-detachable, poisonous reputation – was widely echoed among Kirwan's fanbase. The next sentence, from the same letter writer, would be significant in hindsight: 'And I trust that it may not yet be too late, through the instrumentality of the press, to induce the authorities to hesitate before the consummation of a great crime – the crime of murder – if the man is innocent and a foul stain on the justice of the land.' That rallying call to defend Kirwan was timely.

It emerged that the points of law raised by Butt at the close of the trial would not be reserved for consideration. In other words, the judges considered there to be no need to review any aspect of the decision prior to the execution of the sentence. At the time in Ireland, a review recommended by the trial judge would have been Kirwan's official recourse. The Court of Criminal Appeal did not yet exist, though Isaac Butt himself would make sustained efforts to establish such a court in Ireland, sometimes making reference to this very case. With that legal review avenue cut off, efforts escalated to drum up support for the commutation of Kirwan's death sentence.

There were, at that time, many other letters of support for Kirwan. 'Now, what conceivable motive could the prisoner have had, if guilty of the murder, in first putting his wife's clothes out of the way, and then restoring them to the place where they were found, and were sure to be found, by the Nangles?' asked one writer under the moniker 'W', who supported the theory of epilepsy. Another, 'A Doctor of Divinity', remarked that it appeared from reports that the prisoner had been 'capitally convicted for a crime of which, judging from the evidence reported, he may possibly be as innocent as I am'.

Another significant letter appeared in *The Times* on 23 December, signed by 'A Barrister' and datelined 'Temple' – the London legal district. The letter began by stating that the evidence was not satisfactory, going on to say that there was 'considerable doubt' evident in the minds of the jury. The writer pointed to the timing of the verdict – specifically, after previously saying they couldn't agree, they were able to reach consensus just 30 minutes after being told they'd have to be kept together for the night if they failed to do so. The writer then went, at length, through certain evidence points, digging up doubt.

This letter, we will later see, particularly irritated the jury – but there were many letters, and there's no need to catalogue each one. It is enough to say that there was a substantial volume of voices questioning the verdict. And the letters didn't go completely unchecked. *The Examiner*, a London paper whose vocal critiques of those attacking the verdict were widely reprinted in Irish titles, took umbrage with the letter in *The Times* from 'An Observer', which compared Maria's death with that of the woman whom the writer had seen drowned. *The Examiner* wrote: 'The water in which Mrs Kirwan bathed was not a rapid stream, but a small inlet of the tide which did not ebb and flow at more than the rate of two or three miles an hour, a force which in calm weather could not take an infant off its legs.' The paper, at the time, was billed as an intellectual journal devoted to independent reporting and espousing radical reformist politics, according to the British Newspaper Archive. In the same edition, 18 December, in a piece headlined 'MURDER MADE EASY', *The Examiner* saved some of the same harsh criticism for the coroner's inquest, which the paper said had absorbed 'much and merited blame'. The paper was also in favour of the establishment of a Court of Criminal Appeal; maybe it would save society from the sort of off-the-grid litigation as was occurring in newsprint.

On 1 January, *The Examiner* continued its criticism of the letters in support of Kirwan, the tone and content of many it considered tasteless and insensitive. It referred, explicitly, to a letter from 'T.G.', which appeared in

The Times and included the following: 'Or, perhaps, Mr Kirwan sat on Mrs Kirwan like a night-mare, and killed her so – not much more probable, unless Mr Kirwan were as fat as Daniel Lambert or Mrs Armitage, and Mrs Kirwan as weak as the fasting man at Tutbury.' About the 'odious flippancy', *The Examiner* wrote:

> There is the hideous zest of the Thug in these imaginings; and in most of the letters on the convict's behalf, it is remarkable that no touch of pity ever appears for the victim, who is sometimes treated almost despitefully, as if it were her fault that her previous husband's life were brought in jeopardy. Let it not be supposed that we regard Kirwan's case as one of strong evidence, as it appears reported. But, on the other hand, the arguments against the verdict are sophistical or purely conjectural.

The same paper, in the same edition, floated a theory that was repeated in a number of other journals in the following days: that the fruits of Kirwan's feverish writing from his cell were the very letters proclaiming his innocence, and thus that he was making 'industrious use' of his time. The same article noted a recent milestone achieved by Kirwan's supporters: the death sentence had, indeed, been commuted to life transportation. The lobbyists – as loose as their affiliation may have been – had got their way. But they would not stop there.

In Kirwan's Corner

Newspapers differed on the point of Kirwan's innocence. Broadly, the most extreme positions were divided into two camps. The first camp, largely grouped as 'the London press', considered Kirwan to be an innocent man punished at the hands of an inferior judicial system in a shambolic trial that bordered on conspiracy. The second camp housed those who believed in the wisdom and processes of the Crown institutions and its players in Ireland, and who considered the questioning of the verdict from outside forces to be an attack on justice itself. Many did not wish death upon Kirwan, and recognised the case was not completely solid, but were worried about throwing a jury verdict to the court of public opinion.

Of the newspapers that most favoured Kirwan's innocence, *The Standard* stands out. Its coverage throughout the events that followed the jury's decision provides as good a taste as any of the values and views of the condemned artist's most ardent fans. From the start, the newspaper – staunchly conservative by reputation – had Kirwan's back. On the same day it published Jehu's hypothesis, the paper said the evidence in the case 'would not satisfy a Middlesex jury of the justice of consigning a Field Lane pickpocket to a month upon the treadmill'. It's easy to see through some of the lines in *The Standard*'s leaders why its opponents in the press alleged a flippant tone.

It's also clear why sections of the Irish press were so vigorously stirred. The conduct of the prosecution counsel – their supposed eagerness to see a man convicted, rather than see truth prevail – was a typical target for *The Standard*. '[O]h! How a true English lawyer would blush at the praise of zeal in hunting the life of a fellow creature,' read a leading article on 22 December. It concluded:

> For Mr Kirwan's proved immoralities we have neither sympathy nor indulgence; but has he not suffered for them? Is not the utter ruin of his worldly prospects a punishment? Is not a month in the agony of suspense under the doom of an ignominious death? Is not a blasted character? Are not these some, though it may be an inadequate punishment, without hanging him for a crime that, as we firmly believe, he did not commit?

In its first edition on the first day of the new year, *The Standard* went one further, inferring the concealment of evidence on the part of the prosecution. By then, declarations had emerged from various parties that tended to discredit aspects of the prosecution's story. Among the declarators highlighted were Margaret Caroline Bentley, an acquaintance of Mrs Kirwan who said the latter had known about the affair for years (that the 'criminal engagement' was only recently discovered was never demonstrated in court, the paper pointed out); a servant named Anne Maher, who apparently witnessed Mrs Kirwan having seizures; Mr Kirwan's colleague Arthur Kelly, who corroborated the same; and Maria Crowe, the mother of the deceased, who sang her son-in-law's praises. Supporters also favoured, heavily, the opinion of Dr Alfred Swaine Taylor, who weighed in against the likelihood of the prosecution's story. *The Standard* naturally gave the declarations much consideration. What's more, the newspaper said it was clear from the statements that the information included had been given to the Crown solicitor in advance of the trial. Why, then, were those people not called at trial? Was it an effort to conceal the truth in a bid to secure a conviction?

Intertwined with that scandalous inference was the unmistakable tinge of Irish scepticism that lined much of the commentary in *The Standard*:

One would have thought that even in Ireland, such a case as that of Mr Kirwan might have been tried without the miserable struggle for victory which occasionally disgraces a trial in that unhappy country when some political object is sought to be obtained by the verdict. It was simply a charge of murder, totally unconnected with any sectarian or political question.

And, later in the same piece:

Let any indifferent spectator attend a criminal trial in this country, and he will be impressed by the spirit of fairness which pervades every part of the proceeding; but unhappily in Ireland, the genius loci seems to have perverted one of the most important functions that any human tribunal can exercise into an ignoble strife for victory, in which personal vanity and cunning find their appropriate sphere.

To believe in those declarations, essentially, was to believe in a deep rot Irish justice: 'Supposing them to be true, however, our readers have had quite enough to enable them to judge of the system of a Crown prosecution in Ireland.'

The allegations were soon followed by a letter from William Kemmis, the Crown solicitor at the time of the trial, who flatly denied the mischief alleged by *The Standard*. Kemmis said that the witness who would have provided the proof of the recent discovery of the affair was Teresa Kenny, and he rightly recalled that she did not appear in court when her name was called. This, in the context of the early statements Kenny gave, adds up. In her earliest statement, she clearly states that she did not know of Mr Kirwan's marriage to Maria until six months before her interview. That's somewhat at odds with a later declaration she made, in which she says Maria was aware of the arrangement for 10 years, to the best of her knowledge. It's easy to see the predicament in which Kenny found herself – there was no answer she could give in which her circumstances would be favourable.

There was no corner of the press in which she particularly found refuge – least of all in *The Standard*, as seen in its commentary that ran with Kemmis's letter:

> And who was she? Why, the adulterous partner in sin of the accused for 12 years and more, a period commencing before his marriage. What on earth could she know or testify of the terms upon which lived parties whom she had never seen together into whose house she never dared set foot, even supposing that she was willing to hang by her testimony her paramour for 12 years, the father of seven or eight children and his and their sole support. Who would believe one word from such a miserable degraded outcast, had she presented herself in a witness box in such a cause or who can suppose the Crown solicitor so simple as to expect that she would come forward?

Kemmis's letter addressed the religious aspect, too. Kemmis said the jury was mixed Roman Catholic and Protestant; *The Standard* said it was more like 11:1. That Maria was Catholic and William a Protestant was not insignificant, even if the conservative paper tried to make itself out to be above the politico-religious elements of the discussion.

Concurrent with the campaign of letters and legal work, a meeting was held on 10 January at Anderton's Hotel, Fleet Street, by those in support of Kirwan. *The Standard* labelled them an assortment of 'gentlemen', and the content of the meeting was the usual fare: doubting the evidence; praise of Taylor's opinion; and casual jibes at the Irish. Around that time, another charge of murder – the supposed victim being Richard Downes Bowyer – had resurfaced and been levelled against Kirwan. *The Standard* reported: 'A Gentleman said that a new charge had recently been brought against the prisoner; and it showed strikingly the truth of Dean Swift's remark, namely, that if you put an Irishman on a spit, you would easily find another Irishman to turn him (laughter).'

Otherwise, a single contributor to the meeting reveals at least some further possible information regarding Kirwan's relationships prior to 1852. Christopher Madden, a physician, addressed the group, claiming to have been Teresa Kenny's doctor for one of her pregnancies 12 years prior. At that time, the patient confided that her husband had married another woman for her money, and that they (Kirwan and Maria) lived on unhappy terms. Madden presumably designed this information to demonstrate that the women knew about each other already, thus deflating the prosecution's motive. Actually, if it was true, it probably supplies a better motive: Kirwan was after money and they were on unhappy terms. The contradiction was not picked up.

Jonathan Swift arises again among *The Standard's* musings later the same month, on the 27th, when it identified some 'national peculiarities' that distinguished Irish people from the English:

Swift said, long ago, that what is true everywhere else is not true in Ireland; to this idiosyncrasy rather than to any lesson of experience we willingly ascribe it, and the more atrocious any crime imputed in 'the land of saints' the more probable it appears to the inhabitants. Here and in most, if not all, other parts of the world, we hold that the more enormous any deviation from morality alleged to have been committed, the less readily should we credit its commission. The rule, however, is reversed, as we have said, in Ireland.

Let us see whether we cannot account for the fact in a manner not very unfavourable to the Irish character. The people of Ireland are very imaginative, and not a little vain, and imaginative people are easily caught by the prodigies of a deeply tragical story; and vain people once caught are exceedingly unwilling to confess that they have made fools of themselves or been fooled by others.

Upon no better hypothesis can we explain the furore for the hanging of William Burke Kirwan that appears to have taken possession of great part of the Irish press. We say for hanging the wretched creature guilty of being suspected for the murder of his wife; for though he is condemned to perpetual banishment, we suppose at Norfolk Island, 'the great revenge' of his accusers 'has stomach for much more'.

The discussion around the case eventually became a surrogate for criticism about the national disposition, Ribbonism and even land agitation. The overall message in *The Standard* was clear: the Irish were imaginative, excitable and peculiar – sense would have prevailed in an English court.

In the Green Corner

Not surprisingly, the Irish papers baulked at the idea of Kirwan's crime being of a particularly Irish character. The *Cork Examiner* declared it 'a purely English one'. Not only was the crime attributed to national habits, so too was the morbid interest in the crime: 'We remark that this interest is confined almost exclusively to England. The crime is so like those which usually occur in that country, and so damnable, that by natural affinity it immediately excites speculation and curiosity.'

But the broader hymn sheet of the pro-verdict commentators was a balance of outrage at the attempts in the London press to subvert a jury's decision, and overwhelming confidence in the upstanding judges and jury tasked with considering the case. That said, the pro-verdict group were capable of playing a little dirtier than that. The 'side' was not a monolith, and while the likes of *The Examiner*, the *Cork Examiner* and the *Dublin Evening Packet* – to name a few – kept the arguments civilised, others were a little coarser. *The Nation*, an Irish nationalist weekly, penned a piece chronicling 'the murderer's Christmas' in late December. It included the following passage, which somehow escaped the criticisms based on taste that were levelled at those questioning the verdict: 'Not for [Kirwan] the vision of blooming, happy faces, that flush with joy at the sound of his approaching step; but one of wan, moist visage with tack-strewn hair, oozing blood, that haunts his pillow by night, that shapes itself in the very rays of daylight that penetrate his cell!' *The Nation* was prepared, also, to bring religion into the equation. The paper had 'observed with some amazement that the miserable man's innocence is vindicated with peculiar assiduity and zeal by the Souper interest. We would loth to suggest as the motive cause, that Kirwan is said to have been a person of violent Orange principles, and that Mrs Kirwan became a convert to Catholicity some months before her death – but we believe the facts so to be.'

From the outset, some support for the commutation of Kirwan's sentence was to be expected. There was little appetite, certainly among journals scrambling to exude civility, for capital punishment – and that extended to members of the public. Juries often recommended mercy in murder cases, or simply did not convict due to the weight of the punishment. Consider the following from the *Cork Examiner*: 'It is well known that juries have in certain cases refused to convict on the clearest evidence, simply from being unable to overcome the horror with which they regard the result of their verdict. We do not mean to defend this conduct. We merely allude to the unquestionable fact of its being frequently practised'; or this comment from the *Daily Express*: 'Juries have been known to find a verdict of "not guilty" and at the same time recommend the accused not to do the like again; and this commutation of sentence appears to us quite as great a blunder.'

Just about anybody could get a small number of abolitionists to uphold their case. That went for people who committed crimes that were perhaps considered 'proven' to a greater degree. Among the final public executions in Ireland, prior to their outlawing by the Capital Punishment Act of 1868, were those of two men – Laurence King and Thomas Hayes. The men didn't know each other, but their crimes were packaged side by side in newspaper coverage in 1865, owing to the location – both men were hanged at Tullamore within days of each other – and the distaste for their crimes. Hayes abused and murdered his wife, burying her body in a marsh, and then feigned insanity; King shot an army officer named Lieutenant Henry James Clutterbuck in the back of the head to rob him of a few valuables.

There was not much sympathy for these men. Reporting on the execution of King, who was hanged second, *The Pilot* of Boston, USA, wrote: 'It is unnecessary to observe that if there was little pity felt for the old man about to die for cruelly beating his wife until she expired, there was less for the young but hardened assassin doomed to the halter for the cowardly and based murder of an unoffending and unsuspecting gentleman.' Yet even those men had a memorialist – a single one, a writer named Noble, who appealed fruitlessly to the heart and religious consciousness of the Lord Lieutenant to spare a couple of wayward souls. Though the plea was unsuccessful and both men met the hangman, their case illustrates a wider trend following death sentences in those years: there were some people prepared to beg for anyone's life, if it meant avoiding the moral and societal stain of another sanctioned killing.

Kirwan's supporters had considerable sway compared to the standard jail-gate prayer group. The collection of documents had the official feel of parliamentary reports – and belied the availability of much funds. This, for many newspaper contributors, was outrageous. The supporters were seen by different outlets in quite diverging lights. Compare, for a moment, how *The Standard* and the *Dublin Evening Mail* treated the meeting at Anderton's. The former considered them 'gentlemen' meeting at a hotel; the latter 'a dozen or two of unknown individuals' convening at a 'tavern'.

Of the meeting, *The Mail* wrote on 12 January: 'The convict Kirwan is likely to attain historic fame, not merely as a monster in human form, one of the most venial of whose crimes was the murder for which he has been made amenable to the laws of his country. His name bids fair to be associated with a radical revolution in the system of criminal judicature in Great Britain.' Then, a further dollop of sarcasm: 'Already has his case given occasion for the establishment of a new Court of Criminal Appeal, the first sitting of which was held in a public house in Fleet Street, London, on Wednesday last.' And this, really, was the problem that many had with the efforts being made on Kirwan's behalf. After achieving their apparent first aim – that of saving a man's life from the gallows – they sought full liberty for a convicted wife murderer.

As the *Dublin Evening Packet* put it:

> Their exertions, if they please, produced the commutation: but, not satisfied with that, which out to satisfy all who respect justice, they would have the miscreant murderer of his wife again let loose upon society. It is time the public should arouse itself to a sense of the danger which is threatened. How are the Kirwanites proceeding? Not according to the usage or course of our humane laws, but by outraging the institution of which we should be most proud – trial by jury.

A week later, the same paper commented: 'We do not desire to blacken the character of the wretched convict worse than it is; but we cannot silently look on while any mawkish sentimentality in favour of a criminal is in danger of doing mischief to our whole system of criminal jurisprudence.'

The pro-verdict writers had their own heroes on the letter pages. 'Justitia' was a name associated with one of the most convincing and complete critiques of the counter-theories. It appeared on 13 January in the *Dublin Evening Packet*, and its contents were reprinted elsewhere. 'Justitia' throws cold water on the epilepsy theory for lack of evidence, and pokes holes in the individual declarations. People had come forward and said Kirwan was a model husband

– but why had they not appeared at trial, where they could be cross-examined? The insinuation was that perhaps the declarations were more useful after the trial, when they couldn't be picked apart.

'Justitia' rightly points out that the declaration made by Mrs Crowe did indicate that her son-in-law lived on good terms with her daughter. But it was dated a month before the trial, meaning it was procured in anticipation of the argument that he did not treat her well. The dating of Mrs Crowe's piece adds curiosity to Kirwan's last statement in court, when he declared that his mother-in-law had said her daughter was always treated well by him.

Without delving too much into the medical evidence at this juncture, it would be unfortunate not to mention another champion of the verdict supporters: Dr Thomas G. Geoghegan. A prominent Irish physician and professor of medical jurisprudence at the Royal College of Surgeons, he took a keen interest in the trial and attended in person – which, to be fair, was more than could be said for many of the jury's detractors. In a paper in the *Dublin Medical Press*, championed by the *Freeman's Journal* and elsewhere, he provided an explanation, drawing from pathological and other circumstances, for why Maria must have been murdered, rather than accidentally drowned. Some declared that Geoghegan's paper represented an end to the debate. That would be a large overstatement, but it certainly represented an elevation in terms of the discourse around the case in its focus on the evidence, as opposed to the political and religious elements pulling at the fringes of the facts.

15

CUTTING THROUGH THE NOISE

In the weeks following the verdict, the news media commented upon a number of events relevant to the case, including the commutation and Kirwan's treatment in prison. The latter would be a flashpoint in the press battle. The catalyst for the argument proper was 10 January, when Kirwan was taken from Kilmainham and brought by rail to Spike Island – the infamous, lonely island prison in Cork Harbour – pending his transportation. On board the train he was reportedly saved the embarrassment of prison garb, and instead allowed to wear his own fine clothes and mix with other passengers in the second class carriages. This was a scandal, a demonstration of favour beyond the imagination of some commentators.

Officials themselves took to the columns to clear their names, each broadly denying stories of Kirwan's special privileges and being spared hard labour in lieu of time to paint his beautiful surroundings. One official who put pen to paper was Henry Hitchins, the general inspector of prisons, who reminded newspaper readers that anything that happened outside the prison was outside his jurisdiction, but that he had explicitly informed the governor of Spike Island in a letter that Kirwan was not to receive any special privileges. The very same governor, Richard Grace, wrote his own letter to confirm that no such special treatment was afforded to the celebrity prisoner.

Robert Allison, governor of Kilmainham Gaol, explained Kirwan had been allowed to wear his own top coat over the prison outfit, and his hat over his prison cap, due to how cold the day of his transportation had been. If these officials thought their letters would clear up the issue, they were wrong. The

Dublin Evening Mail was among those for whom the excuse didn't fly:

> He is excused from wearing the prison dress; allowed to provide for his own table; and his daily acts are recorded with respectful accuracy. We should be the last persons to advocate needless trampling upon the wretched, but we submit that this exceptional course of justice is not calculated to raise the credit of its administration among a people who are sufficiently inclined to believe in one law for the poor and another for the rich.

In the case of the commutation, the exact agency and reason for the decision was, at the time, a mystery. The process was questioned by all sides in this heated, languishing debate. A common refrain in newspaper leaders across both islands could be summarised as 'hang him or free him'. If he was guilty, he should hang. But if there was doubt about the conviction, he should be set free. There was understandable confusion about this half-measure approach. Why, and by whom, had Kirwan been commuted?

The players who may or may not have had a hand in it were Philip Crampton and Baron Greene, the judges, as well as Lord Chancellor of Ireland Joseph Napier, and Lord Eglinton, who was the outgoing Lord Lieutenant of Ireland, the position with the final sign-off. The following appeared in the *Dublin Evening Mail*, the *Daily Express* and elsewhere:

> We have learned that the judges who presided at the commission, Mr Justice Crampton and Baron Greene, when the memorial on behalf of Kirwan had been presented to them, gave it as their opinion that no grounds existed for a remission of the capital punishment; but that subsequently, the late Attorney General, Mr Napier, advised Lord Eglinton to exercise the prerogative of mercy and in consequence the life of Kirwan was spared.

Soon after, a letter dated 25 January from John Wynne, the Under-Secretary for Ireland, sought to clarify this issue: 'I beg to inform you that

Lord Eglinton acted on the recommendation of Judge Crampton and Baron Greene and with the concurrence of the late Lord Chancellor, and that he neither solicited nor received the advice of any other person whatsoever.' *The Standard* pounced on that crack of doubt, writing on 27 January: 'The judge doubted, and the jury ought to have doubted, and of course acquitted; but since the getting up of the prosecution has been exposed no rational man can doubt – that is, no rational man out of Ireland.'

Defenders of the verdict simply couldn't understand. The *Dublin Evening Mail* found the letter – with all due respect expressed – unsatisfactory. How could the same man, Crampton, be the one to both recommend the commutation of the sentence and utter the following words, extracted from his long, solemn final address to Kirwan: 'Upon that verdict it is not my province to pronounce any opinion; but after what has been said, I cannot help adding this observation, that I can see no reason or grounds to be dissatisfied with it, and in saying this, I speak the sentiments of my learned brother who sits beside me as well as my own... I cannot hold out to you one ray of hope of pardon on this side of the grave.' There was disbelief that a man of Crampton's standing should abandon his convictions in the face of the controversy. In comments many years later, Eglinton would throw more light on the matter with the benefit of a number of years' separation from his role as Lord Lieutenant, which we will come to. But at that moment, people were left to ponder the motivations of the officials who sought it fit to save Kirwan from the scaffold.

These battles in the newspapers left little room for fact-finding, and much of it tended to contribute to the very noise derided by many in the press. To cover the entire scope of the coverage would require a whole book, but from the taste outlined the reader might see that the interpretations of the evidence at trial really did diverge. Many in support of the verdict promoted Geoghegan's paper, while largely disregarding the declarations in favour of Kirwan. All the while, they scorned the meddling press on the other side of the Irish Sea.

Of course, those same defenders of justice were happy to promote information that supported the jury's decision, while also claiming to find the very discussion of a jury decision to be a tasteless affront to the institutions of justice. On the other hand, those seeking Kirwan's release heavily promoted the declarations as new facts and veered from legitimate arguments surrounding their veracity and the zeal of the solicitor who collected them – yet they were quite happy to scorn the deployment of such zeal on the part of the prosecuting lawyers.

While the debate may not have produced much by way of clarity of fact, it did have utility; the pressure was so intense that members of the jury felt compelled to write a letter justifying exactly why they came upon their verdict. For those eager to understand the jury's decision, it provides very real insight into what evidence was important in the end.

To many, it was simply a mystery how reasonable doubt benefiting Kirwan was not to be identified. Outrage, as we have seen, followed. The *Morning Post* said the verdict had been 'subjected to attacks so unmeasured, so incessant, and so unscrupulous, as almost to force on those responsible for it the unusual course of stating publicly the reasons which led them to their conclusion, and of answering, categorically, the principal allegations which have been urged against their good sense an honesty'. The jury's letter, addressing the wider controversy and some individual writers by whom they were clearly irked, appeared in *Saunders's News-Letter*.

Dated 8 January, the letter is signed by John A. Dennis, the jury foreman, and was purportedly backed by the signatures of 10 other jurors. It's quite long, at nearly 5,000 words, so an edited run-through is provided below. Some of the documents referred to appeared following the verdict; we will examine these further.

The Jury's Letter

The letter begins with a tone of relief. The jurors, themselves against capital punishment, were happy that a man would not be hanged, even if their verdict was the correct one. 'We are thankful for more – that the final decision having been made, we, jurors, are longer bound to silence, and may now, without prejudice to his fate, defend ourselves from the direct charges and imputations which have been cast upon us – a daring and dangerous proceeding, we believe never to have been carried to such extent before, seriously calculated to frustrate the ends of justice, and to damage the administration of the law henceforth.'

The letter notes the huge volume of reaction – 'we have heard of more than have seen or shall be enabled to notice' – before first dealing with the letter from 'A Barrister' in the *London Times*, 23 December. They note, first, his location, before quoting this line: 'I believe that in England you would have to exclude the hypothesis of the deceased having thus met with her death, &c.' The letter comments: 'Certainly this was not written by an English, and scarcely by an honest Irish barrister. These quotations make the design of the letter so palpable, that we may pass rapidly over the matter. We may before doing so say, that on the jury were natives of England, Ireland, and Scotland, and our religious opinions, we find since the trial, were as diversified.'

The jury next took issue with the broad assertion that they came to a hasty conclusion based on a fear of being cooped up overnight, which they flatly denied, as they knew prior to the judge's warning what their fate would be if they did not agree that evening. 'A Barrister' said that they found Kirwan guilty, despite the answer to their question about Dr Adams's testimony ostensibly helping Kirwan's case. The jury disagreed: 'Having explained the nature of the medical testimony of Surgeon Adams, Judge Crampton added, "this testimony, gentlemen, you will observe, altogether excludes the other circumstances of the case, and you will remember too that neither of these gentlemen had seen the body". Others will, perhaps, not find in this passage, which we pledge ourselves is the true one, the tendency the barrister has drawn from his version, which is untrue.' The jury next point out various misstatements contained in the letter from 'A Barrister' – geographical and chronological errors. They note that the letter writer clearly identifies a factor which they believe important: that Kirwan located his wife's clothes quickly in the dark.

The jury's letter next addresses the letter in *The Times* that compared Mrs Kirwan's death with the drowning of a lady in a stream, a comparison the letter writers considered inappropriate. The jury writes: 'He then proceeds to a long questioning as to the evidence of the finding of the clothes, ending like the barrister, in the admission that Kirwan laid his hand readily upon them in the dark. He discusses the probable ways in which the murder may be supposed to have been committed in no very decent terms, such "knocking on the head," and so on; declares that she could not have screamed had a wet sheet been placed over her head, but says nothing of what she might have done before being completely enveloped in a dry one.

'He concludes by asserting that according to the evidence, Kirwan must have been wet to his shoulders in getting to the rock where the body was found, because it was "a very high rock," and "the water one foot nine inches over it," the undisputed fact being that this very high rock rises just 12 inches out of the strand. We merely quote these feet and inches as a specimen of the accuracy in documents in which our characters are so freely discussed. The statement itself goes for nothing; it never was supposed in the jury box that Kirwan was necessarily so deep in the water accomplishing his purpose as it must have been where the body was found, at the hour of seven o'clock.'

The jury's letter continues in this manner, addressing individual accusations in letters as a way of exploring parts of the evidence. Another letter writer they took issue with was 'One who Dissents from the Verdict'. The jury wrote: 'He commences by finding fault with the learned judge in confining the consideration of the jury to the certainty of there being no other persons on the island at the hour when Mrs Kirwan met her death but herself and her husband. Now that this was an admitted fact was clearly proved by the refraining of the counsel for the defence from any contrary supposition, or from pitting any question to any of the witnesses tending to such a supposition. It was clear beyond a doubt that from the time Mr Brew and his party left the island at four o'clock that no one landed on the island between that hour and dark, and Mrs Kirwan certainly died at or about seven o'clock, very shortly after sunset on 6 September.

'The writer then assumes that Kirwan must have waded into the water to the depth of two feet nine inches to have placed the body on the rock where it was found. This is on idle assumption, because no one supposes a murder being committed the body would have been placed by the murderer where it was found. That the body was found attached to that small rock at all can only be accounted for by the catching of the bathing dress upon it. Had it not done so, there was water enough to have carried it further out of the cove with the falling tide. He concludes by saying, "I would have felt it my duty to have given the prisoner the benefit of the doubt which I think I entertain." If we could have conscientiously so discharged ourselves from the obligations of our oaths, we should have been saved a vast deal of anxious labour and the painful alternative. We should, indeed, have been most happy to have given the prisoner and ourselves the benefit of our "well-grounded doubts," so following the instructions of the learned judge.'

The letter addresses another, by 'One of the Panel', and in doing so touches upon the medical evidence for the first time. 'It is true, as he states in the early part of his letter, that there were no marks of violence upon the body – none other than those which according to the medical testimony might not, agreeably to the theory of surgical science, be produced by drowning without violence, because that theory teaches that all mucous parts, or in plain words all portions covered by internal skin, may become gorged with, and discharge blood after death by asphyxia or suffocation, as drowning, the death Mrs Kirwan unquestionably died. Mr Hatchell examined the body, and was therefore enabled to speak as to the extent of the engorgements, so far as that could be ascertained after death; and it appeared from his testimony, as to the state of the body, that the wet soil that it lay in had the effect of preserving the internal portions in a better state for examination than might have been expected at that period, 30 or 31 days from the death – combining what he then saw with the testimony he subsequently heard, in common with Mr Rynd and Mr Adams as to the uterine bleeding, he gave it as his opinion that some violent struggle had immediately preceded death. Mr Rynd and Mr Adams, who did not see the body, and could only have to guide them the descriptions the several witnesses gave, could not speak with the same confidence that Mr Hatchell did; their opinions were confined to theory, and their experience in such supposed cases, which experience they both said had never brought such appearances under their own notice – they had never read, nor had they ever heard of such having been produced in a case of known accidental drowning.'

Next, the jury letter proceeds to the point of the finding of the body and the disagreement over the sheet. 'The two Nangles did not search the Long Hole in the first instance; it was searched in the first instance, or purported to have been searched by Michael Nangle and Kirwan. Patrick Nangle remaining at the boat till they returned and reported an ineffectual search; then, at the suggestion of Patrick Nangle, he, Michael Nangle, and Kirwan proceeded to research the same places, and on this second search Patrick Nangle found the body. When Kirwan first searched the Long Hole with Michael Nangle, as far "as the water would allow them," there could have been, according to the evidence given as to the height of water at the different hours, but three inches of water over the rock on which the body was found on the second search, within an hour, when the rock was dry, and the tide some feet below it.

'Showing that, which no one disputes we believe, and which we never supposed, that Kirwan did not place the body where it was found, the writer calls "disposing of all the suspicious circumstances, almost even the sheet being under the body," this he proceeds to do by saying, "Michael Nangle swore that Kirwan brought the sheet from the rock." He swore no such thing – he swore that "he brought a shawl, and something white like a sheet" – to its being a sheet, or any one particular thing, he could not swear, and though, in the first instance, he said one article was a shawl, it appeared, upon further question, that he only knew this from seeing it subsequently round the head of the deceased, placed so by Kirwan.

'Seeing the two men, Patrick and Michael Nangle, and hearing their evidence, we could form no reasonable doubt of the truth of either of them. They are both elderly men; Michael appears older than Patrick, nor is he, by many degrees, so observant or so intelligent a man; his going on the first search was accidental; Patrick had been given "the bag" to carry to the boat – had he been the one to make the first search, and of the "Long Hole" amongst other places, there can be little doubt, indeed, but that he would have found the body then, when it must have been partially exposed, and the light stronger; the clothes then lay, supposing Kirwan did not remove them during the interval between the two searches, where he so readily found them after the body had been discovered; and Michael Nangle described himself as going all round this rock, down one side and up the other of the cove; this rock, set forth in the various misstatements as in so many different positions, standing about mid-way between the two sides, and towards the upper end of the cove.

'Patrick Nangle's account of his finding the body with the sheet partly under it, and his tying it across the chest and knees, is perfectly consistent with all the circumstances of this particular period, and was so far corroborated, as it could be, by those who gave an account of the state and condition of the body, when brought to Mrs Campbell's – Michael Nangle did not see Patrick Nangle do this, but had it been the sheet Kirwan brought from the rock, and had Mrs Kirwan's body been then to be placed in it, Michael Nangle must have been required to assist; say he did not assist, it is not possible but that he would have observed it being done. The fact of the sheet being tied exactly as Patrick Nangle described, was undoubtedly proved by those who untied the knots he had tied.'

That section is revealing: in the question about which of the two Nangles was the more believable, they had made a very clear decision. The following is also revealing of how much import the jury attached to the evidence that Sherwood found Kenny at Merrion Street after Kirwan's arrest. 'After congratulating himself upon having had the peculiar felicity of "pointing out the finger of Heaven in this case," he concludes by further felicitously directing public sympathy to the fact that Kirwan "had the merit of not deserting his innocent offspring, and the partner of his crime." Perhaps One of the Panel will think that merit much enhanced by the fact sworn to by Sergeant Sherwood, the constabulary sergeant, that some of his "innocent offspring, and the partner of his crime," were living in the house where his deceased wife had resided within a month of her death. How much sooner, how soon after the 5th of July, when they gave up the house at Sandymount, he may have afforded them this protection it is to be regretted, as an interesting feature in this case, that we cannot supply information which might gratify One of the Panel, for further than we have stated did not appear upon the trial.'

The jury, in addressing a letter from Thomas Disney of Carlingford, acknowledges a point central to much of the critique of the verdict: 'Mr Disney not unnaturally says, "This is a conviction for murder where no murder has been proved to have been committed." True, it was not sworn that the body of Mrs Kirwan was the body of a murdered woman. Upon this fact depended the circumstantiality of the case; had that been sworn to there would have been an end of the matter. Proved to have been murdered, she must have been murdered by Kirwan.'

The Standard, not surprisingly, does not escape the glare of the jury: 'An article from a London paper follows this, framed with some editorial dexterity, as a commentary upon a letter of a correspondent, of whom he speaks as a "ripe lawyer" but whose name he is not at liberty to give. This article stigmatises the verdict as "that monstrous verdict, convicting Kirwan of the foulest crime the heart of man can conceive, upon such evidence as would not satisfy a Middlesex jury of the justice of consigning a Field Lane pickpocket to a month upon the treadmill." The writer refers to some other published statements we have not seen, and then he says – "Not only did Mrs Kirwan's father die of epilepsy, but it is now proved by the sworn testimony of an artist and a female servant who lived in the house with her, that she herself had suffered more than one severe epileptic attack. This explains all, and it reflects little credit upon the Crown prosecutors, that though in full possession of the evidence of the unfortunate lady's being subject to epilepsy, they did not tell the truth to the jury. We need not say that the able and learned advocates of the prisoner had not this knowledge, or the accused must have been acquitted."

'Now, that Mrs Kirwan's father died of epilepsy may or may not be true. It was not proved on the trial; it was mentioned by Mr Rynd as a circumstance he had heard in court, and when questioned he said "it was by one of the gentlemen deeply interested for the defence he had been told it." The tale was smiled down and no doubt in a less grave case so useless a trick – not on the part of Mr Rynd, of his prompters we mean – would have been laughed at.'

The jury goes on to say that even if the cause of Maria's father's death was proven, it would not settle the matter – no real evidence of epilepsy was presented. 'We have been furnished with the documents, but we do not believe them; they represent Kirwan to have been present when these so-called fits of epilepsy are said to have occurred; and we cannot believe that if this were the case it would not have been the prepared and not an accidental defence, arising out of evidence on the second day.'

On the supposed screams not being heard by Kirwan due to his distance – 800 yards, as quoted – the jury were not convinced. 'Now, on this subject, we say that, so far as this consideration could have influenced the verdict, it had no weight. We did not believe that Mrs Kirwan died in a fit of epilepsy; nor did we believe that had she so died she could have uttered such repeated screams as were heard at Howth; therefore, all this special pleading falls to the ground.' On Kirwan's behaviour, the jury deemed it suspicious that he was so engrossed by his drawing as to forget about his wife – yet remember to take his bag.

The jury's letter concludes as follows: 'We felt that this defence was due to ourselves as honest and we believe not mistaken men; that it was due to public opinion, so industriously abused, to the ends of truth, and to the sacred character of trial by jury in this country. As far as in us lay we have, to the best of our ability, vindicated both. If we now take a step for which we know of no precedent, happily for the country it is under circumstances rarely, if ever, paralleled; and it has been forced upon us by a repetition of malignity and falsehood from a portion of a press which in either country it is seldom led into or lends itself.

'The object for which it has lent itself in this instance has been accomplished. The life of the murderer is spared, and again, we say, we rejoice; but this might have been accomplished by more legitimate means. If these adopted have obliged to us, in defence of ourselves, to declare as we do, that, upon a full review of all the evidence adduced at the trial and all the reasoning brought to bear upon it since, we firmly adhere to our verdict – solemnly declare that not one rational doubt has been suggested to our minds, that we hold all the circumstances of the case to have been perfectly incompatible with his innocence, and that William Burke Kirwan is guilty of the deliberately planned murder of Maria Kirwan, his late wife, those who have adopted such means to their end are alone to blame. Upon us rests, as we in our consciences are satisfied it should rest, the responsibility the law imposed upon us.'

PART 5

16

BLOODY BILLY KIRWAN

This is a story with long, winding avenues – a good many of them. It's a captivating tragedy whose layers provide the perfect environment in which a researcher could spend many hours and days. The potential for excavating rabbit holes appears endless, but for the purpose of understanding the evidence and the main facts of the story as they pertain to the murder trial of William Kirwan, you, the reader, are now up to speed. The story, in that sense, is finished. The remainder of this book will now analyse and parse the arguments surrounding the validity of certain pieces of evidence, with reference to several key sources, some of which you've encountered already. In these sections, there will be interpretations as old as the case itself; others are brand new. For the empiricist, there may not be much by way of material that can be subjected to anything as stringent as experiment, but there may be ways to illuminate some uncertainties to a larger extent than others.

This case elicited much reaction and, with it, volcanic debate. Facts, such as they are, are distorted, pulled, twisted and corrupted by other interests – certainly as far as the press contributors are concerned. But there is some hope for those of us interested in cutting through the fuzz. It's worth noting that this case, today, would have been wildly different. Certainly less mysterious. With advancements in pathology, toxicology – not to mention DNA, fingerprints, blood analysis and any number of technological capabilities amounting to 'surveillance' – something closer to a set of facts could perhaps be established. In *The Queen* v. *Kirwan*, what the jury was left to decide on was 'circumstantial evidence' – a fact acknowledged several times throughout the trial.

Circumstantial evidence is a tricky concept. It's even trickier to test. Taken individually, a single piece of evidence may not seem particularly compelling, and definitely not sufficient to secure a conviction. But that's not really the idea; the gravity of circumstantial evidence is measured in how the individual pieces stack up together. Declan McGrath, in the textbook *Evidence*, uses the following authoritative description, from Atkins LJ (*Thomas* v. *Jones*, 1921): 'Evidence of independent facts, each of them in itself insufficient to prove the main fact, may yet, either by their cumulative weight or still more by their connection of one with the other as links in a chain, prove the principal fact to be established.' In order to understand legal practitioners' application of circumstantial evidence as it may operate in a court room, it is instructive to consider the metaphor of 'the rope'.

Any single strand of this rope – i.e. each piece of circumstantial evidence – may not on its own be strong enough to secure a conviction, but bound together, those strands have greater strength. To evaluate the body of evidence in a case like this, the rope can be unbound and the strands examined, to see if they merit addition to the rope, so to speak. Each piece must be proven. McGrath highlights the following quote, from *DPP* v. *Nevin*, which came from the Court of Criminal Appeal in its rejection of the submission that a conviction on circumstantial evidence necessitates the abandonment of the presumption of innocence:

> Without ever abandoning the presumption of innocence, the prosecution in proceeding against the applicant on the murder charge is perfectly entitled to rely on any piece of evidence which might be suspicious or uncannily coincidental and such items of evidence cannot just be viewed in isolation of each other. It is the combined effect of the circumstantial evidence which is of importance even though, in respect of each item of such circumstantial evidence, the jury has to consider whether it accepts it or not and also has to consider whether an inference suggested to be drawn from it is warranted or not.

In that sense, it's appropriate to ask: is any given piece of the rope an unambiguous fact? Broadly, for a conviction to be suitable, circumstantial evidence must eliminate all other possibilities consistent with the innocence of the accused, according to McGrath. It must be compelling 'such as to exclude every other reasonable possibility' in the case. With this approach in mind, it is useful to divide the evidence into broad chunks: Kirwan's immoral life and treatment of Maria; the screams heard on the island; the circumstances on the night of Maria's death; and the medical evidence.

Before diving in, it's worth noting that a large portion of the evidence and arguments for/against certain positions came out after the trial, or were included in the prosecution brief from earlier interviews with witnesses who were not called upon at trial, and therefore were not heard by the jury. To that end, the question of 'Did the jury get it right?' is separate to the wider discussion about the evidence. What we're dealing with is the data as it pertains to the story as a whole – before, during and after the trial. With that comes a whole other set of problems: much of the counterarguments came by Kirwan's supporters, and therefore, by design, tend to show him in the best possible light. The efforts of solicitor John Knight Boswell will be referred to multiple times, as will declarations made after the trial. Pamphlets produced in Kirwan's defence will also be looked at, with the two key documents being *Defence of William Bourke Kirwan, Condemned for the Murder of his Wife and Now a Convict in Spike Island* by Boswell, published by Webb & Chapman in Dublin in 1853, and *The Kirwan Case: Illustrating the Danger of Conviction on Circumstantial Evidence and the Necessity of Granting new Trials in Criminal Cases*, published by James Bernard Gilpin in 1853.

Thankfully, for the purpose of fact-finding, some of the evidence has proven to be far more testable than others when it comes to generating untainted information.

Family Secrets

Was William Kirwan a bad man? Does it matter? The jury were reminded repeatedly that the connection between a man's immoral behaviours, such as they can be proven, do not necessarily mean he committed murder. By the same token, they can provide motive, if interpreted in a certain way.

If we travel back to September 1852 – specifically, the 8th – we arrive at the genesis of suspicion. Henry Davis said he was contacted by a party deeply concerned about the events on Ireland's Eye, who came forward having read the inquest report in the newspaper. It was never confirmed who gave the tip-off, but Maria Byrne, the Kirwans' Merrion Street neighbour, is a good candidate. You'll recall Byrne's input so far. We read her initial statement to police, damning in its depiction of Kirwan's cruelty, at the beginning of Part 2. Following the verdict, much doubt was cast over Byrne's version of events. Various declarations were published and referred to in the Kirwan pamphlets.

Maria's mother, Maria Crowe, made a declaration before Pierce Mahony, Clerk of the Crown, on 8 November 1852. Mrs Crowe said Maria told her – and she believed it to be true – 'that there could not be a more industrious, sober or quiet husband than said William B. Kirwan was towards her said daughter,' and that she was well looked after financially. Mrs Crowe recalled her daughter's 'venturesome' bathing – she swam, apparently, to preserve her health, but it worried her mother, who warned her to take more care. On the point of the couple's differing religious persuasions, Mrs Crowe said it was a non-issue. Mrs Crowe also read the statement made by Maria Byrne on 21 September and denied key allegations. On Byrne's story that William was trying to poison Maria with henbane, she said her daughter had actually procured the substance herself – 'a proper and general medicine' that promotes sleep – and taken large quantities.

Mrs Crowe recalled a long conversation with Maria Byrne the previous January. The topic was William Kirwan, about whom Byrne 'spoke in the most derogatory and vindictive language'. Byrne, a widow, said 'Bloody Billy and Hodges and Smith murdered my husband' – when Mrs Crowe asked who the lady meant, the latter said: 'I mean your son-in-law, bloody Billy Kirwan.' Mrs Crowe recalled a time, on or about 13 January, when she heard that Mr Byrne was ill. When Mrs Crowe called to the house, Mrs Byrne led her to a room with tobacco and the means of a celebration of death laid out. 'Mrs Crowe, here is a wake, but no dead man.' Mrs Byrne confirmed her husband was in hospital, but said she hadn't heard from him in three months. 'The Deponent further saith that she entertains no doubt whatsoever on her mind but that said Mrs Byrne has been actuated by base, malicious, revengeful, hostile and unworthy motives towards the said William Kirwan,' reads the text of Mrs Crowe's deposition. Mrs Crowe said her son – the murdered one, according to Mrs Byrne – had emigrated to America with friends, and William had contributed financially to the move. The final passage of this document was a point not lost on the writers of the pamphlets: Mrs Crowe said she attended the Crown solicitor's office on three separate days, and provided them with all of the above details. She was not called upon for examination before the Grand Jury, despite being in attendance.

Another woman to doubt the purity of Maria Byrne's motives was Margaret Caroline Bentley, who said she was well acquainted with Maria Kirwan from infancy. Bentley's declaration would tend to wobble the theory that Teresa and Maria had only recently discovered the existence of the other: '[I]t was with great astonishment I have read in reports of the trial of Mr William Burke Kirwan, that his wife, the late Mrs Kirwan, until within a few months of her death, was unaware of her husband's connection with a woman named Kenny; that to my knowledge, as well as that of several members of her family, the late Mrs Kirwan was fully acquainted thereof before the expiration of one month after her marriage, now more than 12 years ago; that such was in course of conversation frequently alluded to by her, and I often was surprised she exhibited so little excitement or emotion on the subject.' According to Bentley, Maria Kirwan became upset by the situation only once – following meddling by Maria Byrne. Byrne's effect on the deceased was to 'pollute' her mind and 'excite her against her husband, and which, she stated, appeared to her to be the principal object in forcing her acquaintance upon her'. Bentley reported much praise for Mr Kirwan; she said Maria considered her husband's relationship with Teresa Kenny to be 'the only fault of his character'.

Another document highlights the hardship faced by another of this case's most impacted women – Teresa Kenny. Her declaration was taken on 26 January at Capel St Police Court:

I, Teresa Kenny of Dorset-street, in the city of Dublin, spinster, do solemnly and sincerely declare that I was examined by Major Brownrigg, in his office, Lower Castle-yard, some time about 6 October 1852, and previous to the trial of The Queen v. Kirwan, and that in reply to one of the questions put to me, viz. – 'If I was married to Mr. William Burke Kirwan?' I distinctly told him I was not. I declare that I was not married to said William Burke Kirwan, and that I knew of his marriage with the late Mrs Kirwan for the last ten years.

I also declare that the deceased, Mrs Kirwan, from my own knowledge, was aware of his intimacy with me for the last ten years. I declare that when said William Burke Kirwan was first put on his trial some time in November last, I attended pursuant to the summons served on me, and remained in court during the greater part of the day, when the trial was postponed. I declare that the first day when the trial came on in December last, I went to Green Street, but could not get into the court, and that I was most anxious to be examined; I was then suffering from a severe cut across my thumb, which bled until I fainted. I declare that during the trial of said William Burke Kirwan, I was in the house of Mrs Bridget Casey, of No 19, North Anne Street, who generously gave me shelter, and that I was suffering from the effects of such cut, which threatened me with lockjaw, and that this wound and my agitated state of mind produced a low fever, and that for two days I was in bed almost wholly unconscious and insensible, and at which time one of my children was also dangerously ill. I declare that since my name has been brought before the public in connection with Mr Kirwan, I have been hunted and persecuted, and almost driven to madness, not knowing where to find a shelter either for myself or my seven helpless children. I declare that I have been obliged to leave my abode. I succeeded in obtaining lodgings in the house of a Mr Mathews in North King Street, and that I went there with my furniture and children between the hours of seven and eight o'clock of the 31st December last, being New Year's Eve, and that the greater portion of my furniture having been brought up stairs, Mrs Mathews came to me and told me I could not remain; she gave me back the money I deposited; and sooner than be subject to exposure, I left the house; that some of my furniture was broken in the removal from the house, and I and my children were obliged to remain in the street until almost two o'clock in the morning, and that but for the shelter of a covered car, my children would have perished from cold.

That having engaged lodgings in my present abode, a person of the name of Mortimer Redmond, of the detective force, called on me on Friday, the 14th January, inst., in company with another man and a Mrs Bowyer. He said he had a warrant against me for felony of papers, and made search for them, and also for property alleged to have been stolen from Mrs Bowyer in the year 1837. He asked me if I knew anything about the murder of Mr Bowyer, to which I replied that I did not. He also went into the inner room, and in the presence of my son Edward, and my servant, Mary Anne Rochford, said, 'Was I not a foolish woman not to have taken away some of the feather-beds from Kirwan's house?' to which I replied that I never took anything, either papers or property, from Mr Kirwan's house; and I declare that I never did take any papers or property from Mr Kirwan's house, save two newspapers. I declare that about seven o'clock on Sunday evening, the said Mortimer Redmond a second time called upon me, and against my wish intruded himself into my room.

He said he came from Col Browne, to inform me that Mr Kirwan's property was to be sold on the following Friday, and to know if I had any legal claim, and was I not married to Mr Kirwan. He said he had evidence in the Castle of the marriage, and that all he wanted was the name of a witness, and that if I would tell him and admit that I was married, I would be restored to my position in society, and be entitled to Mr Kirwan's property. I replied that I was not married to Mr Kirwan, and that I had told Major Brownrigg so. I then requested said Redmond to leave my room, which he refused. He sat down on the sofa, and said he would not stir until I told him when and how I was married and when I insisted on his quitting and not terrifying my children, he then in a threatening tone and manner said, 'Since you will not give the information I want, I now tell you that Col Browne will put your children in the poorhouse' to which I replied, 'My children are not begging; do with me as you like, but you shall not touch my children, unless it be over my dead body.'

I then insisted on his quitting, and threatened to make him if he would not, when at last he did so. I solemnly declare that some time in the year 1847 my brother, who resides in America, wrote for me to go over to him and that Mr Kirwan urged me to go, and offered to give me any means I required, and that he would either provide for the children here (then four in number), or I might take them with me, and he would give me ample funds for their support and education, which I declined doing, and I solemnly declare that I stated in the office of Mr Kemmis, the crown solicitor, that the responsibility of my intimacy with Kirwan was mine, not his. And I make this solemn declaration at the request of Mr John Knight Boswell, solicitor, conscientiously believing the same to be true, and by virtue of the provisions of an act made and passed, &c.

In a second declaration two days later, Kenny explained her presence in Mr Kirwan's house following the death of Maria. Her sick child, William, needed attention in the city – it was not true that they were living there. She spent two nights sleeping in the house after Kirwan's arrest – 'for the purpose of securing his property'. That Kirwan moved Kenny into the house shortly after Maria's death was a facet of the case which had added great suspicion – and one mentioned by the jury in their letter. Kenny evidently suffered severely following the trial: plastered across the media as the 'other woman', she quickly found herself void of lodgings, and was then allegedly subjected to intimidation by a detective. On that point, Boswell notes that a petition was presented to Earl St Germans – the new Lord Lieutenant –

seeking a public enquiry into Redmond's behaviour. Kenny's statement, not surprisingly considering its inclusion in Boswell's pamphlet, tends to benefit Kirwan's cause, on the face of it: she says Maria was aware of her situation with Kirwan, which deflates the motive somewhat. Equally, Kenny was likely fighting intense pressure from all angles, not least of which was the very real possibility of financial ruin without income from Kirwan.

Kirwan's 'immoral' life, as presented at trial, rested partly upon testimony from a servant of Kenny's, pointing out a time that a strange woman, presumed to be Maria, arrived to make 'inquiries'. The tone and inference of the capacity for deception was undeniable. Was it reasonable for the jury to conclude, based on what they heard from the servant, that the two women knew nothing about each other? At that proximity? For 12 years? That's the way it was framed by the prosecution. The defence flatly disagreed. 'Evidence was given on this point to supply a motive for the crime,' said Isaac Butt of the 'unfortunate connexion', during his own address to the jury. 'Did it supply a motive? The connexion alluded to was not a new one; his wife knew of it, and forgave it, and she and her husband were reconciled.' Perhaps the timing, in the end, didn't matter as much as the existence of the double life itself.

An Old Allegation

The case of Richard Downes Bowyer is a hard one to definitively clear up. Richard's wife, Anne Downes Bowyer, accused Kirwan of murdering Bowyer, who, she said, went missing shortly after they separated late in 1836 – at which point, Kirwan would have been in his early 20s. She also accused Kirwan of stealing property belonging to her husband. Those allegations had been around for some years, but resurfaced in the media in 1853, following Kirwan's very public conviction. Police excavated the grounds at No. 2 Parnell Place, where Kirwan was living at the time of the original allegations. While the seven labourers employed to dig up the garden did not discover the hidden corpse of Richard Downes Boyer, they did find another. The *Kerry Examiner* reported that 'a small coffin, about two or two and a quarter feet long, was discovered buried four feet beneath the surface'. The coffin contained the skeletal remains of a child – but they were deemed to have been there a longer time than warranted suspicion.

Mrs Bowyer's story went that her husband met Kirwan in May 1836, when the young anatomical draftsman operated out of his King Street office. In October that year, the young Kirwan lured the older Bowyer – in his 60s then – to his house at Parnell Place, where Kirwan, his father and two sisters conspired to murder and rob him of his valuable property. Anne said three weeks passed, during which time Kirwan alienated husband from wife, and circulated rumours about her. The younger man allegedly persuaded Bowyer to hand over property he owned in Longford, as well as a bank book containing receipts for lodgements to the sum of about £2,500. The older artist complied. Next, Anne said that one night, between 1 and 2 o'clock, Kirwan entered her home on Mountjoy Street, accompanied by a number of men, who tied up Anne and locked her and a servant away in separate rooms. They took valuable paintings, books and furniture. She claimed that, at the time, a prosecution resulted, which Kirwan escaped through some unspecified legal technicality. Eventually, Anne said a compromise was reached in 1837 after friends of hers threatened further prosecution, and she was granted a £40 annuity for her upkeep. She continued to demand to know the whereabouts of her husband, and called frequently to the house at Parnell Place. This resulted in her being charged with annoyance by Kirwan's father; each time the magistrates heard the peculiarity of her case, she claimed, the charges were thrown out.

In 1843, Anne took out an advertisement seeking information on her husband's whereabouts, alleging that he had 'been removed without my consent and kept concealed from me, by some ill designing person or persons, for the last six years'. Wrapped up in these claims was a story about Kirwan's sister, who, by January 1853, was dead; the woman had apparently told Anne that Richard left the house one night with William and his father, and she afterwards never saw him again. Kirwan had, around that time, apparently seduced a servant girl, and neglected to pay assistants he hired to help paint the ordnance survey maps, feigning poor finances. That was the sum of the allegations that appeared in a number of newspapers, both in Ireland and

Britain, around the second week of January, just about the time when William was moved to Spike Island.

John Knight Boswell produced evidence, and ultimately another pamphlet, with the aim of absolving Kirwan of the Bowyer and Crowe murder claims. The solicitor said he had in his possession a letter from Mr Crowe, addressed to Maria Kirwan, written from where he had emigrated to – Massachusetts – dated 22 October 1852. It's worth remembering that Mrs Crowe was also of the opinion that her son was alive and well. Boswell also apparently managed to locate the missing Bowyer. At least, he discovered where he was buried – and that was not within the grounds of Kirwan's old address at Harold's Cross. The artist had settled in Killeshandra, Co. Cavan, under the name Richard Downes Bowyer Blake. He died there, and was buried, in November 1841. The solicitor produced, in court, a document from the Rev. Mr Martin, Protestant rector of Killeshandra, confirming the same. Boswell also sourced a certificate from the Killeshandra physician who attended to Bowyer on his deathbed.

Extracts from Boswell's pamphlet were published in the press towards the end of January. The extracts told an altogether different story to Anne's: in December 1836, Bowyer arrived to Kirwan's father's residence with a severely bleeding head-wound. Anne had inflicted it, he said. The following day, Bowyer and a number of men – including Kirwan – went to Bowyer's house and took away his furniture. The older artist sold much of the furniture, but kept just enough to furnish a room in the house of a man named Walsh in King Street – where the elder Mr Kirwan also lived. Bowyer and old Mr Kirwan became close friends.

Bowyer also befriended the younger Kirwan, whom he taught to paint. The stipend of £40 was part of a settlement agreed upon as part of separation proceedings; the money came from earnings made by Bowyer on a property in Longford, at Rhine. The rent on the property was sold to Kirwan for £800 as early as 1837; it yielded, according to reports, anything from £130 to £177 per annum. The sale came with the condition that Kirwan continue to pay the £40 annuity to Mrs Bowyer, but she also agreed to 'not molest or annoy her said husband or the said William Burke Kirwan'. Mr Vincent, Kirwan's solicitor, arranged the payments.

Boswell's conclusion was that Anne sought to resume the marriage, against the separation agreement. Richard fled King Street in a bid to avoid her, but she followed him. Bowyer – broadly painted in Boswell's account as a pestered man trying to rid himself of a mentally unwell, abusive woman – stayed at a number of locations around Ireland before settling in Killeshandra, where he died an old man in 1841. On the property that was allegedly stolen, Boswell said he viewed the paintings, accompanied by their owner – a man who had sent them to Kirwan for cleaning. The rare books, he said, were all newly printed editions, and couldn't have been the old volumes that allegedly belonged to Bowyer.

As for the claim that Anne had prosecuted Kirwan after the apparent ransacking, and that he had only escaped conviction by a point of law; Boswell claimed to have debunked that, too. This is where Boswell's argument becomes murky. The solicitor wrote that Mrs Bowyer had prosecuted her husband and William Kirwan for assault in July 1837. During that trial, Boswell reported, Bowyer said he would have been better off cutting his own throat than marrying Anne. Boswell said the Recorder was reported to have noted: 'There is not the least shadow of evidence to cast an imputation on Mr Kirwan' and recommended that Mrs Bowyer accept the proposed annuity and agree to the separation from her husband. Bowyer also pointed repeatedly to Anne's mental state. She had, in the past, been to an asylum and exhibited violence towards her husband. Within the 1837 trial, he noted, expert medical witnesses were produced who agreed upon her unsound mental state, noting her proclivity to 'violence' and 'destruction'.

But that's not really the full story. A reading of the assault trial reports from 1837 gives an altogether more nuanced view of the affair – one in which Anne's account appears a lot more believable than Boswell gave her credit for. For one, the quote by the Recorder listed above is incomplete. Here is the full quote, published in July 1837 in *Saunders's News-Letter* (with the section included by Boswell and reported in newspapers in 1853 in bold):

'The learner Recorder said, that there was no doubt but that the traversers (Mr Kirwan and Mr Bowyer) had acted very imprudently, and that it was a case for a conviction, but what good would that do to the unfortunate woman. **There was not the least shadow of evidence to cast the imputation on Mr Kirwan** of having acted from any sinister motive; he (the Recorder) suggested that they ought to devise some plan of providing for her.' That's not quite how Boswell told it.

In the 1837 case, it was true that men, including Kirwan, had arrived to take Bowyer's belongings – the why and how were the sticking points. Anne, for her part, was exact on the dates and times. A float driver named Matthew Moran had been hired by Kirwan to move the property, and was examined at trial. When they came into the house on Mountjoy Street, they met Anne in the hallway and 'Kirwan asked for a rope to tie her', said Moran. And so, she was tied up. Elizabeth Campbell, Mrs Bowyer's servant, saw her mistress 'forcibly seized by two strong men'. It's quite clear that Anne was restrained while the men – some, according to Mrs Bowyer, disguised – removed the belongings. Besides the furniture, the haul included 87 oil paintings, a looking glass which Kirwan tucked under his arm and a bank book that Mrs Bowyer kept with the Marlborough Street savings bank. A couple of days later, a man came to the door whom she believed wanted to take her to 'Swift's' – meaning Johnathan Swift's, or the lunatic asylum. Dr John Crampton was next sent to the house, but the maid would not let him in. After not being permitted to enter, he issued a certificate stating that he believed Mrs Bowyer to be 'out of her reason'. The doctor said that he saw Anne through the window, pacing up and down – it was on that basis that he decided she was of unsound mind.

Anne herself admitted in 1837 that she had, 15 years prior, been in Dr Gregory's asylum in Finglas 'in consequence of a fever'. It would be a stint leaned upon frequently by Boswell. One man, James Delaney, said he was also employed to move furniture from Mountjoy Street. Delaney claimed to be the one who was 'shut up in the pantry' with Mrs Bowyer, who took a knife and brandished it at him. Insane and violent, or an understandable reaction? Dr Gregory, of the earlier mentioned asylum, deposed that she was at his establishment in July 1823, adding 'she was very violent, and sometimes destructive'.

Mr McDonagh, for the defence in 1837, said Mr Bowyer's case 'was a lesson to old men that they should never marry young wives'. Bowyer said something to his lawyer, who then said, 'He says, that it were better for him that his throat were cut than that he ever married her.' Mr McDonagh said Bowyer suffered 'violent conduct' by his wife, after which he went to Major Sirr, who recommended he arrange to pay her a yearly sum, which she would not accept. He was advised he might take away his furniture – 'and he used no force except what was necessary for that purpose. Whatever was done he avows was done by his direction'. The defence counsel said an intention to assault had not been proven in the case, and that 'a husband is entitled to use a moderate degree of coercion in the management of his family, which was the more allowable in this case, when the woman was supposed to be insane'. At this point, a Mr Walsh spoke to the same effect, quoting Haslam on insanity 'to show that a person nearly insane might conduct themselves with the greatest propriety in a court of justice' – this explained why she was not, then in court, out of her mind, presumably.

Boswell was incorrect on another point. The judge in the 1837 case didn't recommend that Anne accept the money. Rather, he directed the men to make sure she was provided for. In the case, the jury returned a verdict and Bowyer and Kirwan were discharged on their own recognisances, to appear when called upon, and receive the judgement of the court. From the start, they had a legitimate case to answer for, and that much is clear from the very court report, the contents of which Boswell obfuscated.

Anne's main murder allegation does seem substantially unproven – even if Boswell sought to slightly bend some of the facts to suit Kirwan in other ways. But her stint in Dr Gregory's asylum was clearly weaponised to discredit her account. Kirwan did burst into Anne Bowyer's house and tie her up. The men simply felt it was their right to do so. The claims about Anne followed her long after her death. Strickland, in *A Dictionary of Irish Artists*, wrote a brief bio of Richard Downes Bowyer. It concludes: 'Owing to differences with his wife, who was an eccentric woman, and was for a short time in a lunatic asylum, he separated from her; but the constant annoyance he received from her drove him to leave Dublin in 1837, and after moving from place to place he finally settled in Killyshandra, County Cavan, where he lived under the name of Blake. He died there in November, 1841.' And that's her legacy.

Anne died in 1853. Lots of newspapers treated the death as a suicide, though the official verdict at her inquest simply recorded that she was found drowned in a quarry hole at Tubbermore, Co. Dublin. Anne had been obsessed by the issue of her husband's stolen property in her final years. 'It seemed to occupy her thoughts exclusively, particularly since the period of Kirwan's conviction for the murder of his wife,' the inquest heard. She was in the habit of taking long walks. On 7 July 1853, a farmer found Anne's bonnet, shawl and boots at the edge of the quarry hole and raised the alarm.

✦

This isn't the totality of the allegations against Kirwan, but they're the ones most often referenced. Besides the various whispers of murder and seduction, there are far more detailed accusations of painting forgery that emerged when the dust settled, as well as allegations that he attempted to burn documents in his jail cell when authorities came knocking. *The Standard*, which supported Kirwan, commented that to some, he was all but a modern-day Sawney Bean – the legendary cannibalistic clan leader from 1500s Scotland. Whatever about the more pointed allegations of specific crime, what is missing from the above discussions of Kirwan's character and behaviour towards Maria are the testimonies surrounding the incident in Howth – the one referred to by Margaret Campbell, during which raised voices, threats and the violent moving-about of furniture were heard through the closed door of the room in which Maria would eventually lie dead.

Campbell's testimony is imperfect. Through her scattered account, she did the veracity of the story no favours – particularly by omitting the incident in her earliest renditions of the couple's life at Howth. But, unlike the jury, we don't have to rely on Mrs Campbell's evidence to substantiate an instance of domestic violence. The crucial part here is that there are corroborating accounts of a similar character within the brief that was given to the prosecuting counsel – specifically, from Catherine Kelly and Margaret Gillis.

In a sea of half-information, some of the most joined-up evidence on the side of the prosecution resides in the realm of proving that William Kirwan was capable of nefarious acts. That Maria was a victim, in that sense, may be quite a well-supported position. And that's to say nothing of the presumed psychological and emotional trauma that must have been imparted, depending on how much the women knew about – and how each regarded – this 'double life'. The same goes for Anne Bowyer, too; whatever one may think of Bowyer's behaviour, and truthfully we don't know a whole lot beyond second-hand stories, she certainly wasn't treated with overt consideration. As for the declarations that said William treated Maria well? One would presume that the declarants spoke truthfully, and it's likely what they observed and heard from Maria. That does not preclude the fact that he may have been ill-treating her, at least by the time they left for Howth.

Yet the real problem does not lie in satisfying oneself that Kirwan may not have been a good man. The question is – how much does it matter?

17

WHO HEARD WHAT AND WHEN?

H owth has changed radically in some respects. Extensive building in the harbour – including a prominent structure for the Yacht Club reminiscent of a big-top tent, a middle pier, a lifeboat station and spaces for hundreds of cars – took place between then and now. In photographs and images from the late 19th and early 20th century, the location of the sea wall is scarcely believable today, pressed up tight against the main road. In other aspects, Howth hasn't changed one bit. Tourists can still hire a boat and travel to Ireland's Eye, weather permitting. Ken Doyle, of Ireland's Eye Ferries, is the modern-day Nangle – strictly in the occupational sense.

More accurately, he's the modern-day Doyle, another villager who was out on his boat around the island on the day of Maria Kirwan's death. He's mentioned in Nangle's evidence at trial. The name is no coincidence. 'That's my family,' says Ken at the outset of our conversation, quite certain of the ancestral link. Ken has been doing the job a long time, making his first trips in the late 1960s or early 1970s. It's not surprising that the man who runs the ferry service to Ireland's Eye is extremely well acquainted with the most exciting events to ever envelop that very enterprise. The boatman is well versed in the evidence, and like most researchers who come to this case in any detail, Ken is aware of the story's ambiguities.

Much was made of the screams reported around the harbour, and the five witnesses who swore they heard them. It's a part of the story that struck this researcher as unlikely from the outset; you need only visit Howth and look towards the island to be sceptical of the acoustic capabilities between the two points. It was something of a controversial claim then. Owing to his 50-odd years on the job, I ask Ken: does he think it's possible to hear screams coming from the island?

'No, I would have disputed that,' says Ken – or at the very least, he adds, taken it with a pinch of salt. 'You shout from one end of the pier to the next and you can't be heard. I know the Long Hole is probably one of the closest points – the top of the Long Hole where the beach is probably one of the closest points to the land, to the east pier.' Of course, he's correct; a straight line between the 'top' of the Long Hole (the shore side) provides the shortest distance between the pier and the island, at about 1.1km. This is much shorter than the distance from Mrs Singleton's house to the Long Hole, which is likely more than 1.8km. That's the point from where Catherine Flood claimed to have heard the screeches.

'It was said that a boat passing by heard screams, as well,' says Ken, referring to the evidence of Thomas Larkin, who was on the deck of his fishing boat approaching the harbour when he reportedly heard the noises. 'Possibly, with the wind blowing the right direction [you could hear a scream]. The boat was passing, from my reading of it, the west side of the island near the tower. So it was coming that direction. For the voice to carry from the island out to the boat, the wind would have to be coming east. The prevailing wind is southerly/south-westerly.'

On the night, it was repeatedly sworn, the wind was coming from the west, more or less, blowing towards the direction of the scream. The direction of the wind not only casts doubt on Larkin's ability to hear the screams from the Long Hole while he was 20 perches off the island, it would tend to make it even more difficult to catch the sound from any point on the harbour, or further afield. And certainly not the train station, as one witness claimed. In half a century bringing people to the island, you would think Ken Doyle would have had occasion to hear, from the harbour, or surrounding waters, a shout emanating from the island – a passenger who missed a boat, or needed assistance, perhaps. But no. 'I know on our boats, I've been on the island, trying to shout to people on the island to come down because the last boat is going over, and we want to get them back. And they don't really hear you,' says the boatman. 'We're only 100 metres away at the most, you know. We're not a mile and a half away.'

Doyle, while somewhat sceptical, isn't jumping to any conclusions. Not least of all because of the aforementioned building works and the technological developments of industry that add extra noise. As was the case in 1852, it's difficult to be certain at the time of writing; the exact conditions of the harbour on the night could perhaps not be replicated faithfully enough to facilitate a useful experiment. It was tested in the 1850s, however: in the pamphlet produced by Boswell, he mentions these efforts. Men apparently tested the theory and concluded that various loud noises emanating from the island could not be heard on the mainland; that went the same for a rifle shot as it did a loud shout.

It was frequently reported at the time that you could hear shouts coming from the island. Hugh Campbell said it, as did the sergeant, Sherwood, who had only been stationed in Howth about a year, and yet still had occasion to hear them. Another Howth fisherman named John Leland confirmed the same, telling a story about hearing a fare of his whistling from the island. It's not supposed that these people were lying. But even if the shouts were heard from the island, the likelihood that a distant listener could accurately place them as emanating from the Long Hole, and not anywhere in between or from somewhere else on the island, warrants interrogating at the very least.

There's a more basic problem with the evidence surrounding the screams. Drilling down into what those witnesses actually said, things become scattered. Five people officially swore they heard the screams: Thomas Larkin, Hugh Campbell, Alicia Abernethy, John Barrett and Catherine Flood. Each person was interviewed more than once; between those interviews, and between each person, there are some important discrepancies. You've read broad amalgamations of these witnesses' stories already, in Part 1; listed below are some of the key points made by each witness during different interviews, and short notes about where important details diverge.

Thomas Larkin

The fisherman's testimony was probably the most substantial by way of length and detail. It was, really, the one that set off this particular chain of evidence. The basics were that Larkin heard a loud cry, followed by two more, as he sailed his boat between the island and the harbour. The wind, unhelpfully for his testimony, was blowing towards the island, and the direction of the scream. He always maintained that he couldn't tell whether they were the cries of a man or a woman, and though he told his crewmen what he had heard, he didn't feel it necessary to go to the police: Sherwood came to him the following Saturday, after hearing second-hand that Larkin had information.

First Account

The fisherman first estimates that there were five or six minutes between the first scream and the second scream, then on cross-examination says: 'I suppose there was about eight minutes from the time I heard the first bawl until I heard the other two.' He says that conditions were pleasant, but not calm; there was a breeze, and the night was neither rough nor smooth. As for the time, he says it was 'not eight o'clock', and that it was between day and night. In another record, from the Raheny Petty Sessions on 15 September, he says the night was so dark that despite looking in the direction he thought the sounds came from, he couldn't see anything. In this account, he further says the screams occurred between 7 p.m. and 8 p.m.

Second Account

In a similar statement given to the Crown solicitor, Larkin relays the whole story, and this time says it was five or six minutes between the first scream and the second. He says that the evening was fine, and 'the water smooth'. Larkin here estimates that the wind was west-northwest.

At Trial

At trial, *The Freeman's Journal* reports that Larkin says there were five to seven minutes between the first and second cries. According to Armstrong's report, he estimates an interval of two minutes between the second and the last sound. Larkin maintains that the water was smooth and the wind light, and says that 'There could not have been eight minutes between the first and second cry.' In response to Isaac Butt, he concedes that he might have sworn that previously, and his only intention was to be truthful. 'I cannot speak as to minutes,' he says. Instead of saying the island was dark, he now says 'I could have seen a man on the shore if one had been there, but not to know him.' The fisherman refrains from estimating a time frame for the sounds and says the screeches he heard were like calls of distress, rather than someone calling for a boat. According to Armstrong's report, he changes the wind direction very slightly, saying it was northwest.

The Inconsistencies

It's believable that Larkin heard calls. What happens, gradually, over his statements, is the time becomes more ambiguous, and actually earlier. This fits other versions of the screams, as we will soon see. At one point, it was so dark that he couldn't see a person on the island, and 'not eight'; then, it becomes brighter by the time the story gets to trial, and he refrains from offering even a broad chronology.

The sea and conditions become smoother – though not by much – and he does admit the wind was blowing against the direction of the supposed scream. There is the obvious mismatch in the time between the first and second call; it registers anywhere from five to eight minutes. It's not expected that he had a stopwatch, but that aspect does clash with other, much shorter intervals that are reported.

Alicia Abernethy

Abernethy's evidence was the most specific, drawing scepticism. She had the times correct, the location correct, the texture of the screams correct and the gender correct – 'correct' in the sense that they suited the prosecution's story. But, really, her details differed significantly from those shared by most of the other scream witnesses.

First Account

Abernethy says that, a few minutes after 7 o'clock, she 'first heard a violent scream, immediately after I heard a second scream, then a third scream which was quite weakly. I am positive those screams were those of a woman.'

Second Account

Abernethy sticks with a similar time frame: 7.05 p.m. The sound came from the Long Hole, which is 'right opposite' where she lives, and where she was standing. The distance, she estimates, is one mile – or about 1.6km; it's worth noting, too, that the area she lived in would also be elevated from sea level. The interval between the first and second screams expands: she heard 'one dreadful screech, in a few minutes after heard another screech which was not so dreadful.' Then another, 'quite weakly'; she reasserts that it was a woman's voice she heard.

At Trial

Telling her story again, Abernethy confirms she was 'looking at the Long Hole' at the time – her son was out on a yawl and had not returned, and it was getting dark. 'I heard a dreadful screech, to the best of my opinion I heard another screech. I could just see the island at the time.' She swears there were 'about two minutes' between the screams. She then heard a third screech: 'The last scream I took to be that of a person in agony and pain,' she says, 'the first was most dreadful.' It was between day and dark, but she could see the island. Abernethy puts the time of the screams at 7.05 p.m., which she's sure about, because she had just been to a neighbour to ask the time. Here, she adds that she told Sherwood about the screams the following morning, before the inquest.

Inconsistencies

There aren't many changes between the various accounts. But when Abernethy told the court she went out at precisely 7.05 p.m., the defence counsel replied:

'In order to hear the screams, I suppose?' These smaller moments are missing from Armstrong's report of the trial, and underlie the fact that the defence seemed to consider her testimony coincidental and specific beyond belief. And there's reason to be suspicious; at about one mile from the island, she's one of the furthest away – the second furthest – yet the screams resolve in the highest fidelity in this woman's story. They were violent screams, she said, and definitely those of a woman; both of those factors are not necessarily in keeping with the account from Larkin, who was much closer. Abernethy's memory of the time that elapsed between screams wavers slightly – though perhaps not unforgivably so – but the obvious discrepancy on timing is between the account she gave and that of Thomas Larkin.

There is one other issue. Abernethy swore she told Sherwood, on the morning of the inquest, about the screams. To put it bluntly, that does not seem to be the case. It was repeatedly reported in newspapers that a fisherman was the first to raise the alarm about the screams – quite often described as an 'Arklow' fisherman, this unnamed individual uniformly accompanies the first mentions of this piece of evidence in the press. He isn't named, but one must presume it was Larkin to whom the papers referred, although, through his testimony, it does seem he was at Howth on the day Sherwood questioned him; it isn't completely clear.

Sherwood didn't corroborate Abernethy's claim that she told him about hearing such a damning screech on the morning of the inquest. The policeman didn't deny it either, strictly speaking. But when examined by the Crown Solicitor before the trial, Sherwood said he lacked any proof of Kirwan's guilt at the point of the inquest, beyond suspicion and the wet trousers to which he repeatedly referred. If we're to believe Abernethy, the sergeant had already heard about the calls. If indeed he had, it seems unlikely he would consider her story inconsequential; we know that when he heard of Larkin's story second-hand, he thought it appropriate to call upon the man with utmost haste: 'On the evening of Friday the 10th September, I heard that Larkin had stated some circumstances which had occurred at the time of the death of the late Mrs Kirwan. On Saturday 11th I went to Larkin and learned from him that he had heard screeches from the island at the time it was supposed [the] deceased had been murdered.'

Catherine Flood

Catherine's testimony is the least detailed, and does not actually change substantially from one interview to the next.

First Account

In her earliest statement, found within the prosecution brief, Catherine Flood said she heard two screams a little after 7 o'clock after opening the hall door of Mrs Singleton, whose house she was working in, which was situated around the railway terminus. It was a 'dreadful roar in the direction of Ireland's Eye'. About one minute later, she heard one other shout, not as loud as the first. Flood's own house was about 20 perches from Abernethy, on the other side of the harbour. Judging by the descriptions of the witnesses, it's likely that Flood was the furthest away from the Long Hole; the distance as the crow flies is something like 1.8km.

At Trial

Catherine's timing becomes more precise, and more in line with Abernethy's: 'five or six minutes past seven o'clock'. The time has expanded somewhat, to 'a minute or two'. The first scream from Ireland's Eye was 'a very wild scream; the last was cut off in the middle'. The number of screams remains at two, and she heard them after opening the hall door to check how dark it was.

Inconsistencies

Catherine only heard two screams, which clashes with the other witnesses, though that is possibly explained by the fact that she was the furthest away from the island. Her testimony becomes more specific from her initial statement to the trial, and she adds the detail of the scream being 'cut off' on the latter occasion – she's unique in this aspect. She also becomes more confident of the locus of the screams: where first they were from 'the direction' of Ireland's Eye (which could be virtually anywhere in the harbour up to the lighthouse), they later come 'from Ireland's Eye'.

John Barrett

John Barrett was the man whose dray the Nangles used to transport Maria's body to Mrs Campbell's. That was at 11 o'clock. Of course, he spoke with Sherwood owing to his involvement with the grim business on the harbour; but he failed to mention the fact that he had heard calls four hours beforehand on the pier. That statement came later.

First Account

During his first recorded statement, John Barrett says he heard 'a loud screech' from his door at about 7 o'clock – he could not distinguish if it was a man or a woman, but it didn't cause him any mind then: 'It did not then occur to me that it was the cry of a person in distress.' Three or four minutes later, he hears another, not as loud. He walks to the steps on top of the harbour wall, and hears two more screams – lower again. He felt then like it was someone in distress, like someone adrift and calling for assistance.

At Trial

At 'about 7 o'clock', he says he hears two or three screeches from his door, and another two or three when he walks to the pier. The interval between the first he heard at the door and the others was about four minutes. The number of shouts increases again, when he swears that he heard three at the door, and three or four more at the wall. During his testimony, he is asked if he had ever had a conversation with Catherine Flood on the topic. The fisherman says the sergeant came to ask him questions, but he did not tell him about the screeches at first.

Inconsistencies

Barrett would have likely been the second closest person to the Long Hole. His testimony changes somewhat between his first and second account, though his interval between the first and second scream – four minutes – appears internally consistent. It clashes, however, with Abernethy's, Larkin's and Flood's timing. It's also a wonder why he never thought to connect the dots later that same night, or even as he talked to Sherwood the first time. But the main issue here is the number of screams: it ranges from four to seven, and is out of step with other accounts.

Hugh Campbell

The most casual account comes from Hugh Campbell. He was the fish driver, waiting at the harbour wall for the last boats to come in.

First Account

At the Raheny Sessions in September, and before Kirwan's arrest, Campbell swears he heard 'a call' from the island between 7 and 8 o'clock. It sounded, to him, like someone on the island calling for a boat.

Second Account

In a later statement, the calls multiply, though it remains the call of a person looking for a lift, rather than a violent one. Campbell hears the first at the quay wall at about 7 o'clock, then, as he turns to walk back to his house, he hears another. After that, he returns to the wall, where he hears 'more calls'. Ten minutes later, he sees the Nangles' boat going out.

At Trial

There's something of a divide here. The *Freeman's Journal* reported that Campbell now says he heard 'very weak' calls for assistance from the island – or, at least, east of the lighthouse from his position opposite it, at the quay wall. He heard, according to the paper, three cries: the second was three minutes after the first, and the third shortly after. He specified the time further, about 7.30 p.m., and says he said nothing of the cries until he was asked about them. Campbell does not specify how long after the cries the Nangles departed – just that they left after.

According to Armstrong's report, however, he swears hearing 'more than three cries' – and they only 'seemed to come' from the island. He hears the first at about 7 o'clock, according to that account, then after three minutes he hears the second call, then a third shortly after. Half an hour later, he sees the Nangles' boat heading out of the harbour; 'I could not tell whether it was a male or female voice, it was weak, as if of a person waking from sleep.'

Inconsistencies

Campbell's calls multiply from one to 'more than three' – or at least three, depending on the report. The discrepancy was picked up on by Kirwan's supporters. Boswell correctly points out in his pamphlet that Campbell, 'on the 15th day of September last, in the Crown office swore he heard a call; this call, after the lapse of two months, like the story of the three black crows, expanded into three cries. By what magic system of multiplication was this achieved?' The timing of the Nangles' departure extends from 10 minutes to 30 minutes after the calls, according to Armstrong. The characterisation of the screams heard by Campbell is not alarming: the shouts bore the vigour of a person waking from a sleep and calling a boat over. So casual is his interpretation of the noise in the harbour that he remarks to a passing coast guard that someone must be stuck for a lift. Very different from Abernethy's scream of violence – or the cut-off wail heard by Flood. Campbell isn't worried at all – he declines to go to the police; they come to him. The time of the call, too, wobbles a bit, but remains between 7 and 8 o'clock.

What Can We Conclude?

It's hard to know what exactly to make of these testimonies. Some of the differences are not small: Thomas Larkin's interval between scream one and scream two is far longer than any others. John Barrett's overall scream count is more than three times greater than Catherine Flood's. Alicia Abernethy's account is somehow more detailed than Larkin's, despite the large advantage the fisherman had in terms of distance. All manner of characterisations of the scream are present: the sleepy beckon of one who needs a lift; the violent cry of a woman being murdered; and the helpless sailor, gender unspecified, adrift without a paddle. Only one of the five said the scream was a woman's. None thought to go to the police; the police came to them. Really, there should be many more credible witnesses here. The plotting of the players in this instance would have covered an area encompassing most of the main harbour road, and the dwellings therein, not to mention the Nangles and their companions, if indeed the screams occurred before they departed, as Campbell indicated.

Perhaps the reader will believe the discrepancies are the naturally occurring blemishes that arise from multiple viewpoints. It's plausible. On the face of the testimony, however, it's equally plausible they were all listening to different shouts. It would be difficult to come to a conclusion with certainty, given the distances.

What, then, accounts for so many renditions of a similar story? Boswell, perhaps condescendingly to the villagers, suggests a sort of gossip mill effect. He touches, too, on the apparent suspicion of Father Hall, the local priest, towards Kirwan, which would conceivably affect his parishioners. Boswell wrote: 'The reports about the cries magnified to such an extent, that within a month persons from all parts of the hill were found ready to come forward to give evidence about 'cries'. One woman told a gentleman that she heard Mrs Kirwan cry out, 'Oh! what have I done to be murdered?' and when asked where she was at the time, mentioned a locality near three miles distant from the Long Hole. Then was got up the stories of Mrs Kirwan's ghost, which told a doleful tale of how she was murdered by Kirwan, and that all good Christians should avenge her.' Boswell's dismissing of an entire section of the prosecution's case might be flippant, but that aside, the accounts from the witnesses simply don't match up. Authorities, too, were evidently persuaded that there was cross-pollination of stories afoot. Look at the question asked of Barrett – about whether he'd been talking to Flood. Larkin was asked if he knew a 'Mrs Byrne'. In other interviews, namely with Patrick Nangle, a mysterious 'lady in black' – an agent of non-specified meddling, one must presume – comes up. The timing of each player's first account is a curiosity in the domain of potential augmentation of stories: according to the prosecution brief, only two of the five earwitnesses swore information explicitly dated during the earlier September inquiry – Larkin and Campbell.

The timing of the screams is important, too. The earlier Maria's murder, and therefore the screams, the more time Kirwan had to return across the terrain to the landing place. The prosecution's theory must allow time for Kirwan to commit the murder amid a protracted struggle, arrange Maria's body, and possibly hide the clothes before crossing the island. If we take Abernethy's account as gospel, then the prosecution theory is much more likely, as the murder happened at 7.05 p.m. But if we take Nangle's first estimate, that he undertook the 10–15 minute journey at 7.30 p.m., arriving at about 7.40/7.45 p.m., and consider it alongside Larkin's early accounts, that it was 'not eight' – somewhere between 7 and 8 o'clock – yet too dark to see the shore, then we arrive at the possibility that Larkin heard the fishermen shouting for Maria. Or, he may well have heard Patrick Nangle, who swore he let out a shout for Kirwan when the men arrived to the island, at about 7.45 p.m. The men then took to further shouting a few minutes later when they began looking for Maria, which sits neatly with Larkin's testimony of a considerable lapse between the first and second shouts – diminishing in volume as the men moved further from the Martello tower. Pat also noted that he shouted for Mick some thirty minutes after the search began, at which time he could see boats arriving in the harbour, and hear their crew members. It's worth remembering, again, that Larkin was the earwitness closest to the island – by some distance.

In this domain of evidence, as with others, you can construct a formulation of accounts to suit both narratives. In general, screams emanating from an area where a person has been proven beyond doubt to have been murdered are obviously a significant piece of circumstantial evidence. In this instance, though screams were likely heard from some source, there's no real proof that they were Maria's or that they came from the Long Hole. Although, as the jury alluded to in their letter: if there were screams upon the island, from Maria, and they were not caused by Kirwan – it's curious how he would not report hearing them himself. They evidently did not accept excuses for Kirwan having not heard the calls that were based on the peculiar acoustic nature of the island's geography. However, the vast experience of Ken Doyle, the modern-day ferryman, would tell us that hearing a shout from even close distances around Ireland's Eye is not as easy as it may seem.

18

OTHER PIECES IN THE PUZZLE

Secret Weapons

A long, thin blade hidden within an otherwise normal-looking walking implement. It's an irresistible bit of lore connected with this case that has somehow endured. 'Mr Kirwan had a stick of a kind called a tuck stick,' said Patrick Nangle on the first day of the trial. The first public mention of the secret weapon. When asked what that meant, the *Freeman's Journal* says he replied: 'I mean a cane with a sword in it.' In John Simpson Armstrong's report on the trial, he's recorded as saying: 'I mean a stick like a sword cane.' Whatever the exact wording, there's no mistake about what Nangle swore at trial.

The concept of a weapon concealed in Kirwan's walking stick was evidently around before Pat Nangle officially added it into the canon of this crime. We know this because Hatchell explicitly says that he looked for signs of its use when he performed the post-mortem examination, having already heard the stories. As a theory, it tallied with the reported amount of blood, the lack of external injury and had a suitably mysterious quality. The concept would pop up as recently as, at least, 2016, when I myself included it in an archive story for the *Irish Times* based on an account in that newspaper's archive written in the early 20th century. The medical evidence – as is stated in the next chapter – precludes it as a murder weapon, and the mystery cane itself was never brought forward. Extraordinary, considering this line from Pat at trial: 'The private part of her body was greatly cut; the blood would not have flowed if it was otherwise.' Pat steps down from the sword cane theory as questioning progresses. It's probably not necessary to state this, but the sword cane seems to have existed exclusively in the imagination of Pat Nangle. The real question is: what else did?

It makes sense to recall the incident of the sword cane for the purpose of examining Pat Nangle's testimony as a whole, because much rests upon it. Boswell suggested the Nangles had ill will towards Kirwan due to the squabble over payment. The solicitor points to the declaration of a woman named Catherine Brew, who said that in a conversation following the inquest, Pat said: 'If I am called on again, I will pinch him,' meaning Kirwan. This is no secret: Pat himself told the trial about his dissatisfaction with the affair, commenting on his 'bad haul' and confessing that he himself demanded the extra payment, blocking the passage of a horse and dray as he did so. Boswell, in his pamphlet, identifies the 'dray' as the hearse that came to collect Maria's body after the inquest. Boswell writes: '[The Nangles] stopped the hearse when coming into town, and but for the police would not have permitted the body to leave Howth.' It's hard to imagine a level of vindictiveness that would lead a fisherman to construct evidence for the sake of money, but it's not unwarranted to read a level of unreliability into the fabric of the sword cane allegation. And that's important for the next piece of evidence.

The Sheet

The sheet is a battleground. A directly opposing recollection, and one of great importance. Believing the prosecution requires believing the veracity of Pat Nangle's story over Mick's. This is not a case where one testimony is not corroborated; it's a case where another eye witness directly opposed a recollection. As discussed, it's reasonable to believe that Pat disliked Kirwan. His annoyance at the entire saga, and in particular his view on the insufficient payment, are documented. While Mick may have been annoyed, too, he did not mention it in explicit terms.

At the inquest, Pat made no mention of the blood he saw on the body, or the blood on his sail, or the sword cane, or the cat-and-mouse game he apparently played with Kirwan when finding the clothes. The reader might remember that, at trial, Pat said that when he failed to find Maria's clothes, Kirwan went to look himself and returned with a couple of garments. Pat was sent back up for the rest, and swore that he found the items where he was positive he had already looked. The real sticking point arose concerning the sheet. The presence of the sheet underneath Maria suggests something peculiar, if it was a drowning death. Mick said the sheet was brought down by Kirwan after he went to look for Maria's clothes. The presence of the sheet would be suspicious, and actually provides a possible murder weapon if we consider the prosecution's theory that she may have been smothered with fabric.

The division in recollection between the cousins has its origins at the inquest. When Pat reached the part about the sheet, he said Kirwan objected and the fisherman was prevented from saying his piece. He used this interruption as an excuse for why his initial statement did not contain the particulars about the blood on Maria's face or on his sail, and the clothes debacle. Henry Davis, the coroner, later said it was Mick who interrupted at the point of the sheet, and that Kirwan chimed in. It's conceivable that they both interrupted him; whether or not that interruption creates a good reason why, when his testimony resumed, Pat did not mention the various important particulars that began to grow through his recollection, is up to the reader to decide. The injuries, and reports of blood, crop up in Pat's story only during the enquiry in October, while the sword cane arises in his sworn statements for the first time at trial.

The following is from a letter from Alex Boyd, the foreman of the inquest jury, on the topic of those very changes. Bearing in mind that Boyd would be keen to defend the inquest, there is not much here that isn't identifiable through the testimonies themselves: 'It seems to me incredible that, had there been any great flow of blood, the women and the police who saw the body before washing, and who were present at the inquest, would not have mentioned the circumstance. How Nangle, who described so minutely on the inquest the position of the body and all other appearances, omitted to tell us altogether about the sword cane and the sword cut, and about the quantities of blood, which he alleged on the trial, I cannot imagine. I feel satisfied that he gave his testimony to us as one who believed that Mrs Kirwan had been drowned and not murdered. He had told us all he had to say and he so stated to the coroner. There was not the least grounds for his observation on the trial that he was put back at the inquest by Mr Kirwan's directions and prevented giving his evidence. The evidence given by the two Nangles on the inquest, respecting the sheet, was contradictory; the one asserted positively that Mr Kirwan brought down the sheet and a shawl and wrapped the body in it, the other said the sheet was partly under the body when he found it, but he subsequently stated he was confused at the time and could not say whether he might not have been mistaken.'

On the face of it, Mick's story lacks the obvious augmentation that affected Pat's testimonies. Here's Mick's recollection of the situation, from the trial: 'Mr Kirwan went up the rock, and I followed him; he said "here they are"; I then saw Mr Kirwan come down, bringing something white in his hand like a sheet, and also a shawl; he slipped coming down the rock; Pat Nangle and Mr Kirwan were putting the things on her; Mr Kirwan then told Pat Nangle to go up the rock and bring down the clothes, which he did.'

In an earlier statement, Mick said Kirwan had simply gone further up the rock than Pat previously had, hence why he was able to find the clothes. Mick broadly stuck with his story, but as noted in the trial jurors' letter, he mellowed somewhat. At trial, he said 'something like a sheet' instead of 'a sheet'. It was on that difference that the jury staked their claim that he did not swear that the sheet was brought down by Kirwan, which seems like an incredible detail on which to rest such an important decision. At trial, Mick said the items Kirwan brought down were placed on Maria, and then immediately says: 'There were only the sheet and shawl and bathing dress on the body when it was put into the boat.' Mick's recollection is perhaps further questionable because he was a few yards further away from the body.

But the jury, in their letter, discredited Mick's evidence based on the idea that he was less intelligent than Pat – the reader might recall the following: 'Seeing the two men, Patrick and Michael Nangle, and hearing their evidence, we could form no reasonable doubt of the truth of either of them. They are both elderly men; Michael appears older than Patrick, nor is he, by many degrees, so observant or so intelligent a man… Patrick Nangle's account of his finding the body with the sheet partly under it, and his tying it across the chest and knees, is perfectly consistent with all the circumstances of this particular period, and was so far corroborated, as it could be, by those who gave an account of the state and condition of the body, when brought to Mrs Campbell's. Michael Nangle did not see Patrick Nangle do this, but had it been the sheet Kirwan brought from the rock, and had Mrs Kirwan's body been then to be placed in it, Michael Nangle must have been required to assist; say he did not assist, it is not possible but that he would have observed it being done.

The fact of the sheet being tied exactly as Patrick Nangle described, was undoubtedly proved by those who untied the knots he had tied.' This is curious, because it appears Mick did swear that he saw the men 'putting the things on her', and it's clear from any reading that 'something like a sheet' was, well, something like a sheet. At the inquest, he'd sworn explicitly it was a sheet – though he'd been slightly less certain in his statement to the Crown solicitor, when he said he couldn't be certain. In another account, on 8 October, he swore evidence akin to that at trial: 'something white a shift or a sheet'.

At trial, Hayes, one of the prosecution lawyers, relied heavily on the 'passing strange' of Kirwan's ability to locate the clothes quickly when Pat said he could not – and he a fisherman with intimate knowledge of the rocks. Hayes, too, jumps on the wiggle room provided by the shred of doubt in Mick's evidence. He says it was a chemise and not the sheet that Mick saw Kirwan bring down. That the chemise was nowhere to be found was a 'remarkable fact', and he inferred from this that it was in fact the 'something white' brought down from the rock by Kirwan.

That does not square with the fact that the missing chemise was not in the basket, and it was a sheet and a shawl that was found to be tied around the body. Boswell, in his own commentary, figured that the less specific construction of 'something like a sheet' at trial came from efforts to coach Mick between point A, the inquest, and point B, the trial. That's a hard one to stand up, but as we have seen, there was apparent suspicion of various 'coaching' of witnesses. As already mentioned in this section, Pat was asked on 8 October if he knew a 'Mrs Byrne, a lady in black'; a spectre of apparent interference who haunted Howth. It's a curious question, especially when we consider that Kirwan was said by Boswell to have written to Brownrigg shortly after his arrest to claim he was the victim of a conspiracy.

Declarations were made after the trial by people who had talked to the Nangles around the time of the murder, and about the sheet specifically. One such person was Elias George Jackson, who lived in a cottage at Howth around that time. The fishermen, he said, recalled that Kirwan 'appeared ashamed on seeing his wife so exposed, and ran for a sheet to cover her, and that he did cover her with the sheet'. A woman named Marianne Tate declared on 18 December that she had explicitly asked Pat about whether or not the sheet was underneath Maria when they found her, to which he apparently replied: 'God bless you, no, ma'am, it was the poor gentleman who got the sheet to cover his poor wife, and no wonder, as she was quite stripped.' Mrs Campbell declared that she touched the sheet, which was damp but not saturated as if dragged in the sea, when it came off the body; Pat Nangle, however, swore the sheet was wet. Mick's version would have a husband retrieve, presumably, a dry sheet for the purpose.

Mick's story is not perfect, but it did not grow, or become more sanguinary with time. Mick, too, was the first person to vocalise concern about Maria's whereabouts when the men arrived to the island, as Pat returned to the boat. It was Mick who initiated the search. Another difference crops up between the cousins' accounts: Pat failed to mention the blood on Maria's face at the inquest, but it crops up in his various later testimonies. Mick's story lacks this aspect, though it appears that he did not get as close to Maria's body as Pat.

It's hard to infer any malice on Pat Nangle's part. It's conceivable, however, that his imagination and frustration culminated in the synthesis of an increasingly dastardly tale. The point of this section is not to make a villain of Pat Nangle, but to make quite a basic observation: there's no real reason to believe his account over Mick's, and more than enough inconsistency to warrant a pinch of salt. The discrediting of Mick as a witness, even if it's true that he seemed less 'intelligent' than Pat, is a curious tool for the jury to reach for in justifying their preference. Perhaps it's true that Mick was less intelligent than Pat. Perhaps he was just less imaginative. It's not clear why either would be important in considering his story.

Wet Legs

Sherwood claimed to be suspicious of Kirwan from the outset, and much was said of the fact that Kirwan's legs appeared to be wet, to the point of spattering Mrs Campbell's hearth with droplets and producing a steam as he sat by the fire on the night of his wife's death. One person, Catherine McGarr, said in a statement that his India Rubber coat was wet, but nobody corroborated that; if it was wet, it was not wet to the point of arousing suspicion to the extent the legs did. The pamphlet in support of Kirwan notes a large disparity between the timing of the supposed murder (7 p.m. to 7.30 p.m.) and the noticing of the droplets on the stone at least four hours later, if not more. It's supposed, for the saturation to have occurred during the commission of a murder in water, that he had to remain sopping wet, to the point of producing droplets, from the knees down for that entire time. Also, if taken with the supposed struggle and screams, Butt's observation is reasonable: one would suspect his arms to be wet, and his appearance otherwise disrupted – defensive wounds, torn clothes, blood.

There was a shower of rain at about 6.30 p.m., after which Kirwan walked around the island, through knee-high vegetation. The following is taken from surveyor Alfred Jones's pre-trial statement: 'The ground between the place where Mr Kirwan was at 8 o'clock and the Long Hole is covered with nettles, ferns and long grass, some of them several feet in height. No person could go through that ground after rain without getting wet.' In red ink, written next to this point on the prosecution brief is a note that says the Nangles had been cross-examined on that point, and said they were not wet. It's clear which version the prosecution selected to pursue. Jones was the first witness called for the prosecution; he was not asked about this part of his observations.

Thomas Giles swore that he himself got wet to the knees after they brought the boat around to the Long Hole to pick up Kirwan and Maria's body, such was the height of the water at that location. He surmised that because Kirwan stepped into the boat from the rocks, he couldn't have got wet. The Nangles, too, said Kirwan didn't get wet at that point of the story – and maintained that. Kirwan, however, was also on his own for an entire hour, unsupervised, before the men arrived back with the boat.

The Tides

The topic of the height of the water at the time of Maria's death was important to illustrate that the water was relatively shallow for a drowning to have occurred – though, of course, it isn't impossible for a person to drown in shallow water. It was important, too, that the water was going out; it meant that Maria couldn't have drowned further out and then been washed back towards the shallower waters. In short, Alfred Jones's measurements as presented at trial were incorrect. Boswell claimed the height around the time of the alleged murder was closer to six feet deep at 7 o'clock on the night of 6 September, and not two feet nine inches, as sworn at trial (one feet nine inches 'above' the rock, plus the one-foot height of the rock itself).

John Weston Foakes was an engineer who took an unprompted interest in the case after reading about the tide levels in the newspaper – according to his own statement, again used by Kirwan's defenders. Foakes travelled to Ireland's Eye in December to take readings, assisted by Walter Boyd and shown the key areas by Sergeant Sherwood. Foakes recorded data on two days and concluded that the location was subjected to varying heights, owing to the wind. On the first day, at half tide – the stage at which Maria was supposed to have died – he found the water depth over the spot where Maria was discovered to be six feet three inches; on the second, Foakes found the level to be four feet eight inches over where the head and shoulders lay. He claimed he and Boyd tested the waters by swimming a little after half tide: 'When I arrived at about fifty feet from where the body was found, the water being then about up to my breast, I was swept off my feet, and had I not been able to swim, I have no doubt I should have been carried into deep water and against the rocks which cross the channel.' Boyd saved him with the use of a long pole, Foakes claimed. This anecdote, for obvious reasons, was appealing to Boswell.

Samuel Haughton, the distinguished Irish doctor, reverend and scientist who co-authored celebrated textbooks on, among other topics, tides and currents, stepped in some years later with an interpretation of his own. The title of Haughton's work – contained in *Proceedings of the Irish Royal Academy (1836–1869) Volume 7, (1857–1861)* – was 'On the true height of the tide at Ireland's Eye on the evening of the 6th September, 1852, the day of the murder of Mrs Kirwan'. Using the relative height of the measurements at Kingstown, he produced the following table, showing the difference of the height of the tide above the 'Body Rock' – which was accepted as being about one foot high – between the trial version and Haughton's calculations. His was an independent analysis, and he clearly states that he offered no opinion as to the case or the commutation of the sentence; he was simply an expert with direct access to the measurements.

Time	True height above Body Rock	Height alleged at trial	Difference
High water	+ 4.84 feet	+ 7 feet	+ 26 inches
6.30 p.m.	+ 3.11 "	+ 2.5 "	- 7.3 "
7 p.m.	+ 2.37 "	+ 1.75 "	- 7.4 "
7.15 p.m.	+1.85 "	+ 1.375 "	- 5.7 "
7.30 p.m.	+ 1.34 "	+1 "	- 4.0 "
Low water	- 1.86 "	- 2 "	- 1.7 "

In terms of an authority on tides, Haughton is a good bet. The water at the time of Maria's death was between 7.4 and 4 inches deeper when she died compared with the Crown's calculations, if the window of her death is accepted to be between 7 p.m. and 7.30 p.m. The discrepancy may illustrate a negative picture of the prosecution's evidence generally – that they could present false numbers as scientific facts – but the difference is not huge.

The Rest

There are other, smaller evidence fragments that the prosecution put less weight on, but which were discussed. The contents of the various luggage were mentioned a number of times in attempts to account for pieces of clothing. The foreman of the inquest, who saw Mrs Kirwan's basket as it was discovered beside the clothes, described nothing out of the ordinary – 'in it lay, at the bottom, her shawl pin, her garters and on the top her stockings drawn carelessly one inside the other'. There is, also, the issue of the bathing cap – discovered afterwards among the rocks, and which was not with Maria or the clothes on the night of 6 September. It's difficult to conclude much based on that fact alone, though it was a point of interest, and Sherwood produced the same cap at trial. Mr Kirwan's bag, after he left the island, was said to contain some ham, bread and used plates and cutlery. The trial jury's letter mentioned the same bag in the context of a much more important piece of general circumstantial evidence that permeates the entire case: Kirwan's behaviour. They wondered how engrossed a man must be in a sketch to forget that he had not heard from his wife on a darkening island, yet he remembered his bag well enough when he went to meet the fishermen.

The sketch, too, was used by some to indicate that Kirwan had been sketching the sky at the time he said he was. It seems like a lot of weight to put upon the selection and mixing of a hue; any good artist, such as Kirwan, could paint a convincing evening scene from memory. Efforts were made to disprove the insinuation that Kirwan picked a wet portion of the cemetery in which to bury his wife, four days after the inquest, on purpose; information from the man who purported to pick the plot himself, without Kirwan's knowledge, were used by Boswell to dispel that sinister shadow.

Similarly, the idea that Kirwan made the women wash the body in the face of an objection was an injection of malice, though it was apparent that the police had been alerted at that time, and that Sherwood was in the house, witnessing Kirwan drying his clothes. There was also the story that the Kirwans had been due to leave their Howth lodgings the day after Maria's death – counteracted by a declaration made by Mrs Campbell on 27 December. The widow said they planned to stay until November (she had made this point previously in her statement to the Crown solicitor), and further said that a policeman was on the scene when the decision to wash the body was made. She also reported fortifying the women about to wash the body with spirits, and again a second time when they completed the job, at the request of Mr Kirwan, who volunteered his own stock of alcohol for the purpose. Kirwan, she said, was much affected by his wife's death in those days.

Boswell, in his pamphlet, entertained a third man theory, presenting third-hand evidence about a man who swore to another man that Kirwan was innocent, but who had conveniently left Dublin since, without a trace. In theory, it's possible for someone to land on the island without Pat Nangle knowing, even if he denied the same: there are multiple landing points. As a legitimate doubt, it's about as unprovable as it gets. Another story told of a Danish sailor who saw Maria struggling with someone on the beach. Again, nothing solid was forthcoming.

The jury accepted Hatchell's testimony over the two defence doctors; as the man who saw the body, he took precedence over all other medical interpretations. They mention, in particular, the congestion which could only have been caused by a great struggle. It's notable that the judge seemed to consider Hatchell's evidence as broadly allowing both modes of death, because it's evident from the reports that the doctor was not quite so equivocal at the outset of his testimony. The jury also seemed taken with the fact that Kirwan had supposedly moved Teresa into the house shortly after Maria's death. If we believe Kenny's declaration, then she took two of her children there because one of them was sick. But that evidence was not at trial – Kenny did not give evidence at all.

In the absence of that clarification, if indeed it would have been forthcoming, they were left to consider only the fact that Sherwood found Kenny and the two children in the house. They were left, too, to choose between a hastily arranged epilepsy theory and testimony from the doctor who had performed the post-mortem exam. Whether or not Hatchell erred on his medical interpretation is a matter for the next chapter.

19

INTERPRETING THE MEDICAL EVIDENCE

This section, an evaluation of the medical evidence, deals with the most testable information we have. In some instances, as with the previous chapters, the ambiguities that existed then still exist now. However, elsewhere, proclamations of scientific 'fact' can be confidently removed from the equation. The medical evidence also has an important part to play in the genesis of the case itself. Consider the following quote from the jury's letter: 'True, it was not sworn that the body of Mrs Kirwan was the body of a murdered woman. Upon this fact depended the circumstantiality of the case; had that been sworn to there would have been an end of the matter. Proved to have been murdered, she must have been murdered by Kirwan.'

It's quite a stark admission, considering the judge's explicit direction that they acquit if they could not satisfy themselves that Maria had died from violence. But it speaks, again, to the ambiguity at trial. The legal term 'corpus delicti' appears in the press discussion following the trial of William Kirwan. In Latin, it means literally 'body of the crime': it refers broadly to the idea that a crime must be proven to have occurred before a person can be tried for it. It would typically now be considered a requirement that a person be demonstrated to have died of foul play before a murder case commenced; in the case of *The Queen* v. *Kirwan*, due to the combatting and ambiguous medical testimony, it was considered by the jury as simply another strand in the rope. This chapter will quickly go through some of the old medical interpretations. The next will consult modern medical opinion, with a view to trying to clear up the question that precedes all questions: is there pathological evidence that a murder took place?

George Hatchell was given much credit by the jury. The ambiguity in the conclusions of his post-mortem exam, and his own hardening on the subject of the cause of the lethal congestion, left enough room for the prosecution to secure a guilty verdict. There were physicians who took harder lines on the case: the first, in the pro-verdict camp, was Dr Thomas Geoghegan. The second, in what you could deem the anti-verdict cohort, was Dr Alfred Swaine Taylor.

For the Verdict

Thomas Geoghegan was a surgeon and lecturer in medical jurisprudence, whose early work on the case in advising the Crown is present in the extensive brief for the prosecution. In a letter to the Crown solicitor on 25 October 1852, in which he enclosed a detailed medical argument in favour of the murder having taken place, the doctor makes a direct, almost impassioned plea for both himself and Dr Hatchell to be called by the Crown to deliver the medical evidence. It appears, almost, that he was concerned he would not be called. If that's the case, his concern was well-placed. Geoghegan was not called as a witness. His take on the trial was nevertheless made public, appearing in a paper published in the *Dublin Medical Press* of 26 January 1853, and widely circulated in newspapers. Compared with Hatchell's take, his is a more definitive set of conclusions.

The Doctor's Theory

Dr Geoghegan's paper is well-argued, and takes in many factors, not just the direct evidence about the condition of Maria's body. He details the contours of Ireland's Eye with the specificity of someone who has visited. Meticulously, he goes through the medical 'facts'. For the purposes of the paper, it appears Dr Geoghegan uses a different wording of the findings from the examination conducted by Dr Hatchell, to whom he says he is 'indebted' for the account, implying that it may have been furnished directly. It bears a number of small differences to Hatchell's other findings, already discussed. The account mentions, for the first time, that Maria's bladder was empty – a sign, among other things, of an epileptic seizure.

Geoghegan begins his argument by stating Maria's health and discrediting the notion that she had such a fit – citing lack of evidence and, correctly, that Mr Kirwan made no mention of such an important illness at the inquest. Geoghegan mentions the geography of the Long Hole, the dimensions of the 'Body Rock' and his opinion that the body could not have wound up there without interference. He mentions other signs of a protracted struggle, including the extent of the congestion found in Maria's body post-mortem.

Attributing the various bleeding accounts to violence, he describes them as 'those local haemorrhages which sometimes occur where asphyxia has been combined with compression of the neck or chest'. On page three, Geoghegan mentions one of the main thrusts of his argument: the froth at Maria's mouth, and infers that it could only occur where a person had been drowned during a struggle, or 'rising and sinking'. The appearances of the face and condition of the lungs, he said, preclude an epileptic fit as the cause of death.

'The phenomena of drowning present themselves practically under two distinct forms – first where the submersion is continuous from its commencement, and where asphyxia is consequently produced in its most rapid form: secondly, where the drowning person, in possession of consciousness and volition, maintains a more or less protracted struggle rising and sinking for some time beneath the surface of the water. A corresponding and marked contrast exists in the appearances of each. In the former, the face is pale and placid, lips unswollen, and froth is absent from the mouth. Internally, the signs of congestion are comparatively slight and not unusually altogether wanting. Such are the results of numerous practical investigations on the subject by the most eminent medical jurists. Several very careful observations and dissections of the drowned, have led me to the same conclusions.'

The epileptic who falls in the water, Geoghegan surmised, is in the former group. He offers an anecdote, gleaned from another doctor: 'A lunatic female, subject to a modified epilepsy, was found dead and lying on her back in a trough, in which she had been in the habit of washing, and the water in which was about 18 inches deep. The face was pale and perfectly calm, like that of a person in sleep. There was no froth at the mouth, injection of the eyes, or swelling of the lips. The lungs were but slightly congested. A few trivial contusions existed on the posterior part of the body. The appearances and countenance and those of the lungs, in the Kirwan case, were therefore altogether opposed to those of epileptic drowning.'

Geoghegan discusses non-medical evidence. The screams allegedly attributed to an epileptic fit could not have been so; the fit would have meant that Maria fell on her back and had her mouth underwater. Besides, Maria's stomach was empty, meaning the 'full stomach' catalyst was bogus. The doctor doubted Maria drowned at all. The bleeding, in particular, was more consistent with strangulation (or, he conceded, the protracted form of drowning), or compression of the chest, presuming they occurred independent of manual injury. Bleeding of the ears in particular, he stated, occurs in compression of the chest.

Wondering why the prospect of strangulation received little attention by the medical jurists, he said: 'In strangulation, froth is not uncommonly absent, and when present, usually mucous or bloody, smaller in amount and of coarser structure.' Bleeding from the vagina, by the same token, could not have been the result of menstruation: for this, he relies on the characterisation by Anne Lacy that the blood was not the right colour, and his belief that a woman who was menstruating would not go swimming. Added to this, he refers to bleeding following hanging cases and ones in which compression of the chest occurred.

Geoghegan offers the following regarding the lack of strangulation marks: 'The absence of any mark upon the neck is perfectly consistent with strangulation by a soft and broad material.' The doctor invokes a case of his own investigation, in which a man hanged himself with a pocket handkerchief. As for the scratches on Maria's face, they arose from the struggle. Geoghegan concludes with a proposed method of murder: 'On the whole, the conditions of the body, with such of the general fact as are intimately connected with them – as the special depths of water and the nature of the locality – are most consistent with the view that the deceased had been strangled at the land side of the "Body Rock" in very shallow water.'

The pathology indicated murder, he said. The position of the body implicated another person. The 'moral facts' – threats, maltreatment and 'adulterous intercourse with another woman' – dictated who the perpetrator was. The following four points make up the doctor's conclusion on the case.

1. That the death of Mrs Kirwan was not the result of apoplexy, or of epilepsy, nor yet of epileptic or of suicidal drowning.

2. That the combined conditions of the body (both external and internal) were incompatible with drowning unattended by other violence.

3. That the appearances observed may have been produced by strangulation alone, or combined with compression of the chest, or with partial smothering.

4. That they are also consistent with a mixed process of strangulation and submersion, in which the latter condition was not continuous from its commencement.

Some Notes

A couple of notes on Geoghegan's argument are appropriate, given it was championed as the winning narrative. The *Cork Examiner*, in teeing up its coverage of the paper on 31 January, wrote: 'If there ever were any real believers in the possible innocence of Kirwan, amongst the million readers of the evidence adducted upon his trial – which we very much doubt, never having met any – their doubts, or tenderness of conscience needs exist no longer...' Objectively, it falls short of that promise.

Geoghegan never saw the body. Yet he assumes some level of authority over other medical theorisers because of the fact that he attended the trial. Perhaps that is merited to a degree; the material, however, is the same, and it won't be forgotten that the initial work on his position began well in advance of the trial, when he was trying to make sure he was called as a witness. The doctor mentions a number of dubious factors uncritically in building his case. One is that there was a sheet beneath Maria, which is debatable, and reliant upon believing one Nangle over the other, as has been discussed.

Another, more important non-fact is that Maria's nose was broken, or 'crooked', which generally helps his theory of physical intervention. There is no real evidence that facial trauma to this extent was present – the opposite is true and generally accepted: there were no overt marks of violence on Maria's body. That fact was the basis of the entire debate. The scratches and abrasions were smaller injuries, argued over in the context of whether they were inflicted by human intervention, scratching on the stones, or marine life. But presuming Maria's nose was broken is a false injection of more serious signs of violence, and building a theory upon that presumption is a poor foundation for an objective analysis. To be fair to the doctor, it was a detail mentioned at trial. But pulling the thread and locating the source of the information reveals it to be unworthy of any label approaching 'medical fact'. 'Incorrect' may be more appropriate.

Alex Boyd, the foreman of the inquest jury, wrote a letter that contained the following observation: 'the nose was not swollen or bruised, or bent over on the outside of the face…' True, he may have been trying to cover up a poor performance at the inquest. But he is well accompanied in his observation. Hatchell found no fractures during his post-mortem; he mentioned nothing about a 'crooked nose'. Nor did the vast majority of the people who saw Maria after she drowned. To be more specific, throughout the entirety of the material collected as part of the prosecution case, there are at least 10 people who saw the body and swore statements – this number is conservative, and excludes the likes of Margaret Campbell, Thomas Giles and Anne Hannah, who saw the body, but not up close.

Just one of the 10 appears to have mentioned a broken nose in statements made prior to the trial. This person did not appear in the witness box. Catherine McGarr was actually the one who mentioned Maria's nose at the Green Street Courthouse. She – along with Anne Lacy and Mary Robinson – washed the body. It was her first mention of Maria's nose, with Catherine's previous, very detailed statement failing to include such a dramatic injury. There was another woman, however, who did mention a 'bent' nose to the Crown solicitor. Hers is a name you have not heard yet, partially because of her apparently fleeting connection to the case. She was Margaret Doyle.

Doyle ran a small shop, in keeping with the practices of many of the other women whose seafaring husbands were away for stretches. Maria, as she did with many of the other villagers, made an impression on Doyle as she carried out her trade; she was in the habit of purchasing items from Doyle's store. Doyle's sworn statement to the Crown solicitor contains an allusion to Maria's knowledge of a secret life – and suspicion over another woman. It also contains a description of the body, as seen by Doyle, on the morning of the inquest: 'Saw that her nose was bent on one side, saw a dinge in her forehead, the mark of the blood was on the forehead. Saw a mark under her eye as red as the fire...'

And there it is. The sole mention of a broken nose, it appears, to be sworn to the Crown solicitor. If we are to believe the vast minority opinion – that Maria's nose was broken – we must believe, too, that the forehead was 'dinged', and that the medical student missed the facial trauma. As did the policeman. And the doctor who performed the post-mortem examination. And the assisting doctor. And the woman who held the candle up to Maria's face. And the nurse-tender. And the coroner. And the fishermen. And so on.

Many of those people did note Maria's nose, in the context of the foam, without the factor of its breakage. Anne Lacy commented on the nose, only to mention its lack of injury: 'There was no scrape on the nose,' she swore in one statement. Unchecked by the defence, and with absolutely no basis in any fact brought forward by a medical authority – or even a corroborative layperson – Doyle's story about Maria's nose made its way into the courthouse, even if Doyle herself did not. It also makes its way into the realm of 'fact' for the purposes of Geoghegan's argument.

A more basic problem with Dr Geoghegan's theory lies in his central thesis, that the conditions of the body (congestion, foaming at the mouth, etc.) must, without a doubt, have been the result of strangling, or repeated dunking as opposed to constant submersion, and that compression on the chest was a factor. Based on modern expert medical understanding of those appearances, the doctor's position, expressed in such absolute terms, is flawed.

Against the Verdict

There were few other, if any, medical authorities in as good a position as Alfred Swaine Taylor to comment on this case. That's certainly how Boswell presented Taylor's belief that the medical evidence was insufficient to convict Kirwan. Taylor's take on the proceedings – published in February 1853 in the *Dublin Quarterly Journal of Medical Science* – takes up nine pages of Boswell's pamphlet. Also included is a certificate signed by 10 other doctors, which states, based on the description of the body, a belief that many of the conditions were described by decomposition, and that the evidence was 'quite compatible' with death caused by simple drowning or by seizure in the water – 'and we deem it highly probable the latter was the unhappy cause of death in this instance'.

As with Geoghegan's work, I don't intend on including Taylor's input wholesale, but there are some passages that will be useful to highlight. One major difference between Geoghegan and Taylor is their reliance on evidence outside the pathological information. Geoghegan tended to believe that regardless of the lack of marks that would constitute proof, Kirwan must have violently killed Maria – partly because of his understanding regarding various indicators such as the froth on the mouth – and partly because the other 'moral' evidence demanded that conclusion. Like the prosecution, he circumvented the overt lack of physical trauma by suggesting a violent method that would not leave a mark. Taylor, on the other hand, was of the view that defined marks of violence are necessary to prove a violent crime, the damning moral facets notwithstanding.

In comparison with Geoghegan, Taylor offers no specific alternative theory; rather, it's an exercise in pointing out the inconsistencies within the medical conclusions reached by the Crown. In essence, its effect is to show that the prosecution's version of events is unsupported, and that there exists more than a reasonable doubt – one that should have been granted to Kirwan. Atop this assertion is a simple guiding principle: there is no evidence that Maria suffered a violent death. The doctor begins by listing the appearances of the body as noted by Hatchell and Hamilton, the medical student. The delay in Maria's post-mortem examination is highlighted a number of times by Taylor, who makes the point that the delay affected the reliability of the findings, due to the fact that some of the changes noted are the normal effect of decomposition.

Had the examination been conducted within 48 hours of death, the data would be sound; 'In the meantime, because it was not thus and then inspected, conditions of the body, adverse to the presumption of natural death, must not be assumed to have existed in order to work out a charge of murder against a man accused of the crime.' For example, that the 'genital organs were found vascular and injected' meant little, because decompositional changes could account for them. In explaining the bleeding from the vagina, he wonders whether passive menorrhagia or the recurrence of menstruation could have caused it, and considered it difficult to reconcile that observation with a death from violence, in the absence of the other requisite signs of constriction or compression. Taylor clearly sees it as a hazardous factor upon which to determine guilt, a common theme throughout the paper.

In deconstructing the prosecution's version of events, Taylor targets the condition of the lungs and heart, as well as the stomach and the details surrounding the mucus, to disprove death by strangulation or by being drowned by another person. Going one further, he doubts whether Maria can be conclusively demonstrated to have drowned or died from asphyxia at all. The froth observed at her mouth, for example, could have also occurred during an epileptic fit, he says. More generally, Taylor says one of the most striking characteristics of asphyxia is distention of the right cavities of the heart, and of the large blood vessels connected with those cavities, with 'black fluid blood'.

According to his own observation (he was not averse to an anecdote himself) of dead people and experiments on drowned and strangled animals, he calls the above described condition of the heart an 'invariable accompaniment of engorgement or congestion of the vessels of the lungs'. This is at odds with Maria's case as described by Hatchell, who said her heart was empty. The theory of strangulation or smothering by a sheet, Taylor says, is ruled out by the lack of struggle marks – 'the marks of great resistance' and the corresponding marks on Kirwan. The heart, in a strangulation case, would not be empty, but the right cavities should be distended. Taylor writes that if the possibility that the heart emptied as a result of 31 days' decomposition is considered, then the inspection threw no light on the cause of death.

'It is the result of 20 years' experience in the investigation of these cases that the resistance which a healthy and vigorous person can offer to the assault of a murderer, intent upon drowning or suffocating him or her, is in general such as to lead to the infliction of a greater amount of violence than is necessary to ensure the death of the victim,' he wrote. 'The absence of any marks of violence or wounds on the body of Mrs Kirwan, excepting such small abrasions as might have resulted from accident, may be taken in support of the only view which it appears to me can be drawn – namely, that death was not the result of a homicidal drowning or suffocation, but most probably of a fit resulting from natural causes.'

People, while bathing, are often seized with fits, according to Taylor; they can be fatal, or may allow for a short struggle. The seizure could be the result of syncope, apoplexy or epilepsy; in the doctor's opinion, any of those three conditions reconciled all the circumstances in the case of Maria's death.

Some Notes

Taylor's paper is astute, though perhaps less ambitious in its aims than Geoghegan's. That's not necessarily a bad thing. The real merit of Taylor's paper is not in the synthesis of a theory, but in the demonstration of what was not proved, and the implications of the void itself. In purporting to demonstrate that there was no medical evidence that Maria died at the hands of any other person – let alone her husband – it demands questions of the jury, with a realistic view of the real question at stake: in the absence of hard proof, how much should we rely on the 'moral' facts to infer guilt in a case of murder? Or, as Taylor put it, 'A question then arises whether any amount of moral evidence can compensate for a deficiency of proof of the cause of death?'

For Taylor, the answer to that is 'no', there is no amount. This position, it appears, is from a commitment to the integrity of the process, rather than from any sympathy for Kirwan. Taylor refers to the line from the judge's charge, directing the jury to acquit if they could not satisfy themselves that Maria died a violent death. This is a notable direction, when compared, again, with the following line from the jury's letter, written in the aftermath of the trial: 'True, it was not sworn that the body of Mrs Kirwan was the body of a murdered woman. Upon this fact depended the circumstantiality of the case; had that been sworn to there would have been an end of the matter.' Would not this admission, stacked against the judge's direction, seem to be an end to it? By Taylor's logic, it probably would.

There's an interesting divide here, between Geoghegan and Taylor, in that the latter isn't exactly in Kirwan's corner. Rather, he is presenting his observations as an objective view of the case, and demonstrating the dangers of accepting a version of the truth based on conjecture and inconclusive medical evidence. He does not say Kirwan is innocent, nor does he diminish the seriousness or truth behind the 'moral' facts. Taylor acknowledges the risk of potentially letting a guilty person go; a lesser of two evils, which is embedded in the justice system and presumption of innocence. 'Different degrees of evidence satisfy different minds; but a medical witness is bound to base his opinion on medical circumstances,' writes Taylor. 'It may be that some criminals will escape by a strict adherence to this rule, but this is of small importance to society, compared with the punishment of one who is really innocent. Looking at the unsatisfactory nature of the medical evidence of violent death in the case of Kirwan, it would certainly have justified a verdict of Not proven.'

20

THE MODERN EXPERT OPINION

D r Linda Mulligan – Ireland's Chief State Pathologist – interprets the details of death for a living. Where foul play is suspected, it is the remit of the Office of the State Pathologist to provide independent, expert forensic pathological advice with a view to determining the cause of death, for legal purposes. Pathology, of course, is not a new discipline, but the benefit of 170 years of advancement in medicine, science and quality control presents a new opportunity to review the medical facts of the present case. A fresh chance to weigh up the arguments and separate science from moral extrapolation. Having reviewed the medical evidence, Dr Mulligan, in short, is not fully convinced of the prosecution's case – at least where the medical testimony is concerned. 'You're never going to be able to say whether he's innocent or guilty, really,' says Dr Mulligan at the outset of our discussion. 'But, I know in today's justice system, I don't think there would be enough evidence to convict him.'

Before delving into the details, it's vital to remember that much of this story exists, and will always exist, in the unknown. The narrative rests precariously upon interpretations of half-facts and the testimony of people whose expertise varied wildly, depending on who you read. The transcripts scrawled on the yellowed pages comprising the material documenting 'The Ireland's Eye Murder' often present an opportunity for two sides to view the same evidence and land at opposing theories. It makes for breakneck reading. And much reviewing.

That Kirwan was a devious operator when it came to his marital affairs was perhaps demonstrable, and easy to believe. The sketches gleaned from the players on the periphery of the couple's life add up convincingly, as far as this writer is concerned. That he murdered Maria Kirwan in the manner described by the prosecution and accepted by the jury, however, was a conclusion reached based on strands of mostly circumstantial evidence: 'moral' facts mixed with opportunity and propped up by questionable medical testimony. For much of the prosecution's case, there is little we can do to make these topics any clearer. But where the medical evidence is concerned, modern science may be able to untangle at least some of the arguments, even if it cannot provide a step-by-step account of what took place at Ireland's Eye. But nobody can do that.

Four 'officials' of varying degrees of medical expertise saw Mrs Kirwan's body: Henry Davis, James Hamilton, George Hatchell and John Tighe. The input of the latter was a confirmatory appearance, to double down on Hatchell's evidence. Each expert who interpreted the medical facts before, during and after the trial had at their disposal the same material to work with – namely, the notes from the post-mortem examination and the inquest, and the accounts of the smattering of various bystanders who saw the body. In that sense, the raw medical evidence is the same today as it was then – a collection of written accounts.

When Dr Mulligan and I discuss the details of this case, it's with the benefit of much hindsight. Times have changed. The chronology of the process, for one, would be much different in a case like this today. Inquests occur after the criminal trial, whereas they were formerly performed shortly after death, and the evidence used later at the criminal trial – if, indeed, a true bill was found and a trial ultimately went ahead at Assizes. Pathology, too, is now a more refined discipline than it was in the late 19th century. Whatever about modern expertise, the questionable nature of some testimony seems evident, even by standards in 1852. Inconsistencies were not lost on Isaac Butt then, nor are they lost on Dr Mulligan now. 'A lot of the circumstantial evidence from the witnesses is wholly unreliable,' she says, 'and the fact that they changed their stories so much from the inquest to the courtroom – that wouldn't be allowed today.'

There were errors in past medical interpretations surrounding this case. There is, however, an aspect of Dr Geoghegan's paper that rings true: determining drowning as a cause of death is not as straightforward as one might think. Though he posited an unprovable theory of strangulation by a soft object, he was correct to question the assumption that Maria had drowned.

The reference material for pathologists is laden with the possible 'non-specific' features of drowning. In *Simpson's Forensic Medicine, 13th Edition*, the material on drowning reflects the indicative, rather than conclusive, aspects of detecting a drowning death: 'Autopsy findings ascribed to drowning reflect the pathophysiology of submersion and aspiration of the drowning medium. However, none of these findings are diagnostic of drowning or present in all verified drownings, and so the autopsy diagnosis of drowning is one that can cause considerable difficulty.'

In other words, there certainly are factors common to many drownings and which help pathologists like Dr Mulligan reach accurate conclusions, but each factor may not be present in every single case of death by drowning. The assertion put forward by Geoghegan, for example, that froth only appears on the mouth of a victim who has been dunked in and out of the water, is not backed by empirical evidence, and is typical of the overly specific theoretical leaps made by contemporary medical commentators based on fragments. In a body of evidence made up of many small details, the opportunities for such errors were plenty.

Froth and Scratches

The froth, one of the signs of a potential drowning, is the first aspect of the pathology Dr Mulligan points to. Before coming to James Hamilton's evidence, Dr Mulligan says she first read the testimonies of the Howth witnesses. 'While I was reading their descriptions I was thinking: "OK she's got froth in her mouth." That's a non-specific indication of a lot of fluid on the lungs. Pulmonary oedema is what we call it. You see it a lot in drownings, particularly in saltwater drownings, because the concentrated saltwater draws fluid into the lungs from the blood. So, you get massive pulmonary oedema, and that's what causes that froth around the mouth. You also see it in epilepsy sometimes – not always. If it's associated with a seizure, you normally see tongue biting, you'd normally see urinary incontinence. Now, we can't actually rule that out here, because the post-mortem examination wasn't done for several weeks. For nearly a month, in fact.'

Some witnesses called it 'froth'; 'slime' was another descriptor that cropped up. In the reference material, the substance is likened to whisked egg whites. It is not unique to drownings; Dr Mulligan says a pathologist could potentially see the material in acute cardiac deaths. Or, in a death involving barbiturates or central nervous system depressant drugs. Sedatives, in other words. This aspect, for Dr Mulligan, is where the one gaping factor that's missing from the examination – toxicology – could have proven useful.

It's at this point in our conversation that I recall the one element of the body of evidence that could be deemed to approach 'toxicology': reports that Maria had been taking tincture of henbane. Strictly speaking, it was not part of the medical evidence, nor was it brought up at trial as a potential cause of death. But Maria Byrne, whose evidence we have to presume ignited the investigation proper, mentioned it specifically in her statement to Cornelius Egan on 15 September 1852. It is also referenced in Maria Crowe's declaration in November.

Equally, we can probably presume that Maria had alcohol on board – though the source of that is somewhat fickle. Thomas Giles, the third boatman, after quizzing a silent Kirwan in the boat beside the body of his wife, reported that the accused recalled giving Maria three glasses of ale. Dr Mulligan rightly highlights the ambiguities of relying on yarns; the stories lack firm, helpful details – dosage, for instance. Yet, in the absence of firm diagnostic material, the stories are interesting nonetheless. 'If she's taken something (like henbane) – that's a sedative – and she goes swimming? That's automatically going to predispose her to an increased risk of drowning as well,' says Dr Mulligan.

Next, the pathologist notes the small cuts around Maria's eyes and ears. A key piece of evidence. The morning after Maria's death, the coroner and medical student dismissed them swiftly as crab marks, while the women who tended to the body and the prosecution generally denied that possibility. It was a critical point of disagreement, and one of the defining differences of opinion that broadly divided the advocates of a 'drowned' verdict from those who insisted Maria was murdered. On the point of crabs, and based on the written evidence, Dr Mulligan is happy to lend a view derived from her own experience.

'Getting back to the medical evidence, even the laypeople describing the body: they say she's got bleeding from the ears, but she does have scratches and marks on the face and the ears and the medical student and the coroner are both adamant that they're from crabs,' says Dr Mulligan. 'When I was reading their evidence, I thought, "They're obviously from crabs in the sea." I've seen bodies pulled out of the water having just gone in and they have crab marks. So it doesn't necessarily mean she was there for a long time. The crabs usually nibble or pinch the ears, the nose, around the eyes and the genital area, if it's exposed. She was only wearing a bathing gown, so crab injuries could potentially explain the blood from the genital area.'

If the injuries came from another source, such as those picked up from the gravelly shoreline following downward pressure from behind on the head, the resultant marks would be heavier than the light nicks around the eyes and ears described in unison by the onlookers. Obvious bruising around the mouth and nose would be a factor, for example – 'more than small little abrasions or lacerations'.

Based on the external appearances, Dr Mulligan's outlook tends to tally more with that of Taylor, Rynd and Adams: that signs of violence having been inflicted on Maria, judging by the available evidence, are absent. 'I don't think based on their descriptions that there were any external signs of violence here,' says the pathologist.

On the prospect of Pat Nangle's 'sword cane', Dr Mulligan is sceptical: 'If it was a long sword, she didn't have slash marks… I think there was an implication that the sword may have caused the genital injury and the bleeding, but there was no evidence at the post-mortem examination of any penetrating wound anywhere. There was no evidence as far as I could see that

that was used at all. Did they actually find that cane with the sword in it?' A good question. Certainly, they did not. At least, no such cane was physically entered into evidence.

Internal Changes

The scratches and foam at Maria's mouth form just two aspects of the prosecution's case. Another, described by George Hatchell, has to do with internal changes the body went through between the time of death and the day he took the body out of the ground at Glasnevin. The prosecution focused on congestion – of the lungs and vagina in particular – in a bid to demonstrate sudden stoppage of respiration. At this point in our conversation, Dr Mulligan says that the internal changes noted by Hatchell could not be used to determine intent in a drowning death. In keeping with the opinions of other experts at the time as seen in the previous chapter, Dr Mulligan tends to put many of the changes in the body down to the normal consequences of decomposition.

'You can't ever really say accident versus intentional drowning, really,' says Dr Mulligan, speaking about the internal changes observed in the body. 'The swelling of the genital area is described at the post-mortem examination, but the body has been in water (in the grave) for four weeks and has been decomposing for four weeks. Bloating of the abdomen and swelling of the genital area is a decompositional change. It has nothing to do with the drowning; we would often see these changes in a body that's been dead for a couple of weeks. Particularly if it's been lying in a warm climate.

'She has been in a grave covered in water for four weeks and cold water slows down decomposition by a factor of a half. In other words, it will take you twice as long to decompose in cold water, generally. So the changes they're describing are of somebody who has been dead for a couple of weeks. You would expect to see skin discolouration, abdominal bloating, gaseous swelling in the intestines, engorgement of the genital area and slippage of the skin over most of the body.'

As for the dark colouration on the flank of Maria's body, Dr Mulligan puts that down to lividity, or the pooling of blood due to gravity after the stoppage of circulation. If the body was slightly tipping to that side on the shore, or perhaps on the boat, blood would have settled on the lowest possible part. The darkness of the colour may also be a clue to Maria having drowned; having suffered an asphyxial death, Dr Mulligan explains, Maria's blood oxygen level would be low, resulting in a more purple or darker lividity than normal.

The problem with Hatchell's post-mortem examination, as we've seen, was the delay between death and examination. The burial conditions, whereby water was allowed to flow 'freely' onto the body, pouring out of the coffin when it was lifted at Glasnevin, only complicate matters. Modern standards, Dr Mulligan says, would see a post-mortem examination performed within 24 hours of death, ideally. If new evidence arises, and a second look is required then so be it, but that window provides the optimum conditions for accuracy and evidence collection. 'Initially this death wasn't suspicious,' says Dr Mulligan, coming back to the way the case was handled in its early stages. 'Sometimes that happens with us as well, where somebody's brought in and they don't really think it's a suspicious death, but then a day or so later, new evidence arises. Then we (forensic pathologists) have to go back and do a second look or another post-mortem. The reason we try and do our post-mortem examination, especially forensic post-mortem examinations, within the 24 hours is to get the best DNA evidence or any trace evidence that's on the body.

'Even nowadays, this may not have been treated as a suspicious death; it may well have just been done as a routine, non-suspicious-death post-mortem examination. It definitely would have had a post-mortem examination, though; a young woman who drowns in such circumstances will always have a post-mortem examination.'

While not perfect, George Hatchell's post-mortem examination is not useless. Far from it. Dr Mulligan identifies the takeaway points that could be helpful in building a picture of what happened to Maria. 'The main findings I would take from it are: she had no skull fractures, she had no facial bone fractures, she had no hyoid bone damage, there was no real bruising in the neck – and you would still be able to see bruising,' says Dr Mulligan. 'There really wasn't any evidence of external or internal trauma. All of that is fitting with a drowning death; now, whether it was accidental or not – it comes back to the tox. Did he administer to her some extra henbane to make sure she couldn't swim? I don't know; we'll never be able to say that for definite.

'I don't think he's held her down or forcibly held her under the water because generally you'd get either bruising over the top of the scalp or you'd get bruising over the shoulders if somebody's being held down. Again, none of that was described externally on the body, at the time they were making the funeral arrangements, or even at the post-mortem examination. So, there were no real signs of any physical trauma other than the external crab marks, really.'

Quality Control

Today, pathologists have the benefit of advanced techniques. Some of these that are normally employed for drowning cases include diatom testing, which can determine – through the presence in a body of microalgae – whether a person drowned in salt or freshwater. Testing a person's eye fluid for sodium chloride levels can establish the same distinction. In terms of the arguments about whether or not Maria had an epileptic fit, a neuropathologist could have shed light on that through an examination of the brain.

The scant evidence of familial epilepsy mentioned at trial amounted to hearsay. Boswell, in his pamphlet supporting Kirwan, gathered declarations purporting to be from witnesses of Mrs Kirwan's numerous fits. One such declaration, from the servant Anne Maher and dated 16 December 1852, said: 'That she was attracted by loud screaming upstairs, and when she went up she found Mrs Kirwan working in a fit, her arms, hands, and legs working violently as if in convulsions, and froth coming from her mouth; that during her stay with Mr and Mrs Kirwan they lived on very affectionate terms.' This information, remember, came out after the trial and was not available to the jury or brought forward by the defence – nor were any other witnesses produced in a bid to properly substantiate a history of epilepsy. William

Kirwan himself neglected to mention it when he stood before Henry Davis at the inquest. An odd omission, if it's true.

But, if indeed true, a history of seizures would make the possibility that Maria suffered a fit and subsequently drowned a real consideration. 'But again,' says Dr Mulligan, 'because of the limited post-mortem examinations that were done, that is something that is very difficult to prove.' While a possibility in theory, Maria's body lacked some key signs of a grand mal – or tonic-clonic – seizure. More extensive bruising would be expected, as would tongue-biting. The tongue, as it happens, is mentioned along the way. It protruded, Hatchell said, and there were teeth marks as a result. Dr Mulligan notes that bloating of the facial features and protrusion of the tongue is another decompositional change.

Urinary incontinence would be expected, too. Though it was not mentioned at trial, Dr Geoghegan in his 1853 paper did say Maria's urinary bladder was empty; this was a detail apparently furnished to him by Hatchell privately, and not mentioned in any sworn statement or put into the court record. Regardless, an empty bladder would tend to support the notion of an epileptic fit – or, alternatively, the release of urine during the drowning process. Yet another non-specific characteristic, i.e. not diagnostic.

On the topic of epilepsy, it seems like an opportunity to ask Dr Mulligan about the screams. While not strictly a pathology question, the 'screams' heard by the five witnesses at Howth were endlessly dissected: their length, texture, volume, location (somehow), rhythm, frequency and whether or not they could knock a parrot off its perch all became topics of discussion. The 'bawls' were pulled apart and variously appropriated to prove opposing points. The prosecutors say the screams denote murder, while the defence said they accompanied a seizure. They were important, so it seemed odd not to ask the question – even if it did not strictly fit the day's topic of 'pathology'.

'She may well have screamed if she was in danger – screaming doesn't necessarily imply somebody was attacking her,' says Dr Mulligan in a sober view of perhaps one of the more sensationalised sections of the evidence. 'I mean, if you're struggling in the water and you're probably going to shout for help?' It's a clear-headed take, and one that does beg a question not raised by many during the trial: what does a scream really denote? Is everyone who screams being attacked? Or, as Dr Mulligan mentions, would a person who is drowning perhaps let out a scream? And, if she was screaming during an apparent attack, where were the injuries corresponding to said attack? The pathologist's reply highlights a reality about that testimony, which prevails across the many lines of handwritten depositions that form this case file: the screams beg more questions than they answer. In theory, they could prove just about any hypothesis about how Maria died.

'I would imagine that the most likely scenario was that she was drowning and she was screaming for help,' says Dr Mulligan. 'Now, whether he saw her and didn't help her...? We can never know. Pathology doesn't give us handprints on the back when somebody is pushed down the stairs; it doesn't allow us to prove that somebody didn't help a person who was in peril. We can't ever tell that.'

From the discussion of one of the least tangible components of the case, we move on to the foundational characteristics of modern practice – but not the technical aspects or testing. Put DNA aside. And diatoms and the chronological order of the modern mechanics of justice. Perhaps the single most evident advancement in pathology since 1852 is in quality control, within the structure of the processes surrounding post-mortem examinations, and the details gleaned from them. On this topic, Dr Mulligan describes a rigorous procedure for post-mortem examinations, replete with checks, double checks and verification within a peer-reviewed system: 'It's come a long way,' she says. In a sense, Dr Mulligan notes, there wouldn't be much more that could be added today, bar toxicology, better evidence preservation and a much more objective view of the evidence.

The unevenness in the quality of testimony as it tended to vary from person to person has important consequences. Whose word can you trust? I ask the pathologist, for example, about the blood. It flowed freely and in huge quantities, according to the women who washed Maria's body, and the fisherman who came to collect his sail, and the washerwoman left to clean the mess. The flow, in parts of the evidence, was quantified in pints – though, obviously, no measurements were taken.

'You take it with a pinch of salt,' says Dr Mulligan in a bid to contextualise some of the more gory details. 'I will say that the crab marks around the ears, the eyes and the mouth can bleed after death, and they can continue oozing, especially because the body is full of water, so the body fluids are that bit more dilute.' The effect, too, of a quantity of blood mixed with water cannot be ignored: 'A small amount of blood on a white sheet or a cotton sheet will spread; it is going to look very dramatic, so a small amount of blood can actually look like a large amount of blood, especially if it's coming from a few different parts of the body.

'But there is no traumatic injury that would explain blood loss to the extent of large volumes and pints. I would imagine the wetness of the body combined with continuous ooze from the crab injuries probably led to what appeared to be a large amount of blood.'

The trial reports, for a pathologist working now, make for interesting reading, to say the least. While the women who washed the body may have used some 'dramatic licence', the medical expert for the prosecution falls at other hurdles. 'The trial transcript is very funny,' says the pathologist, and not using the word 'funny' for its comedic meaning. In a time before the rigorous verification and replication processes we take for granted, assumptions plucked from minor details are common throughout the records. Dr Mulligan highlights one in particular, used by Hatchell at trial.

'They're making statements like: "The stoppage of respiration must have been combined with pressure of some kind or constriction that caused the sudden stoppage." There's just no evidence of that,' says Dr Mulligan. 'They're making extrapolations, based on maybe what was known at the time.'

Hatchell's performance at trial is hampered not only by some of the theoretical leaps, but also the overt influence his visits to Ireland's Eye appeared to have on his medical opinion. In expanding his knowledge of the scene, he paints himself as both medical expert and surveyor. In one of his pre-trial statements, made following a visit to the island on 15

October, he uses elements of the landscape to inform his analysis. The physician describes water levels and times, and details features of the rocks, theorising at one point that 'the woman must have come by her death at the place where the body was found, as from my knowledge the body could not have floated nor have been removed had she been drowned nearer the place by any water that could have been there at that time of the tide'. The doctor also noted 'a range of stones across the creek where the body lay, from which there were a continuous succession of rocks to low water mark'. His foray into geographical patterns and how they may have affected the presumed placement of the body was, for Dr Mulligan, not particularly within his remit. 'When Hatchell went to the scene, he was talking about this particular rock, and that the body would have to be manually moved to get past that rock,' says Dr Mulligan, adding, 'he's not an expert in tidal movements.' If, in a modern case, a pathologist sat in the witness box and began to veer quite so far from their area of concern, delving into tidal patterns and shoreline geography (at trial, the reader will recall, Butt was quick to block this lane of Hatchell's testimony), it would not be acceptable. 'You'd be ripped to shreds,' are Dr Mulligan's words. 'It really showed that he had been influenced by what was being told to him. Which again slightly mars the evidence.'

It's interesting to note where, in the professional eye, the 'good' information can be separated from the bad. The external examination by the medical student, James Hamilton, has for the better part of two centuries been called into question. He was inexperienced. Out of his depth. Green. This is reflected in the story you've already read, because that is how the story has always gone. Legal experts were quick to dismiss the opinion of the coroner and medical student, and to lean with much more weight on the accounts of non-experts. For Dr Mulligan, conversely, the more reliable evidence is found in the testimonies of the professionals whose opinions were discarded. 'You know,' begins Dr Mulligan as we go through the validity of some of the evidence, 'the external examination done by the medical student was quite good.'

The pathologist puts more stock in the original inquest finding, therefore, than was credited at the time. 'I think if you look at it, the medical student and the coroner were there from the start, assessing the situation. They were the people who decided it was a drowning death and it was all okay,' she says. 'The coroner would have been, by his own admission, a very experienced individual.' And Henry Davis certainly was an experienced individual. He reminded the jury of that fact at trial – he had a decade in the profession under his belt and, within that time, had overseen many drownings.

But the effect of the various biases at work are not lost on Dr Mulligan. We speak about the thought processes of a coroner who perceives the apparent death of the wife of a member of Dublin's upper classes. Perhaps the coroner was quicker to grant the benefit of the doubt. Similarly, when the details of Kirwan's extramarital activities came to light, perhaps people were quick to take it away. But, regardless of the influence of perception, the medical notes speak for themselves.

'Maybe there was a little bit of class bias,' says Dr Mulligan. 'But certainly, I think the medical student's evidence and the coroner's summation were probably the most accurate descriptions. The autopsy was helpful to a point, but Hatchell's interpretation of the injuries then – or, I should say, the findings, were very much based on what he was told when he went to the scene.'

Weighing It Up

Before summing up the pathologist's position on the evidence, it's important to remember the purpose of this review. The medical evidence alone can only contribute to our understanding of the cause of death; it cannot, necessarily, absolve Kirwan. The medical evidence, we now know, indicates that Maria likely did not die the way posited by the prosecution. There is no evidence that anyone physically came in contact with her and caused her death. If she was smothered, facial bruising would probably be present. If Maria was strangled, even with a soft, broad material, there would be some physical evidence: 'Even with a soft ligature, if there was a struggle enough to cause scratches and abrasions to the face (another possible interpretation of the crab injuries) there would be at least some bruising and damage to the neck muscles and possibly to the hyoid bone,' says Dr Mulligan on that point. Besides, froth at the nose and mouth, which became a central factor throughout the medical discussion, is usually absent in strangulation. But it is seen in drowning, and that is how Dr Mulligan would categorise the death of Maria Kirwan.

Circumstantial evidence can often be a vehicle of justice in cases where the remains of a person cannot prove a person's guilt. That was the case in the 19th century and, as demonstrated in recent times, it remains the case. Just because the pathological evidence does not support the prosecution's story is not proof that William Kirwan had no hand in Maria's death. 'We can't rule out that he poisoned her, we can't rule out that he didn't help her,' says Dr Mulligan. However, what we can now say with some confidence is that there was no valid medical proof to definitively say a murder took place on Ireland's Eye on 6 September 1852.

'My feeling is that this was a drowning death,' concludes Dr Mulligan. 'Whether or not she had a seizure that led to the drowning, you can't really tell, but it's a possibility. There's no toxicology; so for example if she did take henbane, then she's got sedatives on board, and that's associated with an increased risk of drowning. The other thing we can't rule out is that he gave her a different drug or a medication or a poison that led to her death, because that was never looked at.

'I think from the accounts you can rule out strangulation, you can pretty much rule out forceful immersion as far as I can see, because there's no evidence of scalp, facial or shoulder bruising. The marks and injuries that are described are very much in keeping with being found on the rough gravelly bed of the sea, as well as crab injuries.

'Apart from that, the cause of death, in my opinion, is drowning, and a seizure may have been a contributing factor. Unless they can prove that he's poisoned her, or contributed some way to her drowning, then I don't think there's any evidence to convict this man. From a purely pathological point of view.'

A Note on Epilepsy

In the absence of evidence of physical intervention causing Maria's drowning, and the prospect of poisoning set aside, considering the possibility of a seizure contributing to Maria's drowning becomes an important task. The prospect that Maria had a seizure was raised somewhat haphazardly on the second day of trial, and then pursued doggedly by Isaac Butt in his questioning of medical witnesses. The medical evidence was intangible and anecdotal, and surely made for an unenviable task on the part of the jury. The arguments focused on whether a person having a seizure can scream more than once, and whether going into the water on a full stomach can provoke a seizure.

Modern expert understandings of epilepsy can clear up these issues, though those two factors alone may not tell the whole story. Some of the most compelling evidence that Maria may have had a proclivity to seizures came out in the post-trial declarations, utilised by Boswell in defence of Kirwan. That brings its own motivational consideration; there is no reason to consider these documents forgeries or falsehoods, but the testimony was not sworn in court or subjected to cross-examination.

The medical understanding of epilepsy has changed dramatically since the mid-19th century. The advent of the electroencephalogram and the drug phenytoin, comparable with the discovery of penicillin for infection in its impact on epilepsy treatment, both occurred in the 20th century. At the time of the trial, official mentions of epilepsy include its tabulation in census reports, where it was denoted as one of a handful of physical causes of 'lunacy' (as opposed to moral causes, which included 'terror', 'joy', 'religious excitement' and 'music', among others). Take the census report for 1851; 100 of the 9,980 recorded 'lunatics or imbeciles' in Ireland were registered with epilepsy as the cause of their affliction.

The report notes that it is impossible to account for everyone in the country who had epilepsy, and that epilepsy does not always equate insanity or imbecility: '[A]s epilepsy does not of necessity, nor in all cases, induce imbecility, and convulsions are frequently but a symptom of disease, we have not thought it necessary, even were it possible, to include the persons so affected among the Insane or Idiotic.' Why would a person suffering from seizures find themselves in an institution, or among some of the 'lunatics' listed as 'at large'?

In the periods surrounding a seizure, a person may experience what are known as peri-ictal psychoses, and have outbursts during periods of confusion. These spells contributed to the characterisation of epilepsy that manifested in these official reports as 'lunacy'. The term 'ictal' means it relates to a period of seizure; the period of behaviour in question might occur before (pre-ictal), during (ictal) or after (postictal) the seizure.

'Peri-ictal' is a term I hadn't encountered previous to conversations with Dr Ronan Kilbride, a Dublin-based consultant with a speciality in neurophysiology. It's true that a definitive answer on whether or not Maria suffered a seizure will always remain out of reach, but an advanced knowledge of the condition can give us something of a road map when assessing older interpretations of epilepsy, and the details of this case in particular.

'An individual may have a seizure and there is epilepsy, a medical disorder where an individual has an enduring or ongoing risk for seizures; there's something inherent about an individual's situation that leaves them at risk for seizures,' says Dr Kilbride at the outset of our discussion about the case. 'Any one of us could have a seizure in the right circumstances, whether it be related to a high fever, prescribed medications, sleep deprivation, alcohol withdrawal, recreational drugs – all sorts of triggers in life can leave somebody at risk of having a seizure at that time. An individual with epilepsy has a perpetuating enduring risk for seizure as a result of the everyday state in which the brain works, where it's at risk of having a seizure.' This is an important distinction, in that it means it is not necessary to prove Maria was a lifelong sufferer of epilepsy to infer that a seizure may have been a factor in her death, although, as we will see, there is some evidence to suggest an enduring condition – depending on whether one chooses to grant weight to the evidence.

The evidence that Maria's father died of epilepsy – if it can be called evidence – would be interesting if its foundation was a little more solid, as epilepsy does have strong heritability. If we evaluate the sticking points at trial, we can quickly dispense with the swimming-on-a-full-stomach theory, which is something of an old wives' tale. Similarly, the 'three screams' theory is not in keeping with the typical mechanics of a tonic-clonic seizure – formerly known as a 'grand mal' seizure.

In the tonic phase, a person loses consciousness, falls and experiences strong spasms of muscle. They may also bite their tongue or inside-cheek. The subsequent clonic phase is denoted by rapidly jerking limbs, followed by a slowing of movement and possible relaxation of the bladder or bowel. Bruises, scratches and grazes are common, as is foaming at the mouth. A person may also experience petechial haemorrhaging – or the bursting of the small blood vessels beneath the skin.

The noise – be it the 'shout', 'bawl' or 'scream' debated upon by the medical minds in 1852 – occurs in the tonic phase. It's not a 'scream' in the traditional sense of the term, in that it doesn't represent a calling out or cry of distress: the 'stirdorous' sound is the physical result of air being pushed through the larynx by the involuntary movement of the diaphragm during muscle contraction. Typically, that occurs once, at the beginning. Three such cries accompanying a tonic-clonic seizure – and ones that could be heard from any kind of distance, let alone against the wind and around a busy harbour's various pieces of maritime furniture – is not a likely outcome.

Screaming may accompany other types of seizures – ones affecting the frontal lobe, for example – but not the classic 'convulsive' seizure alluded to at trial, beyond the first sound. This bursts Butt's bubble, in that regard: if we accept a version of events in which there were multiple screams in rapid succession, they were not likely the calls of a person in the middle of a convulsive fit. It's a big 'if', and relying on the screams in that regard could be hazardous. However, there are different types of seizures, and one does not need to experience a convulsive seizure to increase the risk of drowning.

In the previous section, we read Anne Maher's story about witnessing Maria having a seizure, and the same story was told in a separate post-trial declaration by Arthur Kelly, Kirwan's colleague, who was present on that occasion. Kelly also said he saw Maria have another seizure at the end of June 1852, just before the couple left for Howth: 'I saw the deceased lying on the floor, working in a fit, her arms and legs seeming greatly convulsed, and froth coming from her mouth.' Those declarations, on the face of it, are quite compelling, and bear the appearances of tonic-clonic seizures.

Another similar story was told by Margaret Caroline Bentley, a woman well known to Maria and whose declaration we've already encountered in Chapter 16, though this person did not witness the incident. Around 1850, Maria told Bentley, according to the latter's declaration on 22 December, that she had been attacked 'with a trembling of her entire frame – her knees knocked together, her teeth became clenched, she lost all power to move, and, when she recovered, she was unconscious how long she remained in that state'. Mrs Bentley further adds that Maria said William had walked in during a similar episode, and caught her before she fell. Also, 'she constantly complained of giddiness and pains in her head, accompanied with violent flushings in her face'.

Another former servant, Ellen Malone, said that once, while Maria was bathing, her face turned 'very red' and she became insensible. 'After she got out of the bath, I remarked her putting on her gown, the skirt where the body should have been, and I found that she was quite queer,' reads Malone's declaration, made on 24 December. Similarly, Thomas Harrison, and his son, Thomas Jr (an uncle and cousin of Maria), made a declaration at the College Street Police Office on 22 December, alluding to similar events. Maria, they said, often expressed 'dizziness of sight, confusion of ideas'. The two heard that before she went to Howth, she 'had an attack' that was 'occasioned by a flow of blood to her head'.

The latter stories were dismissed in some quarters of the pro-verdict press as not denoting epilepsy. Dr Geoghegan, as we saw, also sought to debunk the theory of epilepsy based on anecdotal evidence of the post-mortem conditions of a person whose death was contributed to by seizure. We know, too, that Maria was taking medication: tincture of henbane is mentioned throughout the documentation, taken for sleep, according to Maria's mother. Elsewhere are claims she was taking laudanum and comfrey root. In his pamphlet, Boswell claims Maria had scurvy, in a likely attempt to undermine Maria's depiction as a 'healthy woman'.

But some factors described in the declarations are, in fact, quite important when it comes to the epilepsy theory. The flushing noticed on Maria's face is associated with different seizure types – it can occur when a person hyperventilates, or holds their breath during a seizure. Similarly, a seizure affecting the autonomic system, which regulates blood flow and blood vessels, could cause flushing of the face. More importantly, a period of 'confusion' may indicate a person is experiencing a different type of seizure, one that affects only one part of the brain.

'Spells of confusion – that would be a common layman's observation of somebody who might be having what are called "focal seizures",' says Dr Kilbride, adding that such confusional periods may be an indicator that a person may have 'uncontrolled epilepsy'. Generally speaking, accidental death – of which drowning is one of the most common forms – is more frequently seen in people with epilepsy compared with the general population. The same can be said for unwitnessed death. A distinction of 'uncontrolled epilepsy', as opposed to controlled or quiescent epilepsy, carries with it a much higher mortality rate.

The question at the top of this section asked: could Maria have had an epileptic seizure that led to her drowning? The answer, in the absence of the conditions that would prove a murder took place, is yes, it is a possibility. That position is allowed for in the pathological evidence, and our current understanding of epilepsy would say that, on balance, there are no conditions present that preclude a seizure having taken place. While some 'typical' signs of a convulsive seizure – a bitten tongue, for example – appear absent; they are likelihoods, rather than strict criteria for diagnosis. If one goes further and chooses to believe even some of the accounts garnered in the after-trial declarations, it would be reasonable to conclude that Maria had uncontrolled epilepsy – adding further possible meaning to her mother's frequent pleas to her daughter to remain careful while bathing.

By the same token, affording credibility to those accounts further raises the question over the accused man's silence on the topic – a point raised, quite rightly, by Dr Geoghegan and the jury foreman in the vital letter. At trial, the heft of the epilepsy theory was evidently poor, particularly considering the fact that it arose almost by accident. The foreman says it in his letter explicitly: they found it hard to accept that, after months of preparation, they had not made more of an effort to prove such a salient fact. Like all twists in this story, as one part becomes clearer, another fades: if it was true that Maria suffered from seizures, what possible benefit could William gain from keeping his wife's condition a secret from his defence team ahead of his trial for her murder?

PART 6

21

DO I THINK HE DID IT?

Writing this chapter has not been an easy task. I've drafted it a number of times. The exercise is made all the more difficult by the fact that I don't believe the question posed by this chapter's title to be answerable in the absolute sense – rather, it's a game of likelihoods and plausibility. To that end, I would ask the reader to keep in mind that nobody can say exactly what happened on the night of 6 September 1852.

My original remit with this book was a simple one: to research and retell the story. To be engaging. The case was suggested to me as a topic, but I was already familiar with the story. For someone interested in crime and history in Ireland, it's a hard one to avoid. The case had meaning for me, too: I grew up nearby the main locations. That events described in this book are not better known in the locality – bar, of course, among the many local historians – was something I found nearly unbelievable. Certainly, too, there was allure in exploring the characters embodying many local surnames I recognised instantly, but my main motivation hinged on the belief that Maria's story was worth telling again.

I sought to bring some of the lesser-discussed evidence to life: the voices of the Howth people and others who gave texture to the picture, but who were not called at trial, and whose contributions gave more information about Maria's life in the weeks before her death. The problems started early, when I realised there was no single, clean, provable version of the story. Accounts changed, and varied even further between players, presenting far more leeway than you would typically expect in a cache of evidence supporting, eventually, a murder conviction. For me, it was not obvious why one account was given credit over another, and in some cases important details had fatally lightweight origins.

Many hours spent reading the press coverage somewhat solved that puzzle, if it needed solving: some accounts suit some narratives better than others. It's why the Crown and other verdict supporters could elevate Pat Nangle over Mick, or ignore the disparity in the times with the screams, or the lack of physical evidence that a murder even took place. It's why Kirwan's supporters could ignore evidence suggesting the man's capacity for deceit, and why Boswell could bury the fact that Kirwan did act improperly in the case of Anne Bowyer, even if he may not have murdered her husband. There are any number of those marginal, curious decisions of faith.

It's not too difficult to understand the jury's decision, in one sense. They believed Hatchell, as the one doctor giving evidence who had seen Maria's body, and by then he had apparently coloured his interpretation a little to support the side of murder, rather than simple drowning. The doctor said he formed his opinion on the day of the examination, but of course his statements say differently, as we have seen. The jury were not to know that Hatchell's central thesis – that the internal appearances of the body indicated a struggle, or compression – was questionable, to say the bare minimum. The fact that Kirwan's sentence was commuted is worthy of its own consideration. Much commentary was made at the time about the basis for this decision because it appeared to lack consistency of logic.

Was the sentence commuted because someone felt the case was faulty? And if that happened, why should he go to prison at all? Those in favour of the verdict wondered how the outgoing Lord Lieutenant could sign off on such a commutation, and there was disbelief that the judges had recommended it, and much curiosity about the role of the Lord Chancellor. Napier, as it happens, did comment upon the issue in Parliament during a discussion in June 1853 about Butt's court of appeal bill. On the commutation, he said: 'It had been said that this was an unsatisfactory course, for that either the man was guilty of murder or wholly innocent. But, in consequence of the peculiar circumstances of the case, and in the excitement it had occasioned, it was thought the best course to pursue, and the judge who tried the case agreed in that opinion, and, if a mistake had been made, it was on the side of mercy, which no one need regret.'

Lord Eglinton gave his own account of what happened, years later. The former Lord Lieutenant, in no uncertain terms, told the House of Lords that he felt compelled to grant Kirwan's commutation after Crampton and Greene were swayed by the after-trial evidence. Eglinton made these remarks in the summer of 1861, nearly a decade after the trial and just four months before his death, at the age of 49. His comments were reported as follows in *The Standard* on 14 June:

A man named Kirwan was convicted of having murdered his wife, and sentenced to death; but a memorial was presented for commutation of sentence, and the prayer of it was supported by Mr Justice Crampton and Mr Baron Greene, who tried him, upon the ground that there was evidence which had come to light since which, if brought forward at the trial, might have saved the prisoner from conviction. His [the Earl of Eglinton's] impression was that Kirwan should suffer the extreme penalty, but he felt that when the judges who tried him recommended the sentence to be commuted, he was in a difficult position. He felt so strongly, however, that he laid the matter before the Lord Chancellor, saying that if that functionary concurred in thinking with him the sentence should be executed, but otherwise that it should be commuted. The Lord Chancellor concurred with the judges, and the sentence was therefore commuted.

The next he heard of Kirwan was in 1858, and he was then among a batch of convicts who were recommended to be brought from Bermuda and again let loose upon society. He, however, refused to accede to liberating Kirwan and he thought that he was justified in what he did. He rejoiced that he had had this opportunity of clearing himself from an imputation of having done that which he himself felt at the time was

Dublin Libraries
www.southdublinlibraries.ie

wrong, and also of showing how a person who had committed a murder of the most horrible kind could be let loose upon society again.

It's an incredible admission that only throws further doubt on the Crown's version of events; the judges weighed the petition for his release against the evidence they had already heard and the latter did not win out. The after-trial efforts were considered worthy of commuting his sentence by the judges who tried the case. I think them, therefore, worthy of our consideration today.

I'll get to the point. I think the Crown likely got it wrong. I said above that nobody can say for sure what happened on the night of Maria's death – but we can say what probably did not happen. One can conclude, with some confidence, that the prosecution's specific version of events is unviable, for want of evidence that Maria was murdered, let alone following a violent physical intervention. Thomas Geoghegan's post-trial medical argument on that point is, unfortunately for the pursuit of finality, insufficient. Believing that Kirwan forcibly submerged, smothered or strangled Maria is a story that is disproportionate to the evidence; in that sense, the story that secured the conviction lacks substance, judging by what we now know, and the decision to convict on that basis appears flawed. The evidence in the case, overall, seems at least compatible with an accidental drowning of some description.

Does that mean we can say, with any real certainty, that William did not murder Maria? Unfortunately, no. The conviction is problematic to say the least, and while I find the prosecution's story a highly unlikely scenario judging by current expert medical knowledge, in absolute terms we cannot rule out that Kirwan murdered Maria by some other means, including those which would present themselves in a more robust, timely examination containing toxicology, or that he contributed to her death in a more passive, spectatorial way, or through a combination of the above. These alternatives are, unfortunately, unprovable, pending some new piece of long-lost evidence. If William did murder Maria, the prosecution's proof was lacking, and reaching their version of events requires mental, logical and evidential gymnastics. Yet 'unproven' is probably a more suitable label than 'not guilty'.

It's undeniable that Kirwan drips in an indelible suspicion, partly of his own creation. Of course, it's completely possible that William had absolutely nothing to do with his wife's death; but in a game of possibilities, and without a more complete set of data, murder is a difficult event to rule out. The simple fact remains that believing that Kirwan murdered Maria requires accepting that distinct lack of proof. Embracing belief over evidence. Believing the Crown's version of events is even more demanding on the 'moral' evidence, requiring it to bridge the void where the harder proof should be; in that sense, the Crown's version fits perfectly well with what a person might think about William Kirwan, but not so well with the demonstrable facts. To the individual, that may or may not be important: people do not always believe what they can prove. Or, as Alfred Taylor so succinctly put it, different degrees of evidence satisfy different minds. I suspect that remains the case, and readers will come to their own conclusions.

The problems with the Crown's evidence leave us with less closure, not more, and despite the pursuit of clarity, the story remains tragic and ambiguous in equal measure. If indeed there is more to the story, and if there existed some information – a key to unlock a more complete truth about what happened on Ireland's Eye – one suspects it died in obscurity with William Burke Kirwan.

22

A TRIP

On the day I decide to visit, it's a bright, cold morning. I'm thankful for that, if a little worried about a couple of dark clouds threatening the type of unexpected rain that will catch me in the open. I'd always meant to go. Regardless of my own interests, it's a popular spot for tourists, but many times when something so notable is on your doorstep, it's easier to ignore. It'll always be there, and you near it. Of course, despite knowing the case, I'll need the help of someone who knows the land. Equipped with an idea of where I'm going based on helpful pointers and much older material I've read and reread, I set out on a trip I've never taken.

I have the plot number (XD39) and the name of the area I'm headed for (the Garden Section), yet such is the vastness of Glasnevin Cemetery that when I'm given the number, I'm advised to ask for directions on my arrival. It's good advice. A soft-spoken, earnest gentleman gives me a way to walk and the tools to find the grave. I head east-ish, walking in an arc that takes me north, and back west. I read the numbers and letters on the shoulders of the gravestones as discreetly as I can, careful to avoid one pair of mourners and a priest saying mass over a plot next to an elderly lady, sitting on a chair. There are not many people. Squirrels, mostly, and a handful of men driving vehicles around for the upkeep of the graveyard. One man, atop a lawnmower, is going back and forth over the same row some way off in the distance, providing the only real noise besides the brisk wind through the trees lining the pathways.

As I walk, following the coded letters, the man in the lawnmower comes closer and the gravestones become steadily more ancient, sparse and anonymous, with some jutting out at perilous angles from the ground. Where beforehand the numbers were created with neat, machined clarity, they're now less common, and apparently etched by hand on the back of the larger monuments. There's a small rush when I reach the row XD – one I feel somewhat guilty for, but which automatically accompanies the discovery of information. As it happens, it's the row containing the lawnmower man. The numbers descend in a direction that goes broadly north-east to south-west. I walk quickly, counting the headstones and trying to account for the many blank plots, and then I arrive.

Maria Kirwan's plot does not, at the time of writing, have a headstone. Yet it is not unmarked. A wooden cross, well-constructed, stands on the spot. It's heavy wood – decking board, by the looks of it – and it's painted black. Efforts to preserve the structure, besides the weather-resistant paint, are as evident in each nut and bolt and the pieces of metal that offer the structure support. It may not be stone, but it's been built to last. At the top of the cross, a square piece of plastic protects a printed copy of a sketch I recognise: one of Maria Kirwan that survives in the National Library of Ireland, drawn by her husband. Screws keep it in place, and the decorative thumb tacks lovingly arranged at its periphery have paled in the rain, keeping only hints of their former bright colours. At the foot of the cross is a concrete block that provides stability, and a makeshift altar that's perfect for a flower. On the horizontal plain, written in gold ink, are Maria's age, date of death, plot number and the following: 'Died tragically. Ireland's Eye.' Nothing could be truer, no monument more heartfelt.

By the time I find my way, the sun has come out. Looking around, I realise I've come nearly full circle. I'm in the shadow of O'Connell Tower – the prominent structure that looms above the main entrance. Maria's plot is not in an obscure corner of the graveyard, if such a corner even exists among the well-kept rows and columns of Glasnevin Cemetery. I take a brief walk up towards the more prominent resting places, realising that the likes of Eamon de Valera and Jim Larkin are interred less than a minute's stroll away.

Earlier in the project, my research into the newspaper coverage had taken me long past the trial itself: through the auctioning of Kirwan's property, past Teresa Kenny's fruitless efforts to secure financial support from his estate and her targeting by a charlatan named George Darling, who, himself, ended up in prison. Kenny, it is thought, went to America shortly after the trial, possibly with the help of the government, according to reports. Kirwan spent about 27 years in prison, with that time mainly divided between Spike Island and Bermuda. Any tourist to Spike Island will likely encounter the case via a large placard that tells the story. Kirwan's time in prison, and his repeatedly blocked efforts to secure early release on foot of good behaviour, are chronicled in various documents in the National Archives, as well as in books, including *Too Beautiful for Thieves and Pickpockets: A History of the Victorian Convict Prison on Spike Island* by Barra O'Donnabhain and Cal McCarthy; and Suzanne Leeson's *The Kirwan murder case, 1852: a glimpse of the Irish Protestant middle class in the mid-nineteenth century*.

Another, older book, gives further colour to Kirwan's time behind bars. Charles B. Gibson's *Life Among Convicts, Volume II* (1863) tells various dastardly tales of convicts; about Kirwan, Gibson relays rumours that he dissected his own mother upon her death (though Gibson did not believe it himself), and that, in Bermuda, he was suspected to have purposefully given a fellow convict 'some pills that didn't agree with him' – permitted by his special duties at the doctor's station. The following line in Gibson's book provides evidence for his celebrity when he arrived at Bermuda from Spike Island: '"Before you came," said a distinguished housebreaker, raising his palmetto hat and saluting him, "I held the first place in these islands, but I concede that honour to Mr William Burke Kirwan."' There are more details, but perhaps Kirwan's time in prison is a topic for another day. Whatever notoriety he enjoyed petered out by the time of his release on 18 January 1879.

The *Freeman's Journal* reported the event, and the story was subsequently republished elsewhere, marking Kirwan's last real appearance in a news report, bar his name being used as a sort of cultural reference once or twice in the years after. The release report concludes with the following: 'Last week he was liberated, on condition that he should leave the country, and he has sailed, via Queenstown, for America. One who saw him as an aged and very respectable looking gentleman, white haired, bent and feeble and with nothing in his aspect or manner to suggest that he was guilty of the awful tragedy on Ireland's Eye.' And that's how it finished. The story goes then that he joined Teresa Kenny and his children in America, with some sources intimating that he visited Ireland's Eye one last time beforehand. There's no real evidence for that part, beyond that familiar power of rumour and story.

One other report from the jumble of after-the-fact press coverage catches the eye for its revelations about the nature of people and that very same cult of story. In September 1853, it was reported that Ireland's Eye had become an even more popular tourist destination. The following line appeared in the *Dublin Evening Packet* on the 15th – though the same report appeared elsewhere: 'It is a remarkable fact that the "Body Rock" on which the corpse of Mrs Kirwan was found had been totally carried away in small fragments by the English tourists who visited Ireland's Eye during the season.'

Returning to the grave from my tour among the celebrity headstones, I examine the proud, ornate structures neighbouring Maria's plot, the material remnants of the effort and expense of families and friends in mourning. Maria, after her death, was likely one of the most spoken-about people in the country. That in mind, there's a very real, physical inequality that's hard to escape. It's common to hear people say there is undue focus on the criminal when it comes to writing about crimes. It's not incorrect: all historical research is important, but when the focus of any piece must be on the formalities of an investigation and criminal trial – or, in the case of this work, evidence – space gets quickly taken up by discussions about the accoutrement of crime and proof, much of it unpleasant by nature. You try your best to be respectful; elevate important information; cut out undue aggrandising; and above all remember that, regardless of when they died, that long-dead people were just that – people. People who liked to swim and read and who made friends easily and whose mothers warned them to stay safe in the water. People who should have been treated better, and whose death was publicly picked apart and cannibalised in the name of winning arguments.

I'm not surprised to see the cross marking the grave. I spend some time there, not particularly sure what to think or do. While I tried earnestly to treat the material with the eye of a journalist and add clarity where I saw dispute, there is an inescapable sense of emptiness at the realisation that there is somehow less closure, and not more, at the end of that task – one whose weight I felt perpetually. On my way out of the cemetery, I again meet the grass cutter, this time unmounted from his machine and in a position to chat for a moment. Patiently, he tells me it's not unusual that someone marks a grave that has no headstone. I'm not the first person to write about Maria's case – the story is truly out there, and this will not be the only book on the shelf about this sorry tale. I thought about that – the fact that Maria is not totally forgotten – as I admired the makeshift cross. It's hard not to be struck by the warmth that would have accompanied its construction. For those who wish to visit, and who may not have a morning to spend walking through the headstones, these are the co-ordinates, thereabouts (53.370932876683824, -6.276327771673035).

The island, of course, still stands, and will stand above the bay, its craggy faces and strands once the backdrop of a sincerely awful tragedy, a media circus and the gradual forgetting of a person at the hands of time's indifference. Maria Kirwan, meanwhile, lies under a patch of grass in north Dublin, marked only by the goodness of those who feel the sting of sadness between the lines of the yellowed pages that tell this story.